Recollections of a Donegal Man

Packie Manus Byrne at the age of seventy

(*photo: Ray Burmiston*)

Recollections of a Donegal Man

Packie Manus Byrne

compiled and edited by
Stephen Jones

Roger Millington
Lampeter

Éditions Roger Millington
965 Melrose #5 ♦ Montreal, Qc
H4A 2R3 ♦ Canada ♦ (514) 487-7645

Published in the United Kingdom 1989 by

Roger Millington
P.O. Box 7
Lampeter, Dyfed
SA48 7AZ
Wales, U.K.

© Stephen R.M. Jones 1989

British Library Cataloguing-in-Publication Data
Byrne, Packie Manus, *1917-*
    Recollections of a Donegal man.
    1. Irish folk music. Byrne, Packie Manus, 1917
    I. Title II. Jones, Stephen, *1953 July1-*
    781.7415'092'4

ISBN 0 9514764 0 8

Cover design and illustrations by Pierre Renaud
Map prepared by Christian Weber and drawn by Pierre
Renaud
Typesetting by Rive-Sud Typo Service, St-Lambert, Québec
Printed by Payette & Simms, St-Lambert, Québec

CONTENTS

P. Renaud.

INTRODUCTION

Anyone who has ever met Packie Manus Byrne will relish the prospect of this book — as will anyone who has had the pleasure of seeing him perform during his long career, or who is aware of the respect and affection he inspires among lovers of traditional music. But those who have never heard his name before can also rest assured that a rare treat is in store for them.

For Packie Manus is a man of uncommon charm and talent, and the story he tells in these pages is a rich one, full of incident and historical detail, humour and wisdom. It spans the full breadth of the enormous changes that have occurred in the twentieth century, and gives us much to enjoy and ponder on along the way: there are poignant glimpses of a vanished way of life in the isolated crofting community in Donegal where Packie was born; vivid pictures of the bustle and excitement of the old-style country fairs in Ireland; the fun and risks of smuggling cattle and provisions across the border into the North; and many other hilarious incidents in the life of a wanderer who was always on the lookout for adventure. To counterbalance the humour there are hard times and personal losses, and a good deal of food for reflection on how much the modern world has lost in the way of tradition, colour and common sense. Nevertheless, the whole tale remains a celebration of a life enjoyed to the full.

Best of all, this tale is told by a born storyteller whose pleasure in sharing his story is irresistible. The vividness of Packie's words will make it easy for readers to imagine they are hearing the story from his mouth, as I myself heard it during the making of this book, with Packie comfortably seated in an armchair in his North London room, as often as not with a mug of strong tea in his hand, and always with a sparkle in his eye.

The story begins in 1917, in Donegal, a county in the extreme northwest of Ireland that is celebrated for its vigorous folk culture and the spectacular rugged beauty of its mountains and coastline. In the parish of Killybegs, ten miles or so inland from that picturesque fishing port, lies the townland of Corkermore; in those days it was a remote place not accessible by road and composed of eleven small farms or crofts scattered over the sides of a wind-scoured glen. Here, on 18 February of that year, Packie Manus was born, the youngest of the four children of Connell and Maria Byrne.

As in the isolated country areas all over Ireland, the twentieth century was slow to make its impact, and many aspects of life at the time can have changed little for generations[1]. Singing, dancing and storytelling were still the principal forms of entertainment. Packie's parents and many neighbours were noted singers and storytellers, and a fiddle hung on the wall of almost every house. In their leisure hours people went 'rambling' — visiting — in search of entertainment and amusement. Little excuse was needed for the fiddle to be taken down and a vigorous session of dancing to begin. Surprising as it may seem, in those days it was quite usual to find people walking through the area at literally all hours of the night, on their way home from a dance, music session or gathering in a neighbour's house or further afield.

The richness of social life was a vital compensation for the rigours of hill-farming existence. The winters were harsh, and the Atlantic gales frequent and fierce. Ill-health, especially tuberculosis, was always close at hand. The land was poor much poorer than that in some surrounding areas; much of it consisted of treacherous mires, or swamps, and the green fields suitable for hay and cropping had been won by generations of draining, manuring and digging with spades. There was however an abundance of first-class peat bog to provide fuel, and turf (peat) could be sold in the towns or bartered for other commodities.

During the summer months men (and often women and children as well) worked long hours in the fields in order to provide enough food for their families, many of which were large. In the winter, when there was little to be done on the land, many of the men left in search of paid work. Scotland was a popular destination, and Packie's father, before he had children, went there many times. The winter also allowed people to devote more of their

---

1 Some measure of this can be gleaned from an observation that Packie made to me when we visited the folk museum in Glencolumbkille, Donegal, some 16 miles from his birthplace. Here a number of traditional thatched cottages have been built to replicate those of various epochs of the past. Packie pointed out that during his youth the houses in Corkermore were practically identical to the museum cottage dated 1850 — not just the building itself, but the furniture and equipment inside as well — and that this was true as late as 1937, when he left home for the first time.

time to traditional crafts and to music, in both of which fields they were highly skilled.

Naturally enough, in those times people were self-sufficient to a degree that has no parallel today. Indeed, the community as a whole was self-reliant, and neighbours would help one another to weather bad times. There was also great neighbourliness and mutual respect between Catholics and Protestants in the area, as Packie's stories make clear. (This neighbourliness did not, however, restrain them from playing fierce practical jokes on each other, some choice examples of which are recounted by Packie.) All this was part of an approach to life that Packie often refers to as 'the art of survival' — an apt term for what is an important part of the way he himself looks at the world: it encompasses the ability to get by on very little and enjoy life at the same time, an inbred talent for improvisation and self-sufficiency, and the knack of living harmoniously with other people.

This, then, was the community into which Packie Manus was born in 1917: a culture with a traditional heritage and identity which was still flourishing even though it was, as we shall see, on the verge of destruction. Fortunately for us, Packie was an unusually gifted child. In a world where music was such an integral part of life that he describes it as being 'in the air' — something you inhaled and which became part of your nature — he soon emerged as a keen and talented singer and musician.

He began to dance and sing almost as soon as he could walk and, as a child will in such an environment, began to play the instruments at hand without consciously learning how to. In his formative years he eagerly absorbed the songs, tunes and stories that form the basis of his enormous repertoire of traditional material.

Packie went to school in the nearby townland of Croagh from the age of six or seven until he was fourteen. The master, James McDyer, did much more for Packie than school him well in the three Rs. He remained an influence for a number of years after Packie left school, helping him to develop his talent for acting, encouraging him to write, and even arranging an audition which resulted in Packie being offered a job as an actor with the famous Abbey Theatre in Dublin.

After leaving school, Packie lived at home and helped his father and elder brother on the farm until the age of twenty. Droving cattle and sheep around the country for his father gave him a taste for this kind of work, and he later worked in the cattle trade on and off for a number of years.

It was about this time, the early 1930s, that musical fashions began to change, largely as a result of the influence of the radio and recorded music. 'The wireless' was very slow to penetrate to the rural areas like Corkermore, but in the wake of its arrival in the towns came the craze for new types of music. In the 30s and 40s new halls were put up around the county; here, to the music of modern dance bands, the younger people learned to dance the waltz and the foxtrot in place of the old 'sets', highlands, mazurkas and barn dances that for generations had been performed in farmhouse kitchens to the vigorous, earthy sound of the country fiddler. In these same halls Packie gained much early experience as a singer, actor and entertainer, and he is still very well remembered in Donegal for his innumerable appearances on those stages.

In 1937, when he was twenty, Packie left to seek work in England, returning home after a couple of years. He thereby set a pattern of constantly shuttling between the two countries which he followed for the next three decades. The number and diversity of ways in which he has earned his living is astonishing. In England he began working on the railways as a carter, shunter, and platelayer, moving on to be a house carpenter, salesman, steeplejack, circus hand, farm labourer and many other things as the fancy took him. In Ireland he worked with his father and brother on the farm but also became a professional drover and cattle dealer.

Amid all these varied experiences Packie was almost always involved in music and entertainment in some form, whether as a dance-band saxophonist, actor, or variety artist in pubs, cabaret and music hall. When he was still a young man, recordings of him singing traditional songs were frequently broadcast on the wireless — frequently enough, in fact, for his father to get fed up of hearing him — and in the early days of television he was a presenter for traditional-music shows.

Packie Manus has had more than his share of bad health, and in the 1950s spent three years in various hospitals in Ireland recovering from tuberculosis. Music speeded his convalescence, and in the years that followed he entered numerous ballad-singing competitions at festivals of traditional music, frequently taking first place. After his brother's death in 1964 Packie sold their land and moved more permanently to England. In the infancy of the 'folk revival' in Britain, a chance invitation to appear in a festival of folk music resulted in a steady flow of bookings from clubs and festivals, and for the next twenty years Packie became one of the most popular figures on that growing circuit.

From 1971, after a lifetime of constantly moving from one job to the next, he applied himself to holding down a single full-time job as well as performing all over the country several times a week. In 1982 he retired from daytime work and in 1986, approaching the age of 70, he retired from performing only on the orders of his doctor. In 1987 he returned to County Donegal to live in Ardara.

When I first started working with Packie, his stories of life during his youth in the area where he was born — the antiquity of the customs, the self-sufficiency of the people, and the remoteness of the area — gave me the impression that his parents and their neighbours were caught a kind of time trap, in which the crofter's life had remained unchanged for centuries. I soon realized how naive an idea this was. On the one hand, events of enormous significance — the famines, and the era of English landlords — had of course shaped people's lives in quite recent history. (Packie's great-grandparents would have been alive at the time of the famine, and the landlords were still alive in the people's collective memory: even though, in Corkermore and the surrounding townlands at least, it was several generations since the last of them had abandoned the land to their tenants, stories were still told about them in Packie's youth.) After Packie's birth, turbulent events continued to unfold with the struggle for Irish independence and the creation of the Republic in 1922.

On the other hand, methods of work had always been evolving, and some modern technical developments had penetrated, if slowly, as far as rural Donegal. Nevertheless, it is hard to exaggerate the enormity of the changes which occurred after Packie was born, for it was only then that the tentacles of progress really got a grip on the area. Emigration, which had been a fact of life for generations, began to accelerate enormously, with drastic results. When Packie was a boy, there were some thirty dwellings in Corkermore and the three adjoining townlands. Now there are barely half a dozen, and in two of the townlands there is not so much as a single ruined dwelling to be seen.

This exodus alone would have resulted in the destruction of the traditional culture, even without the fatal blow dealt to it by the radio. Along with the invasion of outside cultural influences came sweeping changes in agricultural practice. In place of the self-sufficient subsistence farming that Packie documents, production for sale gradually and all but completely took over. As a result, of course, many of the traditional crafts disappeared. These changes are reflected in people's attitudes, and Packie laments the disappearance of 'the art of survival'.

Part of what makes Packie's story so interesting is that these drastic changes all occurred during his lifetime. He has one foot in the modern world, but the other is planted in a culture that has strong roots in the far-distant past. We feel the force of this connection in his descriptions of a farmhouse kitchen dance, of such characters as Big Pat Byrne, his formidable fiddler great-uncle, or of the old traditions of matchmaking kept alive by his own father. Alongside these and many other echoes of the past, Packie can also recount the sudden arrival of the modern age, typified by the appearance of the first motor vehicle in his area and the first wireless set — and by the reactions of disbelief of older people in each case.

Because Packie straddles both the new and the old worlds, and because he has spent many years shuttling between the contrasting cultures of England and Donegal, he has a keen sense of what was unique about life in the old days and those parts that modern readers will find fascinating. Add to this his rich and varied experience of life, his eye for comic detail, and his gift for telling a story, and we have all the ingredients for a good read. But before we move on to the first chapter, I should give some explanation of how this book came into being.

Friends who read the manuscript commented on the degree of warmth and familiarity they felt towards Packie Manus at the end of his story — as if they had known him for a long time. The warmth is a reaction that Packie naturally inspires in people he meets; the feeling of familiarity is something that, having lived closely with Packie's story for the last three years, I can well appreciate. When we started working on this book together, however, I actually knew him very little.

Like thousands of other people, I first saw Packie performing in a folk club; this was in around 1976, in the Home Counties of England. Packie and the harpist Bonnie Shaljean were the invited guests. The room, a converted stable loft in a very old country pub, was long, low, and packed solid with people. There was no stage, just a small, spotlit semicircular area along one wall hemmed in by tables and chairs. Packie, tall and lean, with his grey hair swept back, cut a fine figure in shirtsleeves and waistcoat, and made a fascinating contrast to the dark-eyed beauty of the young woman at his side. It was impossible not to like a man so completely at ease with himself and with the audience, not to respond to his ready wit and gentle clowning. The memory that persists is of the extraordinary, breathless silence that descended when Packie played the old airs of Ireland on the whistle, its clean, pure notes floating over the metallic ringing of the harp.

Over the next few years I saw Packie a number of times at folk clubs and festivals and struck up a nodding acquaintance with him. But it was not until 1985, when I returned to England after several years abroad, that I got to know him better. One afternoon in the spring of 1985 when I was visiting a friend in London, the flute player Sharon Creasey, she took me around to Packie's house in nearby Kilburn to spend an afternoon of talk and music. I was especially impressed by a number of tunes they played together that Packie had given to Sharon and which were not in general circulation among Irish musicians. Afterwards I suggested to Sharon that she should collect them together and publish them. Her reply was that she thought Packie's life story even more worthy of publication, and that she considered me an ideal person to undertake the task of writing it!

I soon got over my surprise and began to warm to the thought. A long-standing interest in Irish traditional music and a number of years spent working as a publisher's editor gave me, I felt, at least some qualification for the task. A few more afternoons spent listening to Packie's music and stories convinced me that the idea was a good one, and so I asked him what he thought of it. He consented, though with what seemed a distinct lack of enthusiasm. I later discovered that this was not the first, nor even the second time, he had heard such a proposal, but nothing had come of the first two projects. When I began to turn up regularly for taping sessions, however, his interest grew steadily. In case anyone should imagine that our relationship was that of the 'folklorist' with a tape recorder and his 'subject', or that Packie's contribution to the book was merely to talk into a microphone when asked, let me quickly point out otherwise. From the start, Packie had a very clear idea of the way he wanted the book to turn out, and was actively involved throughout the project in selecting and editing the material. As for the microphone, not only did its presence not disturb Packie, but he ignored it completely and just talked to me as he would to any interested listener.

We agreed straight away that the book should be in his own words, as far as possible exactly as he spoke them. I transcribed the tapes I made with an absolute minimum of editing, cutting out unnecessary repetition, inappropriate material — and, at Packie's insistence, some of his more colourful expressions — and then delivered the transcripts to Packie. He read them and made his own editorial adjustments (with admirable skill). He also supplied me with a number of written passages, including several longer stories (the circus escapade in Chapter 19 and the 'Big Mick and Mad Bob' incident in Chapter 24 are examples). Despite their rather more literary tone, these passages are still pure Packie, and blend in well with the rest of the text. (They are also very amusing.)

I then set about organising the material into chapters. This involved juxtaposing sections, editing and cutting as necessary. Some chapters fell easily into place and represent a single taping session almost unaltered. Others, however, were first assembled from innumerable bits and pieces from different taping sessions, and then completed by further sessions with Packie, in which I would ask him to explore further or clarify certain topics, or to provide opening or closing remarks.

The manuscript was not finished until autumn 1987, but most of the taping was done in the summer of 1985; I would visit Packie during the afternoons and evenings. People who know Packie will well be able to imagine that these sessions bore little relation to work or research as these terms are usually understood. They were, of course, hugely enjoyable. To find Packie in a storytelling mood is always a delight, but to have a good excuse for asking him to talk about his whole life for as long as possible was a great privilege.

Getting to know Packie during the making of the book was not merely pleasurable, however; it was also interesting and instructive. His cheerfulness, his balanced, common-sense attitude to good times and bad, his spirit of adventure and his sheer uncomplicated enjoyment of life and human society impressed me deeply. So too did his instinct for living in the present moment, his resourcefulness and his adaptability: even in his old age he continues to exude the 'art of survival'.

As often as not when I turned up at his house he would be in the middle of repairing and restoring furniture (he thought it ridiculous that people would throw out perfectly good pieces that needed only minor repairs), or making wooden instrument cases for friends. At one point he was building an elaborate prop for his stage act that could have come straight from a Heath Robinson cartoon: a brightly decorated stand for an electronic keyboard festooned with whistles, cymbals, hooters and other sound effects ingeniously activated by pedals and levers. His name for the whole affair, which was collapsible and folded neatly into a large wooden case, was 'Packie's Pandemonium'.

He took great delight in modern gadgets, too. I would sometimes find him experimenting with his miniature synthesizer, mischievously playing some ancient Irish air to an automatic bossanova accompaniment, or seeing how close he could get to the sound of the Irish pipes.

Another enviable aspect of Packie's character is the freedom with which he was moved through life, the *Wanderlust* which led him on through so many places and occupations. This trait adds much to the charm of his story, but it also contributed to the difficulty of compiling it. When we started taping, he recounted many incidents and episodes of his life in great detail and yet without being able to give more than the faintest indication of when they had taken place. Frequently he could not say within twenty years when something had happened, nor was it unusual for him to put a date with confidence on an event, only for subsequent evidence to prove him ten or more years wide of the mark. The years between 1940 and 1965 were especially hazy in this regard.

This does not seem surprising when you consider that, as Packie himself reflected, three months was a long time for him to spend in a job, and it takes a lot of spells of two weeks here and two months there to make up twenty years. Nevertheless, in order to assemble the material, we had to have some idea of the chronology of his life, and so we set about piecing one together with the help of known dates — for example, the deaths of members of his family. It was not an easy task, and it lasted as long as we were working together. New facts had a habit of emerging, quite by chance, that threw all our theories into disarray, and to the end there were some pieces of the jigsaw that refused to lie down in the places I tried to fit them.

Another aspect of Packie's character that has had quite a bearing on the contents of this book is his basic modesty about his own talents and achievements. On several occasions, usually when there was no tape recorder in sight, Packie would let slip some remark that opened up a whole new side of his past. An example was the story of his early activities as an actor and playwright, and another is that he was a television presenter for the BBC — a fact he divulged in passing after we had finished the last taping session. A further talent that Packie has glossed over is his songwriting ability: among his compositions are a series of songs about his own home area, and a number of comic songs, one of which was used only recently in a BBC children's television series[2]. Similarly, because Packie's career as a performer on the folk-club circuit is not covered in much detail, readers who have no connection with the folk-music world would never realise how popular a figure he was, and still is, and how much pleasure he has given to thousands of people over two decades of performing. Although he is now retired, at least his records are still available to remind us of his skill as a singer and musician[3].

Packie has made many friends over the course of his life, and I have a feeling he is about to win many more through the medium of these pages. To help bring the printed words to life, readers might like to bear in mind that they were not recounted drily into a microphone, but told with great enthusiasm in a voice that was by turns whimsical, excited, confidential, pensive — all in the beautiful accent of the southern Donegal mountains. May Packie's tales bring as much pleasure in the reading as was had in the telling and the typing!

Stephen Jones
Montreal, May 1989

---

2 For various reasons Packie and I decided not to include any songs or music in the present volume. However, at the time of going to press we are working on a second book that will include tunes and songs, both of Packie's own composition and from his traditional repertoire, together with more stories and anecdotes.

3 See discography at the end of the book.

ACKNOWLEDGMENTS

Thanks are due to people who have helped me in the preparation of this book: to Sharon Creasey, for having the idea that I should do a book with Packie Manus, and for the help, encouragement and hospitality she and her husband Richard so regularly provided; to Dorothy Dodd (and Pete!), for help with the work of transcription; to Adam Nichols, Brendan Walsh and Nancy Lyon, who read the manuscript at different stages and gave much valuable advice and support; to Pádraig Ó Laighin, for verifying the orthography of Irish words used in the text; to Packie and Bridget McGinley of Ardara, who showed me great hospitality and kindness during my visits to Donegal; to my mother, who provided generous refuge in the long months I needed to put the jigsaw together; and lastly, to Packie Manus himself for his hospitality, his patience and his company in the many enjoyable hours we spent working together.

Stephen Jones

In the conversations that went into making this book, I mentioned a lot of people who are dead. It is customary, when you mention a deceased person, to say 'may they rest in peace', 'I hope she's happy', or 'the Lord have mercy on him'. That makes a lot of repetition, so may I say at the beginning that the souls of those that are dead are remembered, and may they all rest in peace. For all who are still alive, long life and the best of luck to them!

Packie Manus Byrne
Ardara, August 1987

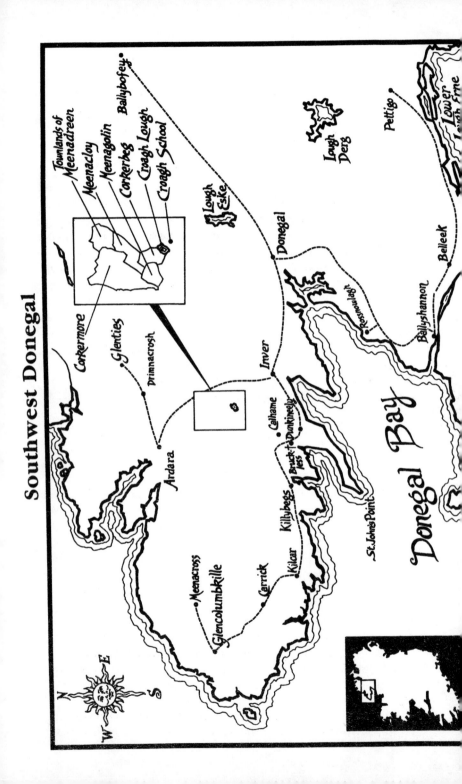

Southwest Donegal

1

OUR LITTLE AREA BACK HOME

If ever you are up in the southwest part of County Donegal, and you're moving in a straight line between the port of Killybegs and the town of Glenties, or between Ardara and Dunkineely, you've a fair chance of trespassing in the area where I was born and brought up — a little townland called Corkermore. Now you won't find it on a map today: the nearest place you might find would be Croagh, which was four or five miles away from our place, where I went to school. But Corkermore was like the hub of a wheel, with Ardara, Killybegs, Dunkineely and Glenties all about the same distance away around the rim of the wheel.

I was born into a time when life, for my parents and the generation above me, was a bit tough. The people back home were all small farmers, crofters. The land was very poor, and they had to work very hard on it to get any kind of a living out of it. There was hardly any money, and they had a method of living, not from each other or off each other, but with each other. Now four or five cows was as much as any farm could support, because the grass wasn't good enough to feed any more, and when some of them would be drawing near calving, say March, April, naturally they wouldn't be giving any milk. There was no danger that the youngsters would go without milk or butter, because some neighbour had cows that were giving milk, and they would hand it out. The same applied if you had a job to do, like hauling something over the mountain and it was too heavy to carry: if you didn't have a horse, well some neighbour would give you a horse for the job.

Very often, when it would come to clipping sheep, a neighbour would come and give a hand. When it came to washing wool or washing yarn, some of the neighbour women would come along and join with my mother. And that applied to everything — building houses, handling cattle, building ditches. Everything was, 'do unto others as you wish others do unto you'.

I don't know if you've ever heard of 'bastings'. That was the first milk from a cow after she would calve. 'Twas yellow milk.

It was distributed around as a sort of gesture, to show the neigh-bours that, well, you won't go short, because this cow has calved, and there's milk. The calf got some of the first milk, but the neigh-bours got the remainder. This milk was different, because when you boiled it, it got solid, it got a bit like yogurt, only it tasted beautiful. You could eat it then with a spoon. You could eat it with a knife and fork, in fact: cut it down and eat it in slices. That was a favourite custom of the people back home, to distribute some of the first milk from the cow.

A lot of the bacon was home cured. If somebody killed a pig, maybe six, seven, twelve of the neighbours would all get bits of that; well then it came around the same way, it came back your turn sometime. That applied in fact in more areas than ours. But like many other customs it died out long ago.

Ah, it was a hard life. They worked hard. Corkermore was a very remote place, and until I was four or five years old there was no road made into the area. There was a sort of a pathway cut through the fields here and there, and quite a bit of it was the bed of the river. You could drive a horse and cart up or down the river, but very often the men wouldn't bother with a horse and cart. They carried almost anything on their backs. And talk about strong men: they used to send their corn away out to a place called Cranny, which was about six or seven Irish miles away from us, to get the corn ground into oatmeal. (Corn, we called it, but it was really oats.) They would carry the bags of corn to the end of the existing road, way beyond the river. A man with a horse and cart would load it and take it away to the mill. And when it would be ground the man with the horse and cart would come along and dump it at the house at the end of the road, about a mile from our place. The meal all came in two-hundredweight — that's sixteen-stone — bags. Every man could pick up a sixteen-stone bag, put it on his shoulder in a rope harness and cross the river on rocks, step from one rock to the other.

People led very simple lives in those days. There were only three things of any importance: work, religion, and music. What was happening in other parts of the world wasn't of any interest to us. Being very largely self-supporting, we didn't have to de-pend on anything outside our own little area. We didn't care whether there was a shop anywhere in the area, excepting we wanted something we really couldn't produce or manufacter our-selves. We had our own potatoes, oatmeal, butter, sweet milk and buttermilk — you name it. The wool came off the sheep, and it was made into clothes, blankets, quilts, and mattresses. People built their own houses, and made a lot of their own furniture too.

Our area was mountainous, although we didn't have any mountain ranges near us; there were high hills, plenty, and rocky slopes, like you'll find in most other parts of Donegal. Now the land varied a lot in quality. It went from good to useless in a few yards. There were some very nice little green fields, sure enough, scattered about here and there, but a few steps out of there and you could find yourself sunk to your knees in a boggy marsh, or standing on a ridge of solid rocks.

Back in the old days before the road was built, a stranger wanting to get to our place wouldn't find it easy. Although, there was one advantage — that everyone you met could tell you the way: because all over west Donegal everyone knew everyone, and the best way to get to their house. But trying to get to our house could be dangerous as well as difficult, because you would have to cross swampy land. And if someone was coming in with animals, that could be very tricky, because if he didn't know the exact route through the moor and along the side of a hill, he could lose the animals, they would go down in the swamps.

Where we lived was a lovely place in the summertime. You could see for miles around, and there would be birds singing all day. Summer evenings were great: the moorcocks and the snipes and the curlews used to come down from the hills to feed on insects and worms in the green land, and they would chatter away for hours on end. But the winters used to be tough, with gale winds off the Atlantic ocean, and cold, sometimes snowdrifts for weeks. Well, 'twas either that or sleety rain.

When I say 'our area', I really mean our townland — the little cluster of houses where we lived. 'Townland' is a word you'll only ever hear in Donegal, Tyrone and Fermanagh. We never used the word 'village'. The English meaning of Corkermore is 'big jail': it comes from the Gaelic word *carcair*, which means prison. Long centuries ago there was two jails close by; we were in the area of the big jail, and about a mile further south there was the *carcair bheag*, the little jail. And within six or seven miles there is the old hedge school, where they used to teach the kids behind the hedges when education was banned in Ireland, and the Mass rocks where the priests used to offer up the Mass when the Catholic religion was banned and the priests were hunted. And over a couple of mountains about four miles away as the crow flies there is the Brahan Walls. *Brachán* is the Irish word for porridge, and that's where they used to make the porridge at the time of the famine. Porridge back home is known as 'stirabout', and that came from the days of the Brahan Walls; there was a pot that would hold about twenty gallons or so, and that was filled every day with relief meal and water and salt and a big fire built under it. You would stir it, and it had to be stirred all the time, because if you let it go it would burn. Some other one then would have a turn about, a stir about, and the porridge became known as 'stirabout'.

Corkermore was a big townland: there were only eleven houses, but they were all scattered, dotted all around the hillside. The houses were all almost identical: one-storey cottages with thatched roofs made of oat straw. From our house you could see up to thirty dwellings, but only three were of Corkermore. There were three more houses about half a mile further down the river, and there were four more straight over the hill behind our place facing the west. The other dwellings you could see were over the river in the townlands of Meenacloy and Meenadreen, and if you moved around a bit from our door you would see little bits of the cluster of houses in the townland of Meenagolin, which was up on top of a hill. The name means in Irish 'the plain of the upper arm', from the shape of the land and the formation of the hills.

Neighbours often dropped in. You never thought to enquire what they wanted, because they didn't want anything, just came in for a chat, and to spread their own news and gather other people's. If someone dropped in from another townland, say from beyond the river — it might be only a mile away, the first word my father would say would be,

'Well, what's the news from your area?'

My father couldn't even wait until somebody would start talking casually about something that had happened, he had to know right away what was the news. Of course, that's the only way news could be spread, by people walking about. It was simple kind of news — someone went over to Scotland, or someone came home from America, or someone sold some sheep, or someone's mare had a foal; or how far people in the area were advanced with crop planting, or cutting turf. World events and politics weren't mentioned so much (owing to the fact that very few people understood either!), and so work was the main topic of conversation. If it so happened that the night before there had been a gathering or a 'big night' (where people gathered to dance, sing and play music) that would be talked about, and who was at this gathering, because everybody knew everybody.

So they would sit around the fire and chat and smoke. My father would caulk his pipe and light it, and when he had it going good he offered it to the visitor. Even they weren't smokers, most people took two or three pulls out of it and handed it back to my father or on to the next person. The women would smoke pipes too, the older ones. They would be clay pipes, and they were usually left over after wakes. Someone would die, and this would be the entertainment for the people who would gather round to sympathise with the bereaved: they were all given clay pipes. They were snow white, and they burned the mouth off you when you tried first time. Then as they went on in years they got more mellow and became blacker, because the soot out of the chimneys and the smoke coming through the stem blackened the pipes till you would think they were wooden pipes, but they weren't. Some people used to break the stem so that they would be hotter. Some of them would have a stem only about two inches long, and they would be holding the bowl almost against their cheek and puffing away like an engine!

Everybody was on first names with each other. So if you were going to visit someone, you would say you were going 'down to Thomas's' — that's Tom Sweeney, our nearest neighbour, or 'down to Pat's' — that was Big Pat Byrne, my father's uncle. The first time you met somebody, you were introduced: 'This is Charlie', and he was Charlie to you the longest day he lived. My father often said, 'It's a waste of time being christened if no-one uses your first name.' The only exceptions were the priests, who were always 'Father so-and-so', and doctors, and the schoolmaster, who was addressed as 'Sir'. Land inspectors and other people like that would be addressed as 'Mr'. In fact a lot of people back home would get a bit insulted if you called them 'Mr' or 'Miss'. My father and mother (may they both rest in peace) only had one name, they were Connell and Maria; but I was christened two names, as a distinction. There might be two or three Packie Byrnes in one area, so naturally they would all have some distinction. I'm known as Packie Manus, or I might have been called Packie Con, after my father. (Packie is short for Patrick, of course. There were quite a few Pats in our area too, but not very many Paddys.)

I was one of four children. I had one brother, Jim (RIP), eight years older than me, and two sisters, Anna (RIP) and Memie. Memie is still alive and living near Ardara. We were a small family by Irish standards, but some of the families in our area had as many as twelve children — nine or ten would be about average, I think.

I knew two families who lived in the same area a few miles from us, and one had sixteen children and the other had seventeen. When they became full-grown they had their own football team! But if you were a visitor to our area, you wouldn't really know how many of a family was in any house, because the neighbour kids were in, and your kids were out in the neighbour's house, and they were eating Lord knows where. It was a kind of a 'one for all and all for one'. If you came across hard times where you were short of anything, all the neighbours gathered and tried to take you back up to their level.

The small children all went about in the bare feet. I didn't own shoes until I was about nine years of age. All the time in bare feet, in all weathers. Weather, funny enough, was something that you never thought of. You had an old overcoat that you put on if it was really raining heavy or if it was bitter cold freezing or something. But I often went barefoot in the snow, oh yes indeed. Do you know what a *whin* is? It's a spine that grows on a thorn bush in our area, and it's as hard as a sewing needle. Well, we could walk through a whin field, and we wouldn't feel it, our feet were so hard: the skin on the soles of our feet was just like leather. We could walk over broken stones — all the roads were broken stones knapped with a hammer — and we could walk on glass, walk on anything. And now, I've got to put on me shoes to go down to open the door, afraid I would step on the slightest little ridge on the carpet!

Times were hard, but people didn't set themselves out to worry about anything; if they did, they would go to pieces altogether, because there was everything in the world to worry about. 'Where's the children's clothes to come from?' A mother would think, 'Well, I'll not worry, because I'll make them.' And she did — she knitted the clothes or cut down the clothes from the bigger ones to fit the smaller ones.

There were worries about money, when bills would come due or the rates on the house would come due, and there would be a worry until that got all scraped up, a shilling here and a shilling there, until it would be made up and paid. But to give them their dues, people never really let it get them down. There's a saying nowadays, 'It'll be all right on the night.' Well the equivalent of that came round in every mind back in the rural areas:

'Don't let it worry you! Everything will be fine!' Or maybe, 'Ah well. God'll help us.'

And he usually did, he didn't let them down!

The hard work kept the people strong and fit, and it generally kept them pretty healthy too. The atmosphere and the climate, the fresh air, helped too. All the childen, from about two years till they would leave school, they all had red faces, summer and winter. In the dead of winter, freezing, that face would be nearly blood-red.

Some of the older people were very knowledgeable in treating complaints with herbs. Indeed my father knew how to treat animals, but some people had a lot of human cures too, like cures for ringworm, which we used to get very often from the cattle. There was herbs that could stop bleeding. They could make up bottles and plasters — in fact there's a fellow still can do it back in our place; he's getting on in years now, but it was a kind of a secret, the cure for ringworm and all these things. I don't know if the secrets have been passed on; probably not.

Some of the women knew all about treating children's and babies' complaints. And talking of women, there was one woman in our area who delivered every baby for about ten miles circle, and believe me in those days the babies used to arrive pretty frequently. I was one of them myself! No doctor, no nurse, no nothing; none of the women ever went into hospital to have a baby. They'd have the baby at home, and this old lady, Mrs Diver, she came around and she delivered the baby, and believe it or not, I hardly ever heard of one of them dying. The baby got its mother's milk, fullstop. The women were healthy, and the women were exercised up to the last minute, and some of them never saw a doctor in their lives.

Mind you, I can't say that there wasn't a fair amount of bad health, because there was. There was a good reason for that. When you're working on a smallholding and you have cattle and sheep to look after, you have to go out in the rain. Everyone didn't have a spare set of clothes to put on when they came in with wet clothes, so they dried their clothes on the body to the heat of the turf fire. Now that is one way of catching bad health. Tuberculosis was really a scourge in those days, and some families lost three or four people in one house from it. That was often caused by abuse, damp clothes and wet feet — because very often you couldn't afford just to get a new pair of shoes if yours started letting in water. Heart attacks were often caused by people carrying more than their own weight. Only the people were strong, they would all die, because the work was hard.

No, it was no paradise back home in the old days. But it struck both ways. There was the good points and the bad ones, and only there were some very good ones, people could not exist. Without going to your neighbour's house and have a bit of a hooley, a song or a couple of tunes or a chat with somebody, or go to a fair or to Mass on Sunday and talk to as many people as you could before you came home — only for all that going on, the work would have killed people.

2

FARM AND FARM LIFE

The old farm that my father had was something like sixty acres. Years later me brother and me bought the farm next door to our own: we used to call it marching — our land and this neighbour's land were marching each other all the way to the top of the hill.

Now in fact these two farms once upon a time had been one, because the farm that Jim and me bought also belonged to one of the Byrnes, who was a cousin of mine. Away back a few generations ago, it was the usual thing in them days for two brothers to share a farm. No matter how small it was they just cut the farm in two and one of them built a house on the bit he was given, and they all worked there quite happily. Probably they worked together in the fields for the rest of their lives. Well, that's what happened to my grandfather: a bit was taken off the farm and given to him, and his brother Big Pat, my gran'uncle, had the other half of the farm. My grandfather didn't have to build a house, because the house that I was born in and brought up in and lived while I was there, was already built before Big Pat and my grandfather's day. I don't know who lived there, but my grandfather just rigged it up and repaired it, and that's where he went to live; got married and brought up a family, one of them being my father.

Big Pat died when I was about fourteen, and then his family scattered away, and none of them ever bothered about working on the farm. So my brother when he grew up, rented it from them, and after a number of years he bought it, and I gave him a hand with it, and it came back to being one farm again. So Jim and me finished up with 180 acres or so.

There was some very good land down along the river, suitable for grazing and cropping, but a lot of it was very poor. Way out the hills it was rough and swampy, where you would find what we called *brughs*, which are mounds of earth, and mires, which is the word we used for swamps. That was not good grazing land for cattle or sheep, and it was quite dangerous land along with being very poor-quality grass. But that's where you got the good turf (that's peat), where you found the mires and the brughs.

The cropping land was all enclosed, of course: if a cow got into a field of potatoes that was the end of it. But we didn't have what you could call fences: there was no money to buy wire, and there was no stones for building walls. So they built earth walls, mounds, which we called 'ditches'. (What would be called a ditch in England was a *seoch*.) The ditches were about five feet high and three feet wide, tapering towards the top, and maybe with a row of young fir trees along the top. They were all built up sod by sod, and that was heavy work, but that was the only way to fence the fields; there were no stones to be got anywhere.

When I was a kid, we had cows for milk, and sheep for wool. We'd also have poultry — lots of fresh eggs, and we used to eat quite a bit of chicken. We kept dogs and cats and all the other animals connected with the farm — which we didn't eat, by the way. In the old days people kept pigs, and I can remember pigs when I was ever so small, but I never remember a pig at our house or at Sweeney's, which was next door.

We grew corn, and potatoes, turnips, and cabbage. All the usual things you'll find on a farm. All chiefly for our own use; we didn't sell anything very much, although in the later years, when me brother and me got to have a bit more land, we used to sell potatoes and things like that. In parts of our county they grew wheat — away down in Letterkenny and the Finn valley area — but we didn't grow any in our area. Mostly oats, and potatoes, and cabbage. Feed the cows on cabbage, and we used to eat cabbage every day.

Everyone had a horse back home; that was an essential part of the farm. They were mostly Irish Draughts. Tough as anything — you couldn't kill them. They weren't really used for riding; it was all wheeled vehicles, and the horse was used for hauling home hay or turf. Our area was a big turf area, and the horse was useful for taking a load of turf into Dunkineely or Bruckless or somewhere and sell it. The horses were also useful for road repairing. There was no such thing as councils repairing roads in the old days. The council tendered out the roads to local people, and they kept the road in repair for three years or so, and the horse was useful for hauling loads of broken stones around.

Yes, the horse was very important — there were very few cars. When I left home in 1937 there mightn't be twenty cars in our whole county, and a few little small lorries. I remember the first motor vehicle to come to our area; I suppose I might have been six years old or so at the time. Now this is hard to believe, because if you knew our area you'd know that it's turf fires, oh for centuries. Well this lorry came in with coal, into the middle of the turf area, because 'twas happened to be one year that the weather was so bad the turf didn't dry. So the neighbours all clubbed up and they bought a ton of coal. Now this was a ton truck that this fellow had, a fellow by the name of Danny McGlynn, and he was appointed the man to deliver this ton of coal.

There was an old man that lived a bit away from us, on the other side of the hill. His name was Paddy Lyons. He happened to be at our place when Danny came down the road in his lorry and across the bridge and started rising up way past our place. Poor old Paddy didn't have very good sight, but he could see this bulk moving along the road, maybe about up to eight or nine miles an hour, and he was staring at this vehicle coming along and he said,

'By the Holy Moses, he has a good horse!'

He thought if a horse could walk at that rate with a load of coal on, it must have been a good one! So my sister explained to him that there was no horse.

'An' what's drawing the cart then?'

She told him anyway as best she could, but no, he wouldn't be made a fool of. That was a black horse! Old Paddy died not long after that, still believing that a horse had been pulling that lorry of coal.

We only ever had one horse on the farm. We hadn't enough land to feed two horses, and anyway the crop wouldn't be all that big. A lot of the land had to be dug with spades and worked by men themselves, because the horse would go down, would be lost in the boggy areas. There was no ploughing done on our farm. My father would work from clear daylight in the morning till it would get dark, till he couldn't see what he was doing, then go to bed and do the same the following day. He had no plough — he had a spade.

Quite often my father would lend a neighbour one of his cows. Mostly where there would be youngsters; if there was three or four youngsters in a house and there was no milk, and my father had a spare cow, not having a lot of good land and feeding, he would be very glad to get a cow fed. Our cow would go to that farm, and they would milk away at that cow and feed her well, because the better they fed her the more milk they got from her, and my father used to get them home in good shape. There would be no money exchanged.

Now the farm animals were sort of like the people. They were! I don't mean to look at, but in their way of thinking, because we never bothered building fences, and the animals would spread about. They would wander in on someone's property, and eat away there. I've seen it that our cattle were probably on someone's farm beyond the river, and there were cattle from beyond the river over eating on our land, and no-one took a blind bit o' notice!

In the evening they would start for home. The cows would come home, to be milked. It was all hand milking, of course. They weren't big milkers like the modern dairy cows. We hadn't the strain to provide a vast amount of milk, for two reasons. One, the grass wasn't strong enough to feed these big dairy cows, and another thing was, the ground wasn't solid enough to hold them up. They would go out and walk on it and down they would go, and you would have to get ropes and spades and dig them out. So we had nearly all Aberdeen Angus — tiny little black polly cattle. They were the principal stock, but there was also Galloways. They were both Scottish animals. I never remember a Friesian in our area in my young days; plenty now though. And Charolais weren't heard of. There would be some Shorthorns, but it would be on the solider land away from the boggy swamps where they would certainly some to grief, because they were heavy, clumsy, and not very intelligent. We couldn't have really anything only these little black tough light cattle.

I've seen the Galloways rummaging about with their noses and putting the snow away off the grass, eating up the grass out of the snow, and they were as happy as could be. And sometimes they would be sunk down in the ground, like a black bundle of rags; you wouldn't see a leg at all, and the belly was sit on the ground and they were reaching as far as they could, and eating the grass all around. And then they would heave themselves up out of this swamp, and they would sink in another one and eat away. I hardly ever remember one being drowned. They had the gift of ploughing out of any predicament.

We had to be very careful walking in those swampy areas, especially in the snow when we would be out looking about the sheep, because sometimes the ice would cover one of these swamps, and then it would snow on top of the ice, and of course the sheep didn't know that there was a swamp there, and they'd carry on ploughing through the snow, and by this time maybe there was a thaw setting in that weakened the ice and down they would go. So we used to do a lot of tramping during snow out in the swamplands, but two men used to put a rope round their waists, whereas if one went down the other was there to take him out of it.

Oh, I went down. There was a fellow who lived next door, Neil Boyle — in fact his son John bought all the land off me in the end, after my brother died — I would be lost, I wouldn't be here today only for him. We were tied together and the ice broke and away I went. You can imagine the kind of swamps they are; it's not really water, it's thick soft black mud like treacle. We used to call it *glár*. There's no telling how deep they are, because some of the turf banks in our area are up to eight and nine feet deep, so if you went to the bottom of that you hadn't a hope.

We didn't have vets or anyone come around to look after cattle. If an animal took what we used to call ill-shock, that was founder, or a bad trembling, my father would go out to the moors, and he knew the kind of herbs to pluck, boil, and give the soup to the animal to drink, and that animal was away in a day or two, away with the others, completely cured. There isn't a complaint, a disease, a mark ever known in the world that there isn't a herb growing to cure it.

The cows were brought in during the winter. There was snow and ice every winter. The sheep wasn't brought in, they were roaming everywhere, but very seldom you would find store cattle lying out in the winter. They would be tied in cattle houses, and eat hay the whole winter; let them out once a day to drink water, and in again and give them more hay. Which made a lot of extra work cutting and saving all this hay — and I remember when there was no mowing machines in our area: the hay was all cut with scythes.

There would be one or two men in each locality that made that their job during the haycutting season; they cut hay on God knows how many farms, they were just haycutters, like the threshers. Everybody's hay would be ready to cut all around the same time, but two or three of these blokes, when they got going, could tumble a field in a day, no trouble, and the next day they were away to some other one, and so on.

Then boys, girls, men, women, all got out to save the hay, and turn it and shake it and make lapcocks out of it. Now making a lapcock was an art in itself. You rolled the hay twice, then you picked it up and you tucked in the bit that was sticking out, and it sat up about the height of the seat of a chair, and it was so soft that the wind blew through it and dried it immediately. That's gone out of fashion long ago, and anyway, I think it only applied in the peat areas and the mossy areas, where the hay is much closer. Our hay would only grow about a foot high or so, and it would grow very close together — more like cotton wool than hay — and you had to work some miracle with it so as that the air would get through.

All the threshing was done by hand, using what we called a flail. It was only two sticks tied together, but in a special way of course. You just can't get a bit of rope and tie two sticks together and use it as a flail. And there was a certain way you swung the flail round: you didn't lift it up and down like beating a carpet, 'cause if you did you would knock the back out of your skull, or you'd kill the bloke opposite. It was interesting to watch two men flailing corn. They stood about ten feet apart, and four sheaves of corn would be laid down between them — usually two one way and two the opposite, with the corn heads overlapping each other. One would swing his flail over his right shoulder and the other would do the same on an offbeat, which meant that the parts of the flails that was in the air, the dangerous parts (they were called the supples), would be away from each other. That was very important, because if they hit in mid-air, it would be serious; like one could lose an eye, or get his skull split, anything could happen. But I've never seen an accident during threshing.

It was the nicest thing for playing music to. I used to play for the threshers, keeping time with the beat; the beat of the sticks made perfect rhythm. And two practised threshers never even had to look at each other. They would start, say, on the very point of the sheaf and they would beat down, swing on down, towards what we called the band — that was the straw that was tied around it to make it into a sheaf. And they could stop dead on; each of them would put down the hand staff, the part of the flail that you held in your hand, and knock the sheaf in on their shoe, and give their foot a tip upwards, and it turned the sheaf right over. The two sheaves came over simultaneously, spot on, and then they would do the other side. The grains flew about everywhere. It was all swept up, put into sacks, taken away and winnowed. This was done on a breezy day: you filled a bucket and held it up so that the corn and chaff came out of the bucket, a little bit at a time. The breeze blew the chaff away, and the corn fell down on a big tarpaulin or a big sheet laid out on the ground.

The fuel for the fires was all turf. Cutting the turf was done in April or May, when you would cut enough for the whole of the coming winter. We used a special spade called a *sleán* with a wing or a flange on one side of the blade. Some had the wing on the right-hand side of the blade, and some had the wing on the left. That was very essential, because everyone doesn't use a shovel the same. Some use it left-handed or left-footed, and some use it right-handed, and if you tried to cut the turf with the wing on the wrong side of the blade, you couldn't do it. The turf would be cut about twelve inches long and four inches square, although they varied a lot depending on the quality of the land you were digging up: if it was what we called easy-to-win turf, you could cut them a bit bigger, because they would dry easily. But if it was the real sticky, solid black turf, you had to cut them smaller so that they wouldn't take so long to dry.

There would be one man shaping the turf with the *sleán*, and as they were cut another man would lift them out on the bank head and build them on a special turf barrow, which had no wings, just a flat bed. Then a third bloke would wheel it out right away on the moor, and 'twould be spread about there, and the elements did the rest. It takes a good while to dry. It wants at least a month before it's properly seasoned to burn. It will burn, but it doesn't make the proper glow, the proper nice blaze until it's at least a month old, and sometimes two, depending on the weather and the quality of the bog.

There was no boggy land at all say from about three miles south of our house — 'twas all becoming good grazing land, good cropping land. So the people who had no boggy land came to cut the turf on people's land in our area. There were people that used to walk from Dunkineely town past our place, that would be over nine English miles, and almost seven Irish miles, to cut turf and to save the turf. They would leave some time in the small hours, and come and do a full day's work, and stay till it would be getting dark, and start for home again. They would pay what they called 'bog trespass', and they paid that every year. There was some places where the owner of the land would be a near-going so-and-so, and he would give them a certain place to stop, they could only cut a bank of a certain width. But my father had so much boggy land that he didn't care how far they went — let them cut out the top of the hill and down the other side, he wasn't a bit worried, and it was ten shillings each year. Then it went to a pound I think. And you know, bog trespass is still going on to this day.

In our area the hay is not so solid or so good for feeding animals as the hay down around Dunkineely town, so come March of course my father would be getting a bit short of hay, and that was one thing that he liked, to have the cattle in good shape. So he would probably have a chat with some man that was cutting turf on our land, and they would make a deal. The man would have hay to spare, and he would give the hay instead of bog trespass.

I remember when the government or the Department of Labour took over a wallop of land in Corkermore, just over the hill from our house. They sent inspectors along to tell the people how to cut turf (or how to cut peat, as they put it) for the government, for distribution to the cities. Well, they happened to come into the wrong area, because everyone, including women, in our area knew exactly how turf were cut. I remember my father and one of these inspectors having a right tearaway about it. Anyway, we all went out to the turf bogs and started cutting the peat our way, let them like it or not. That's how we cut them, it was our way or not at all.

You see, this inspector didn't understand that you could stand on the land and cut these turf one at a time. His idea was that you got an ordinary straight spade instead of a turf spade and you cut facing the turf bank, as we called it, and then you had to cut it out from the other side into little pieces. Instead of using a real turf spade with a lug or a flange on one side, which meant that you could shape a turf each time. Do you know the inspectors didn't know that could be done! They didn't, honest. They thought that people in our area were taking the mickey out of them. Course they were from colleges, and this is what they read in a book, so it must have been right. But I think they got their minds changed, though, because we cut all the turf our way[1].

We were well enough paid by the government for that. It was a nice little job, and along with that, it was the kind of work we knew how to do. It was such satisfaction when these inspectors would come round; we could cut away and ignore them, because they couldn't tell us a thing about cutting turf. We knew it all already, coming down generation after generation for hundreds of years, with turf being cut the same way. To this very day they

---

1 This incident, which took place in 1944, amused Packie sufficiently to prompt him to compose a song about the affair, 'The Bogs of Old Corkermore'. The song was recently unearthed, recorded by a local group, and has become very popular in southwest Donegal.

are cut in that way in some places, although now they have these huge big machines. The land that I sold was at one time all cut by spade and barrow, but now the chap that bought it, John Boyle, has a huge digger for producing these turf. You don't even have to take the sods off the top. It grinds all up, the heather and the bog and bits of sticks and all, and it's put in big sausages away out on the land, and then it's cut into little pieces.

Cutting the turf by hand was heavy work, but it's like everything else, when you're used to it you think nothing of it. Now, the hay used to be cut with scythes, and a man would mow down green grass — up to thirty tons of hay when it would be dry, all cut, bit by bit, with a bladed scythe. You'll get no man fit to do that today. I don't care how well-fed or how strong a man is, if he wasn't brought up with it, he couldn't do it, because that is something that you really cannot learn. That's hereditary, like a singing voice or like loving music. That art comes down through the generations.

Many people nowadays look sideways at the old methods, especially younger people who started using mowing machines or reapers, and machine-cut turf and all that. They think that the past generations were away behind the times, a right shower of old coveys who didn't want to progress. But they couldn't help it. There was no progress, there was nothing in view for them. They couldn't picture a machine that you just sat on and pulled a couple of levers and it cut your turf. They couldn't make themselves believe that anyone could ever manufacture such a thing, or invent a machine to milk a cow, and they didn't know that there was such a thing as a blade that would mow down the hay and the corn for them.

3

LOAVES AND FISHES

When I mentioned work, religion and music as being the principal interests in people's lives, I should have mentioned food! Working on a mountain farm, the work was hard and heavy, and unless you were eating the right kind of food and plenty of it you wouldn't exist.

Me mother done all the baking. And that was good bread and all. It was solid stuff. Made of flour, with a mixture of Indian meal — maize meal — and that was lovely. The meal was bought in, and the flour was bought in. And sometimes the oatmeal would be used with the flour, and it was grand stuff. When you would get that, sometimes hot from the pan, and get plenty of country butter on it, it was a good feed!

The oven was on top of the fire. It wasn't exactly what people today would reckon to be an oven. It was a round pot with a flat bottom, and three legs, and a heavy lid. The bread would be put in this about three inches deep or so, on the bottom of this pot. That would be put over the fire on crooks hung down from a bar in the wall. Then this big heavy lid was put on it and some of the coals from the fire would be picked up and put on top of the lid. The heat came down, and the heat came up; we used a lot of baking soda in the bread, and that made it rise up. My mother had her art off so well that it never touched the lid, but it would come up to within about a half or a quarter of an inch of the lid, and then it got nice and brown on the top. No yeast, just soda, and buttermilk. Sometimes we'd have raisins put in the bread, and ginger, and other little things, and sometimes not. My mother wasn't really all that fond of adding any more ingredients than the bare necessities, but she could make good bread, and so could I.

I remember one time a Scotch woman was visiting in our house; she was a nice enough woman, but she was a real know-all. She thought she knew everything, and one day she decided to show my mother how to bake bread. She probably thought this poor Irishwoman from the back hills of Donegal needed a lesson in cooking, but there was nothing my mother didn't know about baking bread — she did it every single day. Anyway, this Scotch woman demonstrated to my mother how bread was baked where she came from, and my mother, being very polite, agreed with everything she told her. But the funny part came after the bread was baked, because this lady said,

'Now of course the proper way to let this loaf cool is to let it stand outside. That is the way bread should cool, out in the fresh air.'

She went out and left the bread down on the stone wall outside the house. My father, who was sitting smoking his pipe all this time, looked at my mother, and she looked at him. They both knew exactly what was going to happen, and so did we, but no-one said a word. The Scotch woman came back inside the house, and everyone took a cup of tea. We were trying hard to keep from giggling. After a few minutes my father said,

'Well, I'm sure you know all about cooking and you bake a very fine cake of bread, but there's a few things you have to learn about this area.'

'Oh? What do you mean?'

'Go outside and have a look at your bread.'

She went out, and all that was left was a few crumbs and broken pieces. There are lots of grey crows in our area — vicious birds that can peck the eyes out of a newborn lamb — and there were always a few of them hanging about in the trees around the house. The bread hadn't been out there two minutes before they had it smashed into pieces and carried off way out over the fields!

The butter of course was all hand churned. The churns were, some of them, up to about four foot high. Instead of them being barrel-shaped like you would think a churn should be, they were the opposite: they were narrow, they had waists they came in narrow at the middle and then went out wide again. At the top there was a lid with a hole in the centre, and through this hole was a big staff with a wheel on the bottom — like the steering wheel of a car for all the world; all made of timber, of course. You bashed and bashed away with this staff. The wheel was what kept the milk going. It wasn't exactly a wheel, it was a round piece of timber with holes cut until it to let the milk flop up and down, and with the churning and the vibration it turned into butter.

In the summertime the heat would bring the milk on, break it, quicker, but in the wintertime you'd have to pour a kettle of boiling water into it to get it heated up enough for it to break.

You'd have to churn for an hour — more in the wintertime. That butter was lifted out by hand, out of the milk, and well beat to knock all the milk out of it. Then you added salt to it. We didn't like the chore of having to do the churning, because it was monotonous work and it was hard work, but we done it because we were all so fond of the butter! And the buttermilk. We used to drink gallons of that stuff. Slightly sour is putting it mildly — it was very sour!

It was great stuff for calves. When they would go to about two months old or so, you could take them off the sweet milk and put them onto the buttermilk, and they would follow you all over the farm for that. In fact, when they got up to about six or seven months, they would attack you, they'd put up a fight with you. Every time you appeared they came roaring after you, looking for buttermilk!

Breakfast would be very often boiled eggs. Big ducks' eggs, green in colour. Now that sounds funny, but it's true! The shells were green, instead of white or yellow like you would expect eggs to be. They were Irish eggs! There was geese eggs, and turkeys' eggs, and sometimes bacon. And lots of home-made bread, with lots of home-made butter on it, and strong tea.

The tea was very important, because you drank tea all day and all night, and if you felt like it you got up in the middle of the night and drank more tea, 'cause 'twas there! The nearest pub to us was about seven miles, and after a hard day in the fields, to walk fourteen miles for a bottle of Guinness or a pint of beer was a bit out of the question. So we lived on tea instead.

Some places back home, they used to make a big pitcher of tea in the morning, and that sat on the hob all day and all night. Big earthenware pitchers; some were metal too, and some had big teapots. They would take a few coals out of the fire, mush them up and put the teapot sitting on top of the coals, and you would see the lid jumping up and down, with the tea boiling! When you would get a mug of that tea, and a big bit of oaten bread with plenty of home-made butter on it, and maybe if it was available, syrup or treacle spread over the butter, 'twas a good meal.

I remember the bacon hanging in the kitchen — great big half a pig! Mind you, it's my longest memory, because then they became modernised and started taking the pigs to market and buying back the bacon — of course, costing like hell. You know sometimes I still buy a little bit of smoked bacon, and it's horrible! It's not like the kind of smoked bacon we used to have, there's no taste to it. Well, this was different because this was hung up in the peat smoke. You didn't put it into a smokehouse, you hung it up where you were living. The pig was hung inside the chimney, and the fiddle was hung outside!

Lunch was a word that wasn't understood at all back home, it was dinner, and dinner wasn't at six o'clock in the evening like this country, it was between twelve and one in the day. Now, first of all, breakfast would be any time from half-six back, because on the farm you would have to be on the go to get the cows milked and get everything sorted out before going into the fields to work. Then there would be some more tea about half-nine or ten o'clock, and then the dinner at one: potatoes and bacon and cabbage, and maybe fish — oh, several things, whatever was going. About four or half-past so, then there would be more tea, and more home-made bread and butter again, some more tea and bread around seven, and that would be usually all till about ten o'clock at night there was a big pot o' porridge made, and you got bowls of sweet milk and porridge, and you go to bed you could snore like a saw-mill after it.

I still have my porridge. That's what's keeping me alive, in fact, because, well I don't know, I wouldn't eat half-a-pound's-worth in four days of anything else. Eat a bit of bread or biscuits, or boiled eggs, or a bit of bacon, but no bulk of any kind till I make the porridge. And I can eat porridge with anyone, I don't care who they are. I'll have a porridge-eating competition with anyone, and I'll win!

I never saw cheese in our area — it really wasn't the fashion to have cheese. Even if you were out for a day in the town, there was always lots of cheese, but it was the one thing you would never think of ordering. A cheese sandwich wasn't heard of. Egg sandwiches, yes, bacon sandwiches, plenty. And fish — lots and lots of fish.

The fishing boats would be coming in when you would be in the town — in Killybegs in particular — and sometimes you didn't have to buy fish at all. The skipper or somebody belonging to the boat would give you a bag of lovely great big herrings, and mackerels about a foot long, pick five or six real good ones out of the boat and hand them to you.

We also used to get a lot of fish out of the river passing down our place. Fresh salmon, fresh white trout and fresh black trout. We didn't take them with a rod and tackle. No, we'd another way. We used to net them! It was illegal, of course. Away back there were no water keepers and the river really belonged to the people, but then the Board of Fisheries took over and appointed water bailiffs, and if they caught you you were really in the soup, oh yes you were.

According to the bailiffs, you had to catch the fish with a rod and hook and line, which was very difficult, because they're not so dumb, these fish. They can see this miserable-looking fly coming and they know it's a fake!

The rivers back home you see, they're just coming out of the rocks and the mountains. You can see the stones on the bottom just like looking through a window, and you'd see the fish, dozens of them in the summertime, basking there in the clear water. We'd go about it, usually at night time, with a net. The rivers are not all the same depth: they're shallow, then there would be a very deep pool, seven or eight or maybe ten feet deep, then there would be another shallow, or fords, as we used to call them. All you had to do is to have a man on each bank, with the net, what we called a bag net — that means that it was attached to a rope, but it went out like a balloon, like a big bag, in the pool — and the two men walked up the bank pulling this net, and you'll feel the vibration of the rope when a salmon hits the net. As soon as that happens one man throws the rope across the river and the other catches it and starts hauling in, holding onto the two ropes, and when you have the net in you had the salmon lying in the bottom of the net.

With the bag net it wouldn't be caught by the gills. But I rigged up a method of catching them by the gills: I used to set a big net, big open net, in the river and throw in stones, and frighten the fish into it. Well that was *very* illegal, that was set-netting. That was unforgivable. I don't think they would even accept a fine for that, it would be jail. And another thing that was unacceptable too was *proddin'* — catching them with pitchforks. We never did that now: we weren't goody-goodies by any means, but we did draw the line at that. But we did catch no end of them with the nets and with the *dol*s.

A *dol* was a loop made of horsehair. Some young horses would have big long tails, all the way to the ground, so you cut a wallop of hair and twisted it into a nice fine little rope, something thicker than a shoelace. You put a loop on one end and you put the loose end through it so that it would pull — very much like a noose. Now why you used the horsehair was, it would run: horsehair's very slippery stuff, whereas if you done it with an ordinary rope it would be too slow, and fish are very fast, they're all over the place. You would work this down, and the horsehair didn't really make that much impact in the river, it kind of just gradually went down in the water, till you got it down as near the fish's head as you could, and then you gave it a quick backward jerk and it slipped down over his gills, because when a fish is in water his gills are always out, they're not tight against his sides. And that's how we used to *dol* them.

4

CHURCH AND COMMUNITY

There was a mixture of Catholics and Protestants in our part of
Donegal. Some of our nearest neighbours in the townland of Corkermore were Protestants, and there was never any kind of ani-
mosity between people. Everyone in the parish, that is everyone
on the Catholic side, were very devout Catholics. They would be
really worried if they missed Mass for one Sunday, other than having to look after the house. If they missed for any other reason
they would be inwardly worried about that. The most surprising
thing is that that seemed to carry on down through the generations. I remember my grandfather's generation, and that's going
back quite a long way now, and to this day in our area it is the
very same. So that's at least four generations that hasn't changed
one iota. That's the one thing that hasn't changed.

Yes, you were born into the Catholic church, and you were
christened the day after. The little babies would be carried the
seven or eight English miles to the nearest church, and the priest
would baptise them, and christen them — give them a name —
and all. Any day of the week, and any hour of the day.

When we came to about six or so, we were then obliged to
start going to church and to have our first Communion. We were
all dressed up for that. In fact we all got new clothes for first Communion. No white robe: just ordinary clothes, clothes that you
could wear to school — Ganseys and short trousers. Communion meant more than just handing somebody this little sliver of
bread. It meant that everybody was as good as everybody else.
It was a communal spirit, for all hands to be partaking of the very
same morsel. Also, during a Mass, the consecration would liken
this bit of bread to the body of Jesus.

Then, at eight or nine or so there would be Confirmation.
Our church was at Bruckless, and it was a branch of the parish
of Killybegs. There would be no confirmation at our church, only
Killybegs, or at a place called Ardahey in the Inver parish. There
was a day appointed when the bishop would come to confirm
all of us, and we were confirmed then into the church. On that

day we were given a pledge, to abstain from intoxicating liquor till we'd be twenty-one years of age — which we all did. (I don't think I remember anyone ever breaking the Bishop's Pledge. I would be twenty-three or maybe more before ever I'd take a drink.) Then that was it — you were a confirmed Catholic, and that was the end of it.

You had to learn quite a lot about the church, at home, and then in school. (There was no Sunday school — I never heard of that before I came over to England. It was a parish school, of course, and the Protestant kids had their own school. Sometimes, if the Catholic school was away a far distance from a family, and the Protestant school was near, the children would go there.) First of all you learned the basic things — who placed you in the world, and on whose authority are you in this world, which was an essential beginning to understanding what the church really meant. For confirmation it would be a bit more complicated and involved. We would go on to Acts of the Apostles, and Beatitudes, and so many other things. With the result that by the time you were confirmed, you understood the Catholic church almost from A to Z.

So, we all went to church every Sunday, wearing our Sunday best. My father wore a serge suit and a collar and tie. The shirt would be white, maybe with tiny blue strips on it, and the collar was made of stuff called Velisca, which shone like silk. Nearly all the serge suits were blue, and in fact they weren't referred to as suits, it was 'a blue serge'. My mother had a black coat and a round black hat with a few artificial flowers, and high black shoes with high heels, tiny little shoes because she was a very small woman. She used to hitch her skirt up a couple of inches for walking along the road, but when she was at home the skirt came down right to the floor, and I remember being very amused at the sight of the two little points of these tiny shoes peeping out from under her skirt! Those Sunday clothes came off and were put away the minute they got home after Mass.

We used to walk to church, and it was about six Irish miles. In English miles 'twould be seven or eight (and the same distance back again!). In later years, when the roads were made into the backward areas, then horses and jaunting cars came into fashion, and four or five people would climb up into a jaunting car, but when I was young we all used to walk. Every Sunday. It was a two-hour fast walk. That was one thing about being brought up in the mountains: you can walk fast. And no-one brought up in a mountain area is a nice walker. They can cover a lot of ground because they don't take no two steps the same length. They're a lot of the time walking either amongst rocks or on very soft soil: you're going along, you're taking your usual steps, and suddenly you come to a rock which is about a foot or two in height. Naturally you'll have to take one big long step to get around it. Now the same applies to the swampy land. If you're walking on land and it's quite solid, you're taking ordinary steps. You'll come then to a bit of land that would be a swamp and dangerous to step in, and it might be three feet wide: you naturally took a big long step to get over that. Well, that habit still applies when you're going on a road. It does! You'd be walking along, going fine, and suddenly you'd take one big long step, for no reason at all; it's just the way you were brought up! Even to this day I'm not a nice walker.

Eleven o'clock Mass we usually used to come to, and we used to leave at nine in the morning or maybe quarter to nine or so, and we'd be home again, well between chatting the neighbours and everything, we'd be home again about half-past two or three o'clock. We'd come home mad hungry too, after walking all that distance. There was always someone left at home in every house to look after the animals and to have a dinner on the way by the time the others would get back. That person was forgiven.

Not that there was any danger of burglars — that wasn't even heard of, because there wasn't a lock on any door in our area. When we would have the animals tucked away on a winter evening and give them their last feed, and there was a party or a wedding or a hooley or a christening or a country dance, then we would all go.

'Did you close the door?'

'I did.'

'Oh well, that's all right.'

So long as it was closed out, in case of sheep wandering in. But no locks.

There would be a big congregation at church. Our parish alone would be about over twenty English miles long and twelve or fourteen wide, and all the Catholics would converge on the church on a Sunday, and boy, that's where the news would be spread. We would be there maybe half-an-hour or so before Mass time and stand around having a chat. You knew every single one in that church by first name, and everyone knew you by your first name. So it was all a big get-together. Then start for home after. If there were four roads leading away from the church, there would try to be as many people as possible in one big bunch on each road, so that they could chat and swap ideas and talk about cattle and markets and turf and Lord knows what — football!

The youngsters didn't get away with anything on the way to or from church, because there was always somebody keeping an eye on us. And we respected church so much that we knew in our own minds that that was not the place for capering or playing up. Nobody cared what happened on the way coming from school, but church was a different thing; you didn't do any damage at all. Of course, Sunday was a day when you were kind of on your best behaviour.

The old parish priest didn't live at Bruckless. He lived in Killybegs; his name was Canon Sweeney and I don't know much about him because we only saw him once in a blue moon. But the curates were very worldly, good advice-givers. My earliest memory was big Father Sheridan — he was about six feet six, and he was built like a stone wall, with very curly hair. He would be about before Mass on a Sunday, waddling about: 'Hello Charlie, How're ye John, Good morning Mary, Hello Paddy', shouting to everybody. He was just one of themselves. When Mass was over, soon as he could get out of his vestments he would be walking about.

I liked going to church. I did. In those days, the Mass was a very interesting thing, in spite of the fact that it was all in Latin. Nowadays the Catholic Mass is more like just gathering somewhere and the priest has a chat with you. It's not as solemn as it used to be. There was no mucking about in the old days, I can tell you. You prayed with the priest. Nearly everyone had prayerbooks, and you read the Mass in English out of your prayerbook while the priest was doing it in Latin on the altar. It was rather nice.

I liked church still better after Confirmation, when I was singing in the choir. I was a choir member for years, and I used to walk from home to the church an evening a week or so to have practice. I was the furthest, the others were from around the church area. We didn't wear vestments in the choir; the only ones that had to wear vestments or special apparel were the Mass servers, the altar boys that attended to the priest's needs — we called them the clerks. I never done that, though I could, I had it all learned. It was always youngsters from near the church that did that.

Taking it all round, you know, church was all a very nice, homely, friendly thing. It was a great way of creating comradeship, or really getting to know people. When we were kids, we could sit around at home, and we could name and picture the spots in the church where everyone sat. We knew everyone so well. The priests themselves, standing at the altar, knew every face.

Now that applied in all religions. I'm not saying the Catholics were friendlier than the others, because they weren't. Talk now about the troubles in Ulster where Catholics and Protestants are killing each other. The way we walked to church, on that track there were a lot of non-Catholics — there were Presbyterians, Methodists, Church of Ireland — but you shouted hello to everybody and everybody shouted hello to you. There were lots of what we called spring wells on the way, because there was no piped water. There was one family in particular, the Deans, they were very strong Protestants, and they always left cups out at the well for the Catholics to have a drink in the warm weather.

Always St Patrick's day would be the Catholics' day, over home. Now there would be a demonstration of pipe bands and flute bands in the towns — Dunkineely, Ardara, or maybe Killybegs. Nearly all the Catholics would turn up as a kind of a duty to Saint Patrick. Now the twelfth of July was the Protestants' day, and all the Protestants would go away for that day, as a kind of a tribute to the Battle of the Boyne. Mostly to a town called Rossnowlagh, to the south of Donegal town. There was a Protestant family called Shaw lived over the hill from us. Old Tommy himself would come to ask my father if he was going away for St Patrick's Parade.

'Well, I think I'll go.'

'Well, don't worry, I'll keep an eye on things till you get back.'

And if Tommy was going away on his big day, the twelfth of July, we would be ordered: 'Have a look at Tommy's cattle when you're out lad.'

People had to live like that, because if they weren't like that they wouldn't survive. You had to be dependent on your neighbour. Now in those days we all used just little paraffin-oil lamps with a globe on, and that light in so many houses would be left burning all night. This was before the roads were built in our area, and there was one special reason for that: in the event of someone losing their way on the moors, and the moors being so treacherous with these swamps and all. Everyone that was moving at night knew exactly whose light that was, and whose light this was, and they knew, 'If I walk straight for that light, I'll be safe, that's solid land between here and there.' It would be pitch dark of course, no lights anywhere only these lights shining out of windows.

Even yet, I could stand out on the hill above the old house where I was born, and I could name every light. That is, up until twelve o'clock at night: now they're all put out because there's no need for them. They have roads and you don't need to walk on the dangerous land any more. But there was no end of lights kept going all night, just so that someone could get their bearings and know where they were. That was part of the mountain hospitality. Mountain people you know, they have a strange way really of living — it seems strange to people who wasn't brought up with it. Now in fact you have much the same way of living in the Appalachian mountains of America, and in the north of Scotland. They still live like that — doing something for some other one.

And you know, a lot of that tradition still applies, even to me, and I'm an old man away from all that for one-and-a-half generations and living here in Kilburn. I would ask no better fun than going over and chatting that bloke across the road. He knows me and he'll always come around, yapping across the fence, and if he wants anything done I don't mind doing it. And the families next door, one of them is Indian — very nice people: it applies everywhere, if only people would set themselves down to it.

Back in the old days you hardly ever heard of someone damaging property or doing wrong to a neighbour. There might be one case in ten years, and you can be certain that whoever done it would only do it once. He would never do it twice, because he would get such a hiding, he would no more than hell think of doing anything like that again.

Quite honestly, things were not stolen. You'd be working out in the field all day and you would just walk in at night and leave the tools you were working with. It might be a spade, a scythe, a pitchfork, whatever it might be: you left it there in the field and went back in the morning and it was there. When we were small, we never touched any other one's property. When we grew up, we didn't mind so much: like if we were in a house rambling at night and it started pouring rain by the time we were coming home, we'd see an overcoat hung about, put it on, and away we went. We left it back the following night or maybe a week from that. The bloke that owned the coat might come home with some other one's coat on! That was not thought of as stealing, it was an accepted thing and showed that we were friends. We wouldn't put on an enemy's coat!

Really stealing something was very serious, but not quite as serious as selling a wrong animal — a bad horse or cow. When you sold a horse, we used to say that you 'engaged' the horse to be sound and a good worker. If it turned out that he was sickly or a bad worker, that was called 'breach of warranty', and that was serious, because the people really depended on their animals. They had their own special way of settling rows and arguments, and many a bare-fist fight took place in fairs — cattle markets and sheep markets. That was how the dispute was settled.

I remember a case one time: a fellow came down from near Derry, I think he was from St Johnstown. It was coming near the ploughing time of year and he wanted a couple of horses to do ploughing. There was this fly-boy in our area who was a sort of a horse dealer, and he had a horse in a fair at Ardara, and this bloke came round. It looked a strong horse, and in good condition and all, but he was a bad one — a real bad worker, and he wasn't all that sound anyway. The deal started about the price of the horse.

'Will you engage him?'

'Aye, I'll engage him all right. He's a strong horse.'

'Well,' says the bloke that was buying him, 'I can see he's a strong horse.'

The seller says, 'He's a very useful horse for land.'

'Well, that's what I want him for.'

'I'll tell you what, you will never get a better horse on land, because for taking in hay, and putting out manure, the like of this horse you never saw in your life!'

That's what horses in our area were mostly used for: one of the principal jobs in the months of March and April was to draw out all the winter's manure out of the yard and the cowhouses and spread it on the land, and stack some of it away for putting on crops. And then for drawing in the hay and the corn in September time.

So, your man bought the horse, gave a good price for him. When he tried him on the plough, the horse wouldn't work. So he came back to the seller, and he said,

'That horse that you sold me will not work. I tried him single, I tried him double, I tried him in the centre of a trio: it's no good, he just refuses to work.'

'Well,' the seller says, 'There was no word at all about work when you bought the horse!'

Your man was looking puzzled. 'I understood you to say that this was as good a horse as ever was born for putting out manure and taking in hay.'

'How's he eating?'

'Oh, I never saw one could eat like him!'

'And is it coming out the other end all right?'

'It is. Why?'

'That's what I told you — for taking in hay and putting out manure: I'll bet you never saw a horse in your life could eat or shit as much!'

He thought he had got away with it, but he didn't. He had to take the horse back. Oh, it was my longest memory, but it was a good laugh in our area for a long time.

But most disagreements were trivial matters, like trespassing animals, broken fences, or maybe malicious gossip. You might hear of one court case or two in a year, but that would be something big, concerning land or the tenancy of a house, that couldn't be settled in a pub, like a row over an animal could. They didn't believe in going to court over something that could be settled by someone in a pub acting as a kind of a mediator. And anyway, it was more interesting than sitting in a dry courtroom. My father was never inside a courtroom in his life, and neither was my brother.

Very often the mediator would be the landlord of the pub. He'd be the go-between, and he would also act as judge and jury. If you wanted to buy an animal from me, and we were sitting in this man's pub, he would do the dividing: if you offered me, say, fifty pound, and I was stuck at fifty-five, he would make it fifty-two. He tried to get the deal clinched before he would let us out. There were two reasons: one was, it was making him popular with the dealers, and another was, he'd sell a couple of rounds of booze afterwards. He would also settle arguments: it was into his barrow to have people friendly, because then they would buy drinks for each other. None of them liked a row on their premises. If I sold you a bad working horse, the publican would try to persuade me to take back the horse and give you your money, and sell the horse to somebody 'up the country' — that was far away behind the mountain! There was usually some way out of it.

Sometimes the local doctor or the police sergeant would take a hand. I remember one dispute that arose in Dunkineely on a fair day. It was between two neighbours about land — whose job it was to build the fences. The sergeant was in the town on the day. He settled it for them. He said, look, you fellows are talking about taking each other to court, and nobody's ever won a court case. So why don't we just go into so-and-so's pub and settle it there. So they did, and the sergeant put both sides of the story. He did it all very cool, without getting excited, and they agreed that he was talking a bit of sense, and they ended up having a drink together.

The nearest police (or guards, as we called them) to our place was about seven miles away. There was three policemen and a sergeant in Dunkineely, which was our police district. You hardly ever saw them unless you went into town, and they were standing about chatting to people. All they had to do in those days was come round with census forms, and get everyone's name down. They would sign dole tickets and keep an eye open for cruelty to animals such as working unshod horses or donkeys, which usually meant a heavy fine on the offender. They would come around to see if there were any unlicensed bulls or unlicensed dogs in the area. Probably sit down and have a cup of tea and the dog sitting staring at them and they would forget to ask about it! Maybe one or two of the guards would go out the road on a Sunday night, to see if there were people riding bicycles without lights. That was about their biggest headache.

There weren't so many troublemakers, because the people were great believers in making the punishment fit the crime. I am all for that; people tell me I am wrong, but I think that if somebody is bad enough to do a very mean, dirty trick, do equally the same amount of a dirty trick on them. An eye for an eye and a tooth for a tooth. Troublemakers were a bit afraid to cause any trouble. It was kind of a home-made law, like if someone rode roughshod over anyone that wasn't standing in a corner, they hadn't so much of a living after. They didn't have a great time, because they would know that the neighbours weren't too fond of them, and eventually they'd be beaten up and nobody knew how it happened. ('Standing in a corner' was an old saying back home: if you're standing in a corner, no-one can walk over you. Someone might advise you, 'If you're going to deal with that man, you'd be as well to stand in a corner.')

If a young fellow in an area would get a bit big-headed, or maybe fancy some man's wife and start giving her a bit of a hassle, well, he would be as well to move out of the area. Some of them didn't and suffered. It didn't really have to be that the woman was agreeable. Even if it was noticed that the man was paying her more attention than his own wife, that could start a little spark. And that spark would kindle on until finally he'd get a little reminder one night to teach him a lesson.

I never in my life had to clobber anyone for molesting my sisters, because no-one ever did hassle them. If they did, knowing my sisters, they wouldn't get away with it. I have belted one or two in my time for other reasons, but the girls could take care of themselves, no worry in that respect. People treated women very respectfully. If you went into a house and a lot of girls were in there, you didn't throw yourself about. You demurely sat in some corner and you didn't make yourself forward until the dancing or the singing would start. You behaved yourself to show respect for the company. If there was a lot of booze at a party, especially poteen, there might be one or two blokes that became a bit boisterous and threw their weight about. But they soon became educated to the ways of the area, and after a couple of hidings they started acting normally.

No, our area was pretty peaceful during my time. But back before my time, in the last century, it appears things sometimes got a lot rougher. When I was young I heard many stories told about disputes and feuds between families long ago, including some of my own ancestors. There are several very interesting stories that I could tell, but I won't, because people in our area have long memories, and some things are best left to lie.

But before my time there was what you could call vigilante work going on, definitely, and maybe up until around the time I was born and into this century. There were people that skidaddled, or went away to America, and were never heard of again. Indeed there was more than one person killed in those times.

One of the things that could be the cause of that was putting an eye on your neighbour's wife. That was breaking a very strict commandment. Thou shalt not covet thy neighbour's wife. And the same applied for another commandment: thou shalt not covet thy neighbour's goods — your neighbour's sheep, cattle, or kids (although you would treat them as your own). But there were one or two that overlooked that advice, and weren't the better for it.

In my time there was one man: it was supposed that he went to America, but nobody was ever sure of that. He could have been killed. I was very young at the time. It was supposed that he stole cattle. I don't know how the hell you could steal cattle in our area. What would you do with them. Everyone knew every other one's cattle. If I was passing along and I saw two heifers belonging to you in some other one's field, naturally the first time I met you I would say,

'Do you know there's two of your heifers in so-and-so's field?'

'Aye — I lost them two or three days ago!' And he would go and get them.

I suppose nowadays, people wouldn't report these things. But in our day, you did. You told your neighbour if you saw somebody do something against him. And very often then you gave him a hand to deal with whoever done the misdemeanour.

Another incident that happened before my time — like I only have this second- or third-hand. There was supposed to be a bloke that was fond of somebody's wife. This bloke disappeared — nobody knew where he went. Mostly it was thought that he went to Scotland. But the strange thing was, there was a man's arm found in the estuary, a few hundred yards from the tide, where the river meets the sea. Now nobody had lost an arm! Some one or two put out that it could be this bloke. Now they probably knew that it was; but when they took the harm out of it by saying 'it could be', they were not implicating themselves or involving themselves in making any kind of judgment. But the arm was found all right. It was thought that the arms had been cut off to probably get the body into a small enough box to be carried about unnoticed. Very likely the river ran where the person was buried in soft land or swampy land, and wore the land away from where the grave was, and that one arm became dislodged and went away with the water. But it was sort of hushed up, in case it was this bloke that had disappeared.

Only about five or six years ago there was a body found in the Cushgrahan bogs about a mile or so from our house, on the main Donegal-Ardara road. (*Cois Screathain* is the Gaelic for a desolate area.) It was a woman's body, and it was perfectly preserved by the bog, with all its flesh and hair. When I went home for a holiday, everyone was talking about it. I could stand at our house and look straight across where the bog was cut, where it was found. People back home can give a good guess how fast boggy land will grow, and by the depth of the turf over the body, people reckoned she would be there for nearly two hundred years. She had both her arms!

I did know one or two men that got good hidings, and I knew one or two that disappeared and were found later on in Scotland or England, but they couldn't go back and live at home. People back home never forget these old happenings. If somebody was beaten up, say today, and he went to Scotland, and after twenty or thirty years he thought, oh, nobody will remember: they would. And the old people will pass it on to the younger ones, and the younger ones will remember. That stems from centuries ago.

5

SCHOOL AND SCHOOLING

Our nearest school was at Croagh, about four English miles or so away. I mentioned English miles and Irish miles before: there is a difference, which is that it takes much longer to walk an Irish mile than an English mile. Now very few people believe this, but it's true! There's 1760 yards in an English mile, and there's 2240 in an Irish mile. Now, the school would be four miles by the road, we used to say 'around the road', but we never bothered the road, we always went over the hill, and when there were hard enough frosts we crossed the lake on the ice, which wasn't a safe thing to do, but we used to do it anyway. Away back before my time there were two young schoolgoers drowned in the lake.

The school itself was entirely different to schools nowadays. There were no computers or anything like that! And there was no central heating. It was a dingy, cold place when I was there, and it was many years before it was properly repaired and modernised. The water used to come in round the chimneys and pour down the wall, and there was a big crack in the back wall where the snow blew in when it would be drifting snow. It was very cold. We used to put a few turf under our oxter — that means under our arm — along with the books, and walk the four miles way over the hill to school, and put them couple of turf in a box behind the door when we would go in, and that would keep the school heated for the whole day. Next day you done the same: every child brought a few turf.

People then got a bit enlightened and discovered that there were an easier way of doing it than that: somebody would bring a load of turf and dump it at the school, and the kids would take in the load of turf and dump it in the box; and that was the rule up until I left home in 1937.

We'd start school between six and seven years of age, because being so far from school, the kids had to be fairly strong to survive, and the winters were really rough — a lot rougher than they are now back home. Oh yes, I've seen snowdrifts far deeper than houses, and there used to be a lot of rain in the wintertime. Then the summertime would be nice weather the whole summer, an occasional little shower here and there just to keep the grass growing, but nearly always nice weather. Which is entirely the opposite nowadays back home.

There was one master, one teacher: James McDyer — he lived just out across the road. His sister was also teaching the infants, they would be anything up to between six and eight, but there was one headmaster. He was headmaster, footmaster, he was the lot, and he done all the teaching, and there was an average of a hundred and forty on the roll. And there was some discipline in our school: he kept the whole lot in order, all in one room. The infants would be behind a little partition, but it was the same room.

We had the same teacher all through the school. He knew all about us, and we knew all about him. Old McDyer was not a bad fiddle player, and he was a good singer. At times he could be good fun, but he'd a big long canewood rod, and he'd give you a right good bleaching if you done anything out of the way, and then make you stand with your nose against the wall for about an hour. Yes, and he turned out doctors and politicians and lots of priests — all started their education with old James McDyer.

The parish priest was the boss. The day he'd be coming there of course we'd be all scrubbed and washed and everything, because he would send word that he was coming round on Wednesday or whatever day. He would arrive and have a talk with some of the kids, and the master would be on his best behaviour. Then the schools inspector would call round once in a while to see that the education was going on properly, and I'm telling you that schoolmasters in the old days had it rough. Talk about them being badly paid now: there were farm labourers getting more than the schoolteachers.

Take the like of old James McDyer that taught me, say with an average of a hundred and twenty every day, and the whole lot of us weren't little angels either, if we got away with it: he was working hard from about quarter to ten or ten o'clock, and steady on then to three — we would be let home at three, having so far to go. He was continually on the alert trying to keep this lot in control. And he kept us in control: if there was any fighting or any mischief or such like, he dealt with it. He took the offender out, maybe sometimes out to the porch, and gave him a good drubbing. I don't care what anyone says, the cane will work in schools.

There was so many things used to happen on the way home
from school. Never anything on the way going, because it was
a hard race to get there in time, having so far to go. Tree climb-
ing: that was one thing that we were pretty good at. We could
go up any kind of a tree, even a tree without branches. Put your
arms round it and up we would go, one foot after the other —
bare feet of course.

Coming home in the summer time used to be fun. We would
have a bath in the lake: get out of all our clothes, and have a pud-
dle about, and try to swim. Some of us were up to fourteen years
of age, and the boys would get out of all their clothes, and the
girls never took a blind bit of notice. And the same applied if the
girls were going to have a bathe in the lake. It was just the way
they were brought up. Like a flock of birds. Males and females
did mix a lot better, because they didn't understand the real meaning of sex, or the real meaning of being nasty towards somebody.

There would be cases where some girl would best you with
her schoolbag, or you would pull some girl's hair, or if you were
sitting behind two girls in school (they all had long hair in those
days), you tied their hair together, or tied their hair to the back
of their seat. When they got up there was a row of course, but
if you were a good runner you escaped! Indeed we got into fights
and trouble on the way home from school, but we never talked
about it at home, and we never mentioned it around the school
the following day, because if old McDyer thought that there was
any fighting or caper going on, we would suffer. And he was no
worse than my father and mother would be if I came home with
a black eye and said, 'So-and-so beat me'.

'Well, hard luck lad. You're learning to stand your own, boy,
so take it.'

And if a kid went to his father and told him a sad tale, that
father didn't run to the house where the chap lived that done the
damage and raise hell there. He didn't bother his head.

'Boys will be boys', that's what most of them would say. 'Let
them fight it out, they're learning to grow up.'

I think because the children were let go to do whatever they
liked, it did leave youngsters that they grew up more enlightened
in how to get along with people. How to avoid getting into trouble, and how to handle yourself if you did. If you couldn't fight
you ran, and if you couldn't run you stood your ground and you
done your best. Get out of it one way or the other!

People in the area always took an interest in the schools. Like, if the school wanted some repairs, well you couldn't just be waiting for a tradesman to come and do it: so some handyman — and nearly every man in our area was a handyman because he had to be — would go and do a little job, repair the school door or something. Oh yes, living was a kind of a combined effort. And it was an effort really. But they all survived.

Going to school wasn't compulsory when I first started and by the time I left it was. The kids would leave school at every age until the compulsory education came into being; then they had to stay to fourteen. Now my father never went to school in his life — not one day, because as soon as he was seven or eight he was away working with farmers. He was working horses and digging with spades and mowing hay with scythes when he was about twelve or thirteen years, and it never done him a bit of harm. He'd no read or write or anything. If you showed him his own name he wouldn't know what it was. But he knew all about living. He had a gift: he could buy and sell anything. We used to have great fun with him, when me brother or me would come home from a fair, in later years when he stopped going (fairs were what we used to call the old-style cattle, sheep and horse markets back home). He'd ask,

'Did you see so-and-so at the fair?' (naming some of his old friends).

'Aye, did. He was sellin' sheep.'

'Oh aye, what kind of sheep were they?'

'Yows.'

'How many had he?'

Well, we used to give him an awkward number, say seven or thirteen, and we sometimes deliberately used to give him the wrong price, say three pounds seventeen and sixpence each, or something like that. And he would tell us how much that was. He could reckon up. All he had to do was just think.

He could look at a stack of turf, away off the road, he wouldn't even have to leave the road, he'd be looking into somebody's moorland, and he'd see that stack of turf, and he would say,

'Hmm, there's twenty horse-loads in that.'

And that's what would be in it. He couldn't read or write, but he could learn songs as quick as you would sing them, and tunes. He never played an instrument, but he could lilt. He was a jigger. He heard a tune about twice and he had it picked up. Had it right, too.

Now one thing my father could read, and that was a clock. Although he was also pretty good at judging the time by the sun. When I first went to school there was no clock in our house, and my brothers and sisters went to school nearly all their school days without a timepiece in the house. Our house faced the east, and in the morning my father could go very near the time by judging a spot on the floor where the sun shone through the window, where one bar of the window would be making a shadow on the floor — and then working according to the time of year it was. The only snag was, if it was a wet day or a gloomy day, he was cropped!

And no end of people, when they would be out cutting the turf, one would say to the other,

'I'm getting hungry, is it coming near dinner time do you think?'

And they would stick the spade perpendicular into the ground and use it as a sundial, stand back and say,

'It must be; it's half-twelve anyway.'

And they would be right. But I remember in our house the first clock we ever owned, of any kind. I would be seven or eight, I suppose. It cost five shillings, and we called them pandy clocks, because they were just the shape of a porringer, of a pandy, with two bells on the top and a little hammer between the bells. My parents could read the time, because if they were going in to Donegal or Mountcharles or anywhere, they would take good stock of the Inver church clock. There was a clock on that spire for long years before I was born. Many of the people might not be fit to write their own name, but they knew the time on the clock, and if you put any amount of figures with a £ sign before it, they'd tell you what that was! You wouldn't fool them anyway as far as figures, money and weight was concerned.

Do you know they used to sell hay and potatoes, oats and turf, and they never used scales? They never used any weighing machine. Oh no, it was guessed. And if you put it on a weighing machine after, it was dead on. And they could judge, by lifting an armful of hay, what weight it was. They could lift exactly fourteen pounds weight, they called that a 'stone', in their arms, and eight of them was put on a side and that was a hundredweight of hay. There was no argument at all about it.

They used to make their own potato baskets — 'creels', we called them, fashioned on the shape of donkey creels, only that these were made of fine willow rods. And they could make them the exact size, water-level on top, to hold one hundredweight of potatoes, without any measurement, without any rule, without anything. They drove the standards in the ground, and they worked and worked this lattice of these willow rods round and round, and put holes that you could grip on the sides, and when that creel was finished and filled with potatoes and then the potatoes were put on the scale: there was one hundredweight of potatoes. They didn't even have to think about this, they had a mental picture of the finished article before they started, and the hands done exactly what the brain told them. But if you gave them a ruler and said, 'I want that made now forty-two inches by twenty-nine', or something, they couldn't do it.

Some in my father's generation did go to school, but a lot of them didn't, because they just couldn't afford to go to school. As soon as they were fit to do anything at all they were away looking after cattle for richer people and so on like that. My father's people were not very poor, but they were the 'underclass', they were the people who did all the work for the people who could afford to pay.

At school we learned the basics — reading, writing, spelling, counting, geometry, and catechism. We didn't really have a lot of good education like geography or shorthand or grammar — we never left school good enough to just walk into a good position in offices or anything like that. Which I suppose wasn't a bad thing. I don't regret being a worker; no way. At least I did learn the art of survival, which I'm afraid is really behind the door nowaday. We could survive on any damn thing when we left school.

Some children would go on from school to college — only a few, mind ye. Maybe their parents were fairly well off — mostly the well-off people got the top of what was going. Now amongst the children, and amongst the grown-ups, there was no such thing as class. You didn't look on somebody as, 'Oh, he's a step above me.' You looked at somebody and you thought, 'Well, we're equal. I'm as good as him.' And he thought, 'Oh, that fellow's as good as me.' But in spite of that, we were always the working lot, and we were never rich enough to get pushed ahead. But from our school alone there would be dozens of men and women who got into really good jobs. A lot of priests, a lot of schoolteachers, and quite a few doctors, and there were even politicians, and ministers of state and all this, came out of our school.

Our area was an English-speaking area, but everybody in the area could understand and speak Irish in my day. There are ones there today that don't. Me father and mother both could talk Irish, but English was the language that was spoken at home. The only time my parents fell into Irish was if they were talking about something that they didn't want us to pick up, because they knew that we didn't have anything near the kind of Irish that they had. My mother could work around it, when she'd be telling something to me father, and make it so obscure that we wouldn't understand it, and we learned Irish at school! I could talk, rhyme off, in Irish, but it's a long time since I did. If I got time enough to think first, I could still chat somebody in Gaelic, but it would take me a very long time.

There was lots of Irish spoken, but as far as we younger ones were concerned, English was our language. If somebody ever said, 'Oh, why don't you talk Irish?', well we could; but we didn't do it if we got away with it, because I think we understood that eventually there was only the one thing for us — emigration. We knew that even when we were at school, because so many of our brothers and sisters had to emigrate, so naturally we knew when we grew up that we would be treated the same. Therefore we kind of concentrated on the English, because we had enough sense to know that without the English we were nowhere.

Irish is a lovely language, and I'm very fond of it. But to be quite honest, learning the Irish in school could be a curse other than an advantage. It left a lot of children that they had neither English nor Irish, because they were trying to cram too much into their heads at the same time. They say you cannot serve two masters; well, you cannot serve two educations either. You have to have one prominent one, and in the *Gaeltacht*, the compulsory Irish areas, the children there had to learn Gaelic along with the English. We did too, but not to the extent that the children in the *Gaeltacht* had to deal with it, and (I know it's not a very patriotic gesture to think this) in those days it was a waste of time, simply because when they left school there was only one thing for them, and that was emigration. They had either to go to Americay, or go to England or Scotland, where there was no Gaelic-speaking, and they weren't educated enough in English to get any kind of a reasonable job, so they were given all the mucky jobs.

I remember after the war I was working in King's Lynn, up in Norfolk, and the time of year came to open the sugar factory. We were working in the factory, putting in floors and doing up the pipes and all that to get ready for the opening. They were recruiting men in Ireland, in Connemara in fact, to go over to King's Lynn to work in the sugar factory. So, me being Irish and what they thought was a good Irish speaker, I was sent over to Dublin to meet them. This was right after the war, when things were really booming in England and people thought, oh, the war's over and everything's going great.

I didn't of course understand a lot of the Gaelic the lads were speaking that I met in Dublin, because the West Country language is entirely different to ours, and when they arrived over in King's Lynn, fine, strong, clever men, the kind of jobs they got was wheeling the leaves of the beet out of the factory, and working in what we called the stone catcher, having to wear waders up to their waist, and all that, because their English wasn't good enough. I was put on the carbonating tanks, and had to keep account of all the juice: every tank I put through had to be accounted for, and the amount of lime and all, and make it up at the end and so on. These lads would say to me,

'How did you get in there?'

Because I could count in English and I could talk in English and I could think in English. There was no point in writing anything for them in English because they couldn't understand it. Really nice fellows, and their lives spoiled because they didn't have enough English.

6

FAMILY

As far as I know, away back in the old penal days, the Byrnes who were my ancestors came over to Ireland from Scotland. They came from Kinlochleven, which is way above Glencoe; if you were going from Glasgow to Fort William, you would pass through Kinlochleven. They came over, and quite a few of them settled down on the east coast, down around Wicklow, and Waterford, and today around there and in Dublin you'll find thousands of Byrne families; some, but only a few, of them went to the west of Ireland, round Mayo and I think Galway.

My immediate relations (going back many generations) carried on to a place called Glencolumbkille, way in at the point of Donegal, and settled down there. There were quite a few blacksmiths amongst them, and to this very day, in the town of Ardara, the blacksmith is a Byrne, a very distant relation of mine, and that's maybe twelve generations since the Byrne blacksmiths lived in Glencolumbkille. Some of the Byrnes of course emigrated, and there are a lot of policemen in New York called Byrne! Why they all settled in New York I don't know, but a lot of them became policemen.

My mother's family, they were Donegal bred and born. Gallagher and O'Donnell are very prominent names in Donegal. They were small sheep and cattle farmers from away back Lord knows when. And they're still very much in evidence today. In 1985 I went home for a visit with a few young musician friends of mine, and we were doing a little concert at the Abbey Hotel in Donegal. It's a rather posh place, and the audience seemed to be a bit subdued, a bit too well behaved, so Ralph Jordan, for the sake of breaking the monotony, said to them:

'Packie tells me he has quite a few cousins and relations around here. Are any of them here tonight?'

And just like a forest, hands went up. There was one side farthest away from the stage, and the whole line along the wall were all relations of mine. They would be chiefly Gallaghers and Gallagher relations — though there might be some Byrnes and McGinleys too. It wouldn't be a very safe place for anybody to start taking the mickey out of me, because they are nearly all big hefty men. I am six feet tall, and I used to be a good bit heavier than I am now, but I was only a weakling beside some of them.

The Byrnes were very strong too. My father was really a strong man in his day. I suppose too strong, and that's why he got into bad health. He wasn't afraid of getting wet, or sweating and working hard; he worked from clear to dark, summer and winter.

My father never followed up any trade other than land. He could build a bit of a wall all right, but he wasn't a builder or a carpenter or anything like that. He was a very good man on the land — manual labour, that's real hard work with a spade or a scythe. He used to work for other people too — going back before I was born. He used to hire himself to other farmers to work on their land — mowing hay and cutting turf and planting potatoes with spades.

He didn't have to go to hiring fairs to get work because people around knew that he was a good worker, and they would hire him. I think that the average wage in those days was a shilling per day. And that was a day, from clear to dark: it wasn't leave off at five in the afternoon — they worked till ten at night in the summertime. For a shilling.

He would do the work on his own land when he could, like when he came home in the evening. And if there was some time that the people that hired him didn't have a lot to do, he would rush home and do a bit on his own land. If he was kept late, he would very often work on his own land by the light of the moon. So it's no wonder that he got into bad health. Maybe at nine o'clock in the morning it would be a downpour of rain. He would get wet. Them clothes would be on till one or two o'clock the following morning, where either the moon would set or he would get so tired he wasn't fit to carry on. And by that time the clothes were dry again.

He also worked on the railway for a time, when they were making the line from Donegal into Killybegs. He would be labouring — levelling mounds, and laying down the road first before the rails were going on. The railway never passed Killybegs, that was the terminus. They had a big turntable — drive the engine in and that spun it around, and hook it to the other end of the train and away back. I think there was only two trains belonging to our line — 'twas a narrow gauge. So for that my father would have to walk into Killybegs every day. They didn't go around the road, they went as the crow flies, because they knew every inch of the moors and the fields, and I suppose as the crow flies it would be seven miles.

Besides being hired and working on the railway, me father also went over to Scotland to work. That would be wintertime — he wouldn't go in the summer, because he had to be about home to work on his own land a few hours at a time. I don't know how often he went, it was before my time, but he must have gone several times. He used to tell good stories about being in Scotland. He worked in Fort William, and he worked in Ardrossen, which is down in the Glasgow area, and he worked on the Clyde for a while, when they were building shipping piers, wheeling concrete at the port. He worked for a farmer in Scotland for a term, but that was down in Lanarkshire, I think, in East Kilbride. He was only one of the dozens and dozens that used to go.

When the children arrived, my father had to take a lot more out of the little bit of land that he had, because there were a few extra mouths to feed, and he had to plant more potatoes, and more corn and cabbages. So the going to Scotland and being hired out had to stop; that ended before I was born.

My father's and mother's family lived about five miles apart. My father and mother probably got together through what they called rambling. My father and his cronies would be going around; everywhere he heard of a dance or a ceili or a music session, he was there, and probably my mother was there singing or something, and that's how they met. They knew each other and each other's people, of course. The Gallaghers were sheep owners and small landowners, just the same as my father was.

My father was a marvellous character. He was well liked because he would oblige anyone. He never set out to be a popular man, but he was very genuine. He would give a little bit of a song, and would talk nice to everyone, and he could settle arguments, and was a bit of a matchmaker, which made him as popular as any of the small farmers around our own area.

He made it a kind of a law that you treated everyone the same. In his eyes there was no such thing as one better than another, and there was no such thing as religious differences or political differences. It didn't mean a thing who anybody was, they were equal to the person he met five minutes before that. Nearly everyone in the area was like that, mind you. It was so remarkable in big fairs, like at Dunkineely, which was our market town. Cattle dealers would come in from Fermanagh, Tyrone, Derry, all over the North, to buy cattle, and they wouldn't be sucked up to. No-one would give them special treatment or do this or that for them because he thought, oh if I do something for this dealer maybe he'll buy a couple of cattle from me. No, damn that for a caper, they would think! If he came round and asked ye to sell the cattle, sure; and you wrangled the last sixpence out of him. Which of course is the proper way to live — there's too much creeping going on nowadays.

Yes, me father and most of the people in our area had pretty strict ideas about things like that. Another thing they didn't believe in was credit. Of course, you could go to a shop where you were a regular customer, and if you wanted a bag of flour and you didn't have the money for it, that was all right, because something happened that you had the money to pay for it the next time you came in: probably you would sell a basket full of eggs or butter, or sheep or cattle. So you could get a leniency like that, but you would never buy anything on HP. There were chaps used to come around selling things, and a woman from over the hill bought a clock, and it was really a lovely clock. She didn't have the money, so she had to sign a document saying she would be willing to pay so much a month. So the news came round that she had bought the clock, and my father, being a bit nosy, wanted to see it, so he went to visit her. He came home, and he told us,

'Ah, it's a smashing clock, no doubt about it. I wish I could afford one like it!'

Well, this woman must have told my mother that she got it on the never-never, because she said to him,

'You could afford it the way she got it.'

So the next time that woman came to our house my father told her what to do with the clock:

'Leave the bloody thing back with the bloke that you got it from! I wouldn't have it in the house if I were you, 'cause you'll be paying the longest day you live.'

You'd think she had signed away a thousand pounds, the way he talked, but maybe the clock had cost fifteen shillings or something like that. But that was too much for him. If you hadn't a clock, other than get it on HP you could always go up and look at the sun and guess the time.

But my father never really got excited about anything. If something wasn't done today, it would be done tomorrow. It was so noticeable in the harvest time, when the hay and the corn would be for saving. It would probably start off a wet morning. Even

me mother shouldn't be as interested in hay and corn as she would
be in the housework, she would be a bit excited about this, that
that hay won't be got gathered up today. His story was, 'Hmm,
it's pouring. But if it clears up in the afternoon we might get that
field done!' He had that kind of a way of getting along that things
like that didn't sink in with him — he didn't like getting excited
about things that don't happen.

He also had this way with him that, it didn't matter what trouble we got into, he could talk the other person out of doing us
any damage — including me mother! Because she was really strict
and a believer in discipline. She was a tiny little woman but she
could deliver a hefty wallop. I remember that well, being on the
receiving end pretty frequently.

I was always closer to my father than my mother in a way,
because I was always more like him. She was very efficient: she
had her thumb on everything. We didn't really contradict her. She
wasn't the kind of woman you could argue with, because she was
usually right. It's harder to get along with people that are right
all the time. I like people to be right occasionally, like I am, but
I like people to be as wrong as me once in a while, and that's saying something! My father wasn't right all the time. There was room
for improvement in his mind at all times. Like if he was telling
you about somebody that died long long years ago, if there was
a bit that he didn't remember exactly, just off the top of his head
he made up the bit and the story carried on just the same. And
very often it would be more interesting than if it was the truth.

Now I have a bit of that tendency in me, I have to admit! But
I'm also like my father because I don't like to get worried if things
don't happen. If someone is coming round to see me and they
don't turn up, well, probably something happened that they
couldn't come. But if my mother was expecting a visitor, of course
she would have the little house shining because there was strangers
coming. And she would be out, staring along the road to see if
they were arriving. I remember her standing outside the house
looking. You could see over two mile of the road from our house
right along the side of the hill.

But my mother was a good woman and we admired her. She
looked after the money and everything to do with the house, because my father couldn't be bothered with handling money. My
mother took charge of everything in the line of shopping — excepting buying and selling cattle; my father was the boss in that.
But when he came home from a fair, he just emptied his pockets

on the table. She put everything away in a quiet place. She had her own little places for hiding things that we couldn't get at, like spare tobaccay. We had travelling shops coming around — people with horses and carts came around with groceries and sold them at the doors, and she'd probably buy an extra ounce or two of tobaccay. We sometimes found that, because we were all chewing tobaccay like good ones when we were nine or ten years of age, but she succeeded sometimes in finding a place that we couldn't discover! When my father ran out of tobaccay, instead of sending somebody away to the shop, she would produce this tobaccay, from nowhere, we thought.

My mother also had the gift of making a meal. A visitor once said that she could make a dinner out of a doormat. It was a slight exaggeration of course, but she was a good cook all right.

I owe my mother a lot. She brought me up. . .not right, because that would be impossible! but she brought me up in a way that all my life I've been fit to look after myself. If there was something to be done, I was told to do it, and I did do it, because quite honestly I was too much afraid to not do it. And by being afraid to not do it, I was getting the education of seeing how it was done first hand.

Say when I was a young lad, and me mother would notice that a button was about to drop off my trousers or coat or whatever it might be, she would say,

'Come on! Get a needle and thread and put that button back on again.'

So I would be making some excuse, but she would have none of that. She always used to say,

'It could happen that you'll have to do it some day anyway, so you may as well start now.'

Well, my father was different. He was easy-going. If he told me to do something and I didn't do it right away, he would say,

'Ah, well, it'll be time enough, you'll probably get at it tomorrow.'

But we were very fond of my mother. She was a good woman, and a hard worker. She was a great little character, and as tiny as could be. She knew her way about, like, she was no fool. And she was cheerful; she never stopped laughing. And her sister Anne was the same. Anne used to come to visit us, and they were as like one another as two eggs. Anne was a little bit bigger than my mother, and a bit more sturdy built, but I suppose just as thin. When them two got together, you would hear them laughing if you were down at the river from our house, and that was a good few hundred yards.

I don't know how many brothers and sisters my mother had. Anne married a man named O'Donnell, and they brought up I think nine kids. And their brother Patrick had twelve kids; there was ten men, and about eight of them were full grown at the same time. Then they started going away to America, one of them died, and a couple came here to England, and got married and scattered about. 'Twould be pretty hard to gather them up now.

In spite of the fact that my mother used to chide us once in a while, we were never really afraid of her, and we were never afraid of my father. She was strict about some things, like smoking. I could smoke in the house about the time I left school, but at about the age of nine or ten she used to be a wee bit crabby about it. Very often my father would be sitting in front of the fire, filling the pipe and cutting the tobaccay, and of course I would be somewhere very near. He would be keeping his eye on her, and he'd cut off a bit of tobaccay and slip it to me, and he would never miss a movement of his arm — his arm would move same as he was cutting the tobaccay and slip this bit to me, and I would roll it up in paper and sometime we would both be out, I would get a match from him. He would light the pipe and I would light the fag made out of newspaper.

The funny thing about it is, that being so opposite in everything (even in education, because she was a very good reader and writer and he could do neither), my mother and father could get along perfectly. It was the best thing ever happened that they were so opposite, because if they were both very easy-going, we would be useless. I would be a useless man today, because I wouldn't be fit to look after myself or to get along in the world. They sort of complemented each other.

The Gallaghers were all pretty bright, they had a lot more education — reading, writing, counting — than my father's people. But my father's people were more enlightened and more bright in the ways of the world. Nobody ever won an argument with my father, because he worked around it some way like a solicitor would do, or a detective if he was questioning you. He worked around it some way that you tripped yourself up in the end, so he had the last laugh.

My younger sister Memie grew up a bit like my mother in that respect. She likes things done. Anna was a bit different, she was a bit more like me. She could take life a bit easy. But she died very young, of tuberculosis. It was 1944, when she was thirty-two. She left five kids behind her, but the little baby died too. Anna's husband was a man the name of Patrick Keeney, and he was a very good fiddle player, one of the principal fiddle players at country-house dances in the area. And strangely enough, Memie married a man of exactly the same name, and he was a very good weaver. They went to live in the parish of Ardara, where Memie lives still, in the same house.

My brother Jim was an entirely different character to me, and he was different to anyone in the family. Because he had his head screwed on. In spite of the fact that my father was bright enough in reckoning up money and planning for the future, he still wasn't as bright as Jim. Jim never had to write down anything. If the time of year came when heifers or cows would be served by the bull, everyone would write that down in case they'd forget it, but he could remember the date. And he could remember the age of every animal in our whole area, the neighbour's animals and all, and if he done something like thatching a house, he could tell you the date and the day of the week it was when he thatched that house. He wasn't as interested in music and singing as I was, but for being wide awake in the line of making a living and working and all that, he was pretty keen.

He never married. He might have married, if he had a' lived, because he had a girlfriend, but bad health put an end to that. He died of a heart attack at the age of fifty-three, in 1964. We were working together at the time.

Now I mentioned just now that my father was a bit of a match-maker. He wasn't a professional matchmaker, but he took a delight in that kind of thing, and he wasn't the only one: there was several around our area. And I'll tell you what, some of them had pretty successful ventures too, into the matrimonial area. They didn't really want themselves known as matchmakers, because they would then probably be asked to do something. It was a bit of a hobby! They were let go and do it on their own, and they got a great kick out of this, and if they saw then that a marriage result-ed, well that was the greatest thing in the world.

It would very likely be older people who didn't trouble get-ting married in their younger days or when they should, and then the years wore on and they found that they were either living alone or they weren't very happy with the brother or sister or whoever it was, and they would decide they would get married. My father would have a very quiet chat with this bloke, probably maybe in his own house, and there would be a drop of whiskey on the job. Then, somebody always knew where there was a fitting woman for this man. And one night, the bottle of whiskey would be corked and put in the pocket, and away over the mountains or wherever this girl lived. My father would probably go first on his own, with one or two of the neighbour men that were in on the deal too, and sort of break the ice about this chap that wanted a woman. Fair enough, he would be invited along, and in lots of cases it worked.

There were also, mind ye, matching fairs. There was hiring fairs, and there were matching fairs too, where likely bachelors would go. There were a lot of marriages resulted from the harvest fair in Glenties, and now they're starting it up again. But I remember it going very strong. The ballad sellers and the matchmakers would be there.

The matchmaking was a great thing really. They'll say that people couldn't be happy unless they know each other for a very long time. That's rubbish, because no-one ever heard of two separating that was put together like that, through matchmaking. They were happy as could be. They both knew what they wanted, and along with that they were suited to each other. You only married within your own circle. If you were a small farmer, you went out of your way to marry a small farmer's daughter, to be kind of on the same level. If a doctor's son wanted to get married, he'd try to get in on the level of marrying a doctor's daughter, or a politician's daughter, or something like that. There was no reason then for disagreement, because one was equal to the other. Of course divorce, it isn't yet heard of, but in those days people didn't know the meaning of the word.

In a crofting area where there's not much money or land to spare, getting married and finding a place to live could be a problem, but there were several ways of overcoming it. One was emigration — you could marry then as you fancied. Or if you made up your mind to stay at home, and your brothers and sisters made up their minds to get out of the area, well then you married, because you had a ready-made home, probably a farm. In the old days, back before my time, a farm would sometimes be divided up between two sons, like I was telling you happened between my grandfather and Big Pat. That didn't happen so much in my time, but there was another method, called cottering.

Very often, two or three farms running 'longside' would be bought up by one reasonably well-to-do farmer, and there would be a house on each of these little smallholdings. Of course, then, he would want some men to work on his land. Some young bloke got married in the area and didn't have enough work to do on his brother's farm or his father's farm, so he went to live in this spare house and worked for that farmer. He was a cotter. In most cases, he could stay there for the rest of his life, even when he would retire. The father would probably be dead, and his sons couldn't care less what happened to the houses or the land or anything. They were into the motor-car age and probably emigration — fed up of the weather at home.

It was also not unusual for two brothers to get married and bring their wives in to live with the father and the mother. Which meant that at the very least there would be three men and three women in one house. And lots of children! Because that was the follow-up of getting married — sometimes more than a dozen of them. They weren't big houses, but people knew how to live with each other, because there was no alternative. You could put as high as five kids in a double bed, so that was one way of overcoming bedroom space — pile them in there!

When I was young, people didn't really consider that a young married couple needed to be on their own. The father and mother of the person that was moving into another family would accept that it was a normal thing to do, especially if it applied to a female. In most cases, with the exceptions of a very few, when the daughter-in-law moved in, the old lady thought, right, I've had my day and I've done my best, and now it's up to you: you carry on. Again, they had to be like that, because if they weren't it's possible the daughter-in-law would pack her case and get out of it. Which meant that the old lady was on her own, and probably she was getting a bit old and a bit past doing the hard work that is required to keep a smallholding together. The cows had to be milked and fed, and a lot of the women worked on the land at the hay and the corn and gathering the potatoes. The old woman would probably think it over for a long time, and finally she would think, oh well, I know I'm not going to live for ever and this is a young, strong woman; I moved in forty or fifty years ago and the same as she was, so let her now do the same as I had to do. Give her the reins and let her get on with it.

But there were exceptions — I've heard of one or two — where the old woman had still tried to rule the roost. People say that two queen bees are too many in one hive and that's true. It would finish up not so nice. The old people who were causing the trouble would be left on their own, and would live there until the neighbours found the last of them dead in the house. They would discover that they couldn't go on no longer and they'd just go to bed and die.

But those were rare cases. The marrying and moving in was the principal means of really keeping up the population: because a woman that moved in could have say, seven, eight kids. Instead of if she moved in to her own house, and having to look after, on her own, three or four kids, she would say, 'Full stop, that's it, I'm not having any more.' But because grandma was there and she looked after the kids, she could have a baby every year. It didn't turn a hair on her; she was getting on with her work, but she never had to bother all that much about the kids. The old folks were useful for looking after the kids and keeping them out of mischief.

7

WEDDINGS, WAKES,
AND ALL THIS CAPER

Weddings were good fun in the old days. They're still, mind ye, big things; but what they do now, they book a hotel rump and stump — that hotel is the property of the wedding party for the one day, two days, three days, whatever it might be. Big hotels like The Abbey in Donegal, and The Highlands in Glenties. Everyone connected with the bride's people or the groom's people all agree on this hotel, and they all have their heads together about the band that they will book, and the variety acts and all. It's really like one big concert or festival now, whereas in the old days the weddings were all held in the bride's home. And that's where the fun used to be.

I often heard my dad say when he was married there was something like twenty-two horse-drawn vehicles that picked up the people here and there and brought them all back home. It was always a chase from the church to the bride's home — who had the best horse. Them horses got some abuse: have to gallop with about six or seven people on a flat-bed van, or a jaunting car or a trap. Then the horses would be tied to trees for the whole night while the dancing and singing was going on. There would be a blanket thrown over them, because there would be a rake of smoke going out of them with the drive that they had from the church.

The first away from the church had a good chance, because the roads were pretty narrow, and if you were first you could keep all the others back, because the jaunting cars are wider than ordinary horse-drawn carts, so all you had to do was sort of zigzag your horse, and no-one could get past you. The first at the bride's house always got a big glass of whiskey — well, full of a cup or something of whiskey. They used to fake it really: somebody with a slow horse would try and get away from the church first and hold back the lot! And all of them dying for a drink of whiskey.

It was all paid for by the bride's family, of course. Mind you, the entertainment would be free. I used to be invited to weddings, to sing and act the eejit, and on more than one occasion I was the chief barman. My mother and father were very often invited to sing too. We'd sing all night, and probably part of all day, and we'd never, never get paid, oh no. Get plenty to eat and plenty to drink. I wasn't drinking at the time but my mother liked a little tot of whiskey, not a lot, but me father could drink a bit too, so they were quite happy to go. I was quite happy to be with them, and my sisters used to go too. My brother Jim never really was into that, and he was a marvellous singer, and about the best whistler I ever heard in my life. He could whistle like birds or anything. But he was always too interested in cattle and horses and land. He was a very thrifty little man. He went out to dances and all that, but if he went to a wedding he would be home again about three o'clock in the morning (which is unheard of) because he'd have to be on the move in the morning looking after cattle.

Weddings used to carry on for sometimes two or three, maybe four days. I was at a wedding myself, and it started about four o'clock in the afternoon of the day of the wedding, and it finished up sometime in the small hours of the third day after. People would stay up and dance, oh crikey yes; dance and drink. It was a known fact that some of them would go home and sleep for about two hours and get up and come back again. And drink more. Whilst there was whiskey or poteen or Guinness going, they wouldn't leave. When all was eaten up and all was drank they'd leave.

Now as well as all the dancing and drinking and merrymaking, people would very often play little tricks at weddings. All doors in our area open in, that was in case of a big fall of snow. Well, sometimes the door might be tied on the outside; a lot of the houses had only one door, and the people that were in there would have to stay in for a few hours maybe. Little funny things like that.

Sometimes the caper that was done, people today wouldn't think it was so amusing. In our area there were little red ants that sting like hell, almost as bad as a bee sting. There was one couple got married quite a distance away from us. The bride's house was a strange shape, because instead of the rooms being one after the other like they are in all the old houses back home, this house was in two parts, with two sloping roofs instead of one. The bed that was made up for the bride and groom was in the back one of these two rooms, so some clever so-and-so got the full of a cocoa box of these little red ants and put them in the bed. The news was spread about, and it was decided that people would leave early — say about two or three o'clock in the morning. Naturally the newly-weds were anxious to go to bed, so they did, and they got into this mess of these stinging ants, and it nearly drove them out of their minds.

Oh yes, people thought that kind of thing was funny. But there were only a few in any area that would do the like of that. There were always a few — we used to call them 'blackguards' — that were up to all the trickery that was going, and if anything out of the way was done, they would be suspected. It was like the police following up somebody with a bad name, if you get the name of a crook in the eyes of the police: so if you got the name of being a blackguard back home in the old days, you were branded that way and you had no way out of it. So you might as well carry on your good name! The people who had the tricks played on them wouldn't like it, but they accepted it. Today it wouldn't be accepted, it would be open war, but in those days things like that were accepted.

The funerals were a bit more solemn than the weddings, and at least one representative from each family for miles and miles around went to a funeral. Everyone in the townland stopped work for the two days of the wake while the remains was in the house at home, no-one worked. Even in the middle of summer when the hay had to be saved and all, you didn't work if one of your neighbours had just died. The relations of the deceased never had to bother their heads about anything: the neighbour men would go away to the churchyard, they'd dig the grave — there was no undertakers of course — and somebody would be appointed with his horse and van or sidecar or whatever it might be, to take the remains, and the neighbours would all walk after that right to the graveyard.

At some wakes, there used to be a bit of fun too, you know, oh yes, playing games and doing tricks and all this caper. I remember one place where this old woman died, she lived alone, and we all went there and stayed up all night — like that was a rule that someone stayed there day and night, the room where the remains were was never empty. There was always someone there, and one stayed until another came in and so on and sometimes the place would be packed. But this particular wake anyway there was no-one to feel sorry because she didn't have any close relations. But she had two lovely fiddles. There was this fellow called Peter McGrath and myself got the two fiddles going, played the fiddles at the wake. Well, it didn't do any harm really. Some of the older people around raised a few eyebrows when they heard of it, but 'twas fun while it lasted.

Another thing at wakes too was going out amongst the neighbours, unknowing to the neighbours like, and pinching one of their chickens or a duck or maybe a goose, and have a big pot of soup about three or four o'clock in the morning. Two or three lads would go out with flashlamps and blind a chicken and grab it and take it back. The womenfolk or the young girls would have the pot nicely washed and the water bubbling; pluck the chicken and dump him in, have a nice wallop of soup! Yes, we used to do that regular.

But I think the best time of the year was what we called the putting in of the hay, that was drawing in the hay. Now they didn't have haysheds or no buildings to store the hay in: the hay was built in big long stacks and then thatched over like the roof of a house, and roped down. We used to have some fun building haystacks.

I remember one haystack we were building, oh indeed my father was there and he was one of the ringleaders; this man that owned this hay, he had a beautiful ladder, brand-new, 'twas about 25 or 30 feet long. The ladders would be all gathered from the neighbourhood so as that four or five men could be thatching at the same time, because the stack was drawn in, built, thatched, roped, finished, all in one day. So when it came to the evening time to do the thatching, this man's ladder was lost; no-one knew where it was. Well a few did but they weren't going to tell, including me and my father. The man was really worried, he could not figure out where his ladder was, and he told everywhere that his ladder was stolen. He told the guards that his ladder was stolen, and they were out looking for the ladder, out on bicycles and questioning likely subjects and all.

But when it came to using the hay, around October when this man started taking the hay out of this big stack he came on his ladder. The ladder was built in the stack of hay! And the hay was beaten down, tramped down in between the rungs of the ladder, so he couldn't get it out. He used and used away at the hay and naturally the stack was getting shorter, and there was the ladder sticking out, and it was there the whole winter, till the month of March, till he had the last dash off the haystack and he could lift out the ladder, and by that time it got so much abused from rain and snow and all, it was almost rotten!

Until the day he died he was never told who was responsible for that. Three or four of us done that while the rest were in the house and having a meal. The rooms were small and the tables were small, so very often they would eat in two lots. So we said, oh, we'll stay, go on, you fellows were earlier than us. And he was so proud and careful of that ladder. He wouldn't leave it in the sun because it would warp, he wouldn't leave it out in the rain because the timber would get soggy, and in spite of that it was out the whole winter.

There was another case: this bloke, he was the first in our area to wear Wellington boots, which we just called rubber boots. Wellington boots weren't really the fashion in the old days — the men all wore hobnailed boots, and what they called *searacháns* (that was pieces of hay rope or little leather straps tied around the trousers below the knee to save the wear on the knees of the trousers, and to lift the bottoms out of the muck and the dew, and to keep you from tripping over the trousers while you were working or carrying something). So, this fellow got a pair of Wellington boots and everyone was admiring them and they were so useful: you could walk through wet meadowland, you could walk through swamps, oh they were the greatest thing. He was a very good haystack builder, this bloke, but he always built in the stockinged feet. Wading through soft hay all day with Wellington boots is a bit tiresome, so he took them off and put them away behind a clump of trees or little bushes that was growing near the haystack. I wasn't in on this deal, but I think my father was. When it came towards late afternoon and the stack was finished, your man came down; having the stack finished he was admiring his work. He went over to the clump but there were no Wellingtons. The Wellingtons were built in the haystack.

Now if they were built anywhere near the working end of the haystack, he could have them earlier in the year, but they were put right at what we called the stern, which was the far end that would not be touched because that was facing the storm — like there was a method in all this: in our area all the storm comes from the west and the south-west, so if you're building a haystack you put this stern end, very well built and raked and padded down and very well thatched, towards the storm, so that the hay wouldn't get damaged, and you worked out of what we called

the sheltry end, the mouth, and worked backwards. So he had
to go the whole long winter without Wellingtons, he was back
to the hobnailed boots again, and oh he was in a right bad way
about that. He didn't get them till maybe the end of March.

Oh, there used to be some funny things done. And they wer-
en't done out of spite — the man who lost the ladder was very
well liked in the area. But nobody took much notice because that
kind of thing was expected. Then there would be a little dance,
a little country-house hooley, at that farmer's house that night,
and all the caper that was done during the day was forgiven. Especially after a few drinks, dances, songs, tunes and stories, all
in the company of pretty young girls.

Christmas wasn't really the big time over there for kids that it is
in this country. Oh, we recognised it all right, it was the birth of
Jesus, but we never had toys you know. I never had a toy in my
life — no such things as guns or cameras or watches. We had our
own sort of toys: pet lambs, and there were calves, and there was
chickens, and everything like that. There would be a good Christmas dinner, I'll say that, and lots of jollifications and a few drinks
and all, but nothing to a great extent — it wouldn't be talked about
for half the year the way it is here. The New Year was quite a big
time, and I think a lot of that came from the continuous movement of people from Scotland to our own area and vice versa.
The Scots people don't reckon all that much to Christmas, but
New Year's a big time with them. The same applied to us when
I was a kid. New Year's Day was a day nobody worked, and everyone went to church, and there were dances everywhere on New
Year's night.

Nobody took a blind bit of notice of birthdays. I knew I was
born on the eighteenth of February, but I always thought of it
about a month or two after it was over! There were no birthday
presents, there was nothing like that. Presents weren't really the
in thing in our area. The kind of presents that you would give
somebody, if it was the time of year when they might be short
of seed, putting potatoes in the ground to grow for the following
year, a present would be a bag of potatoes or something. There
was no such thing as buying clothes or anything like that: that
wasn't heard of. I don't know if the people would accept anything like that, but if it was anything connected with what they
needed to live, they accepted it and they were very grateful. It
wouldn't be a very valuable present you could afford anyway, so

it was much cheaper and more useful to give somebody a creel full of Swede turnips, or basket of heads of cabbage, or bag of potatoes, or hay for their cattle.

8

WE MADE A LIFETIME OF IT: MUSIC, DANCING AND SINGING

The music was a very important part of people's lives in my younger days back home. It was part of growing up for the children, and it was part of passing on for the very old people, and for the in-betweens it was part of their pastime. In fact it was the principal pastime whenever there was no work to be done, especially in the winter evenings, and on Sundays: music, singing and dancing. There was nothing else: we didn't have televisions or radios or anything.

I remember the first wireless ever to come into our area. It belonged to the old schoolmaster, McDyer; one day he took us over to the house to show us this great invention. It was as big as a fridge. McDyer told us that this bloke was in Dublin that was talking. We didn't believe a word of that! Well, eventually I suppose we were convinced, because very often we used to go there late at night and listen to the wireless outside his window. We did that that he wouldn't know we were out late at night. But my father wasn't so easily persuaded. How could somebody talk in Dublin and we could hear it in West Donegal? Even after he heard it he couldn't make up his mind about it for a long time — for quite a few years, in fact, until my brother bought one.

The radio made a sort of a dent in our tradition when ordinary people started buying them. It moved in, and when it did, a lot of the tradition moved out. The younger people didn't bother playing music, they didn't have to learn to play instruments no more, because there it was, all ready-made, and they'd much rather sit listening to somebody playing down in Dublin behind microphones.

But when I was a kid there was no radio. It was all traditional music, and what we called traditional dances — mostly Scottish dances like highlands, and also sets of quadrilles, and there was polkas and mazurkas and all that, and barn dances, what we used to call 'Germans'.

We connected every traditional tune with a fiddle, because we heard them played on a fiddle. Fiddles were the principal instruments in Donegal and Tyrone, and I think Fermanagh too. Probably more than half the houses in our area and in other areas round about, there would be a fiddle hanging on the wall above the hearth. When I was about ten or eleven, flutes and accordions and other instruments came in and the modern dance bands started coming into the areas, and even then any instrument that wasn't playing a traditional tune wasn't worth listening to. We never imagined that one day the other music would become more important.

I don't remember the first instrument I ever played. Whistle, or mouth organ, I suppose. I started both around the same time. My father and mother were singers. Neither of them played. My mother used to play a little bit on a whistle, but we used to laugh at her because she wasn't a good whistle player. My father never played any instrument, but he was a smashing singer — when he was fit to sing, but he suffered from asthma and he very often wasn't fit to sing. But we weren't short of musicians around the area — nearly all fiddle players. There were a few melodeon players and a few fluters but you never bothered listening to them if there was a good fiddle player in the house. If I came home from a gathering, my father would never say, 'What music?' He would say,

'Who played the fiddle?'

I would rather make up a name from somewhere far away than admit that I danced to a flute or a melodeon or something. If my father heard a fiddler play a tune very well he would say,

'He could take music out of a fresh loaf!'

I won't repeat what he used to say if he heard a bad musician.

Very few women played fiddles. It was a strange thing about that — the women reckoned that it would be beneath them to play fiddles with the men. There were funny ideas about music and the men just did not like to have the women playing as good as they did: they were always afraid of a thing like that. Of course, the women came out to parties and hooleys and rambling houses, but some men thought the woman's place was in the home: 'Let her bake a cake of bread instead of playing a tune on the fiddle.' That was very much on their minds.

The women accepted all that. But when it came to singing, of course, the men had to take a back seat. My mother, in fact, when she would start singing, well the men would have to shut up, and the fiddles would go silent; and the same for my grand-aunt, Big Bridget Sweeney, or Biddy Sweeney — she could sing like a thrush. And there was the old lady that brought us all into the world, Mrs Diver, she was a very nice singer, and several of the old women back home.

Them two were getting on in years in my time, and so they didn't drop in to the hooleys and country-house dances and sing there. But they would be invited along to special evenings. Probably the women that were invited would do an afternoon and up to about eight o'clock doing quilting, or blanket hemming, or carding wool and spinning, and then sit around and have plenty tea and a few more songs. I can remember them so well, I can picture their faces. Biddy Sweeney was very tall, and a fine-looking woman. Her hair was combed straight back and tied in a bun. She was very regimental — sat as straight as could be — and she had a beautiful voice. Mrs Diver was also nice-looking, but she wasn't as tall as Biddy Sweeney. She was a very homely-looking lady.

It was really nice when you would get four or five of them together, quilting or something, sewing up and down from top to bottom: they'd probably all be singing in unison. They knew nothing about harmony, but they could make a real good job of the melody, decorations and all. And even the younger girls like my sisters, they were very much into embroidery and doing very intricate patterns on handkerchiefs and things, and you'd get three or four of them sitting around and they'd be singing at the tops of their voices and working away at the embroidery. That sort of came automatically to them, too. They never took their mind off the embroidery — they were still going like hell and making a good job of it but the song kind of came naturally.

They didn't have any particular songs for that — chiefly they were traditional songs, of course. But before my time, as far as I've heard, they had special songs for each job, and the waulking songs for the stretching, pressing and folding of the homespun. And away down in north Donegal they used these waulking songs and working songs, but not so much nowadays. They're probably still used in the north of Scotland, I don't know.

There was another Biddy Sweeney, who lived in the next house to ours, but she was not a near relation of Big Bridget. She was a nice singer, and a smashing good lilter — she used to lilt for dancing. A woman that lived in the next house to that again, she could sing, and her daughters could sing. There was also girls that lived across the river in Meenadreen, the Hegartys: there was four houses in a row of Hegartys, and they were good singers too.

People ask me, how did I learn to play or sing. Well, that's another thing that I don't know. You see, in tradition you don't really learn to sing, you don't learn to play. You pick up the instrument, and you keep at it until you knock a tune out of it. When the songs are all around you — they're sort of 'in the air', as the saying goes — and you hear them sung in different houses on different nights, you have no excuse: they're going to get into your mind anyway. If you have any ear in the world for music, the song will penetrate, and the tune will.

Nowadays back home, people don't know if they can sing or not because they never tried. But in my young days everyone had a go, and some of course failed the test, but the ones that found they could sing, they would make a lifetime of it.

Another singer that I remember, although it's my longest memory, was a man named Jim Doody. Now he could sing, and he had some songs too. He worked for a man called Joe Dorrian, who was also a lovely singer. They were very welcome visitors at any gathering. They lived straight across the river from our house, in the townland of Meenacloy. The Dorrians were all very good singers. I think that Jim Doody was a native of Derry, and he came down our way in his young days, and he stayed there living with this Joe Dorrian and Joe's sister. They were very popular, and I got quite a few songs from them.

Yes, the songs were in the air, and me being very interested in music, I listened very carefully. Like if someone sang a song that I never heard before, I would try to pick that song up by hearing it once. I wouldn't naturally be fit to pick it up, but I would only have to hear it a few times. I would get the follow-on of the story, get the path of the story; then if there were words that I didn't pick up listening to the singer, well I would improvise, put in a few words of my own here and there — which was, although I didn't know it at the time, a very traditional thing, going back centuries. And still is — there are people still doing that, and I do it myself if there's a line that I can't remember, make one up as I go along.

I think there's one advantage that people who cannot read music have: they depend on their memory, and their memory gets a lot sharper. There's a lot to be said for reading and writing music — it's beautiful to be able to write music. But then on the other hand, if you can't read music, it keeps your brain a wee bit more alert, to make yourself remember something.

I picked up a lot of my songs from my mother when I used to card the wool when she was spinning. She sang all the time as she was spinning, one song after another, most of them in time with the rise and fall of the pedal board. Although some of the traditional songs had no timing, no strict rhythm, which I didn't like so much in them days, but I have since discovered that they are the real stories put to music; they can be listened to as someone telling a story, whereas if they were put to a dance tune, that takes from the substance of the story. To this day I would rather listen to someone singing in freestyle.

A lot of the songs that we had came from Scotland. The men from our area who went over to Scotland to work brought back a lot of songs and circulated them in our area at home and we picked them up. Songs would be picked up at fairs, too. When I was at school there was street singers at every fair, taking up their pitches, and performers of every kind, and as well as the ballad singers there would be four or five ballad sellers at the fair: there were a family called McGee who used to come around to the fairs in our part of Donegal.

The ballad sellers were my favourites, because they all used to sing the ballad, and then they would sell it to you — penny sheets. I was very young then; I would be at a fair with my father or with some neighbour, and they gave me a few pennies for doing a turn for them, handling cattle, and I was away to buy these ballad sheets. I would come home with a whole bundle of them. I got a lot of songs from that. My mother used to be waiting for me, to see what songs I would bring home and for me to have a go at them. Well, she knew nearly all of them. I would think I had a capture — two or three of these songs that I never heard; but she could sing them for me, and she had the air. There was only the words written out, because very few people could read and write music. So I had a good chance, because my mother knew the airs to these songs. By the time I was a grown man the ballad sellers had disappeared. They were going up until 1936 or thereabout. I would say they died out then completely.

I would get songs from people me own age too, of course, like Charlie Waters, who was a beautiful singer and a good friend of mine. He had a world of good songs. I remember one time Charlie and me got caught in the snow in my sister Memie's house. It was back in the mountains in a place called Glendoan. Memie was about to have a baby, and so she was away in hospital, and her husband Patrick was away too. Charlie and me went there to keep the place in some kind of shape. The storm started and the snow started — *Glendoan* means 'deep glen' — and we got stuck and had to stay for three days.

We weren't so badly off; there was a cow, so we had milk, and we had potatoes. Mind ye, it took a long time to boil them, because we had to cut green branches off a tree to make a fire — we couldn't get out to the bog to the turf stacks. We didn't go hungry, but the food was pretty meagre. Cocoa and under-cooked potatoes, and they don't go well together! Charlie tried making some bread, but it never cooked properly, and the middle of it was like an iceberg. So, we sat about in the house with our overcoats on and sang songs to pass the time. I learned a good few songs in them three days, and so did Charlie. We were writing down the words with pencils and writing paper.

I don't know when I started dancing. I know I was dancing highlands and polkas and mazurkas and all that long before I went to school. I suppose I would be four or five when I started dancing properly, or maybe more. My brother and sisters were older than me, and they were all very good dancers, so like picking up the songs, the dancing was also in the air. My mother was a great dancer, my father danced too — like the singing, when he was fit to dance. The whole thing sort of came down through the generations, and when something is in the blood, it's not difficult to make a better job of it, whereas if it wasn't there already it takes a long time. First you have to get it installed inside yourself, you have to get it into the blood before you can do any job with it.

I've heard a lot of traditional musicians in my time, and I can always tell the people that were brought up with it and the people that learned it as a chore — to learn this music was something that they set themselves out to do. I'm not saying that the people who picked it up from their parents were always better musicians, but there was something about it that just gave you the idea, oh aye, it's in his hands or in his blood or it's in the head all right. Even to this day if I'm in a folk club or at a festival or somewhere, and someone picks up an instrument to play it, and if it's anything like a flute or a fiddle or a whistle or something that I was brought up with, I'm nearly always right when I say, 'Ah, that came down through the generations!'

It's just there's a feeling about it. And there's a lot of that feeling in Ireland, especially around the Dublin area, and the West Country, they used to call it the 'nyah' — there was this kind of a little twist in the voice, and in the way the words were put to the notes of the tune, and the decorations, which is very natural when you're born into that kind of music, or when you pick it up when you're very young; whereas very often that does not exist in the people who learn to sing or play when they're full grown. They do decorations and they do twiddlies, but funny enough you can tell if it grew in the hands or if it was brought in artificially.

Talking about reading and writing music: we learned all our tunes by ear, of course — we never saw such a thing as a book of tunes written down, and if we did none of us would be fit to read them. To this day I can't read a note of music myself — and later on I'll tell you a story about how that caused me a very embarrassing moment a few years after. But I remember there was one time when they were opening a new school over a few miles away from us. The parish priest and all the clergymen were going to be there, and they were bringing a piano player all the way from Derry — thirty miles or so — to play for this opening. My father didn't go for some reason, but Pat Hegarty, one of the Hegartys from Meenadreen, who was a great friend of my father, he went specially to hear this piano player. On the following morning he came to visit my father to tell him all about the happenings of the night before. My father of course wanted to know all about this famous piano player, and Pat said,

'She can play none! I don't think she had any idea of the tune she was playing. At least I never heard it!'

My father took the pipe out of his mouth and said, 'Is that so?'

'Aye, that's so. Do you know, she had to read it out of a book!'

'She *what*?'

So Pat had to say it again, because my father didn't know that tunes were ever written.

'Oh well,' he said, 'I'm glad I didn't go if that was the only way she could play.'

So singing and making music was the most natural thing in the world for us, because we grew up with it. I can remember my first public appearance: it was when I was between five and six I suppose, at a school concert. I was given half-a-crown after, and that convinced me it was my life — I was making money! It wasn't a competition, it was because I was so damned tiny, a lit-

tle five-year old, probably in the bare feet with a knitted jersey
and trousers. I don't know who donated the half-crown, there
was probably a collection.

> See the pretty snowflakes falling from the sky
> On the walls and housetops soft and thick they lie
> On the window ledges, on the branches bare,
> See how fast they're gathering, they're filling all the air.

> Little Robin Redbreast comes hopping to the door
> Because in the long summer days he lays not up a store,
> He knows that he'll get plenty whenever winter comes,
> And there he is a-hopping and a-digging for his crumbs!

That was what I sung, and I got half-a-crown for it. I was singing around the house long before that, and everyone that could
get a clout at me was doing it, because I was a right nuisance, but
I think that was my first professional stint!

I got on from that; I used to be playing whistles and mouth
organs. My Uncle Patrick was a marvellous whistle player. That
was me mother's brother. He used to come to visit us very often,
and I would always hide, because I was afraid of him. If I played
a bum note he'd clout me! The people were very strict about music
in those days. It had to be done right, because it was an insult
to the traditional tune if you didn't play it as well as the listener
thought it should be played.

When I was a bit older, before I left home, I used to travel
quite a bit to concerts here and there. I was quite a bit in de-
mand, and I don't know why, but I was, to appear at concerts
and give a few songs and so on, like that. Yes, we covered quite
a few miles now — there was several of us used to go around like
that, anywhere that there was. . . they called them concerts, but
really they were just a gathering of singers and musicians in a hall
somewhere. Usually for parochial purposes, for repair of a
church or a school, and we all gave ourselves as free, of course,
there was no fee. We weren't drinking at the time — not one in
the bunch. But we had plenty tea and plenty t'eat, get free transport — what more did we want? Probably load the whole lot on
an open lorry and away in the middle of the night, raining or not,
'twas all the same!

I was going to concerts when I was still at school. Nearly all
the concerts were held on Friday night, so therefore we didn't
have to worry about going to school the next day. We got a few
hours extra in bed every Saturday. Because we had four or five

English miles to go to school and would have to be up really early in the morning. So Saturday was a godsend.

Yes, the music and the songs were really important to us. Sometimes, you know, I would wake in the night with a song or a tune going round in my head. 'Twould be mostly a tune that I had heard for the first time and it would just click — part of it would sink in. I would have no thought of it when I went to bed, but I would wake with this tune turning round in my head and I was stuck with it! Probably it wouldn't be exactly as I heard it played, but as my father would say, the bones of it would be there. In fact that still happens: to this very day I can wake in the middle of the night thinking of an old song or tune, and that finishes my night's sleep!

And very often on a breezy day I could hear a tune in the rustling of a tree. In fact a lot of the old tunes were composed from that: some fiddle player would hear music in the roar of the waves or something, and he would sit down and make a tune out of it. That used to happen to me especially if I was up late the night before and didn't get much sleep. The following day I would be doing something and this music would come out of a tree near me. And I wasn't the only one, there was lots of us like that.

That song or that tune that you heard the previous night or a couple of days before was the only new thing in your mind. Nowadays that could not happen, because if you heard a tune last night, you turn on the radio or the television today, and that'll put it completely out of your mind, you might never think of it again. Without any other distractions like radio or television, yesterday's tune was still fresh in the memory.

In our life, music was number one. As far as I was concerned, anyway, that was the most important thing. Finding enough food was a second consideration. We always did though. I used to really pity people who couldn't sing or couldn't play an instrument or couldn't pick up a tune. I used to think, what have they? I didn't know there was anything else. I thought they were lost for life because they couldn't play.

9

A COUNTRY-HOUSE HOOLEY

People played music chiefly at night — they were too busy working during the daytime — unless on Sunday. There might be little music sessions on Sunday, because no-one worked on Sunday: no-one done any farm work other than tend animals or something like that that couldn't be helped, but you never went out to make hay or dig potatoes on Sunday. That was a day of rest. You went to church first, and then you had the rest of the day for chatting the neighbours and for visiting — rambling, raking we used to call it back home. Our house was one of the principal rambling houses in the area, and we used to have a lot of country-house hooleys and little parties.

Sunday night would be the principal night for the dance, not Saturday night. Saturday was the night when you left everything ready for the next day. If it was the time of year when you dug the potatoes as you used them, you dug as much on Saturday as done you Sunday, and several other things like that. Anyway, everyone had to get up on Sunday morning to go to church, so you couldn't be too late on Saturday night. But Sunday night there were dances everywhere, because no-one gave a hoot about the rest of the week.

There used to be plenty of dancing sessions that would happen just off the cuff, without anything being organised or anybody being invited. A few girls would come into a certain house, just to be together and to work on embroidery ('sprigging'), or whatever was to be done. A few men would come in, and if there wasn't a fiddle in that house there was one next door, and somebody ran out and took in the fiddle, and there was nearly always a fiddle player in the company, and there would be some dancing. It wouldn't maybe start until about eleven o'clock. They used to be smashing nights, because on an organised night you would usually get too many people, and the house would be so packed that there would be hardly be room for dancing. In those days the dancing took up some room — it wasn't standing the same ground like a diesel engine running, like they do now! Really they want-

ed a bit of space in those days, for the 'sets', and highlands and
mazurkas and barn dances.

Then we used to have the organised nights, which we called
'big nights', especially when there would be a few visitors in the
area. There would be two or three big nights organised in their
honour, to give them a chance to meet the locals, and to see the
customs. The musicians would be appointed three or four days
in advance. The girls would be invited for miles and miles around.
There was no need to ask the men, because they would follow
the girls, they would come anyway. But all the girls would be invited, and if they weren't invited they didn't go.

We all looked forward to the big nights. There was the dancing, and the singing, and the music, and of course the females,
and along with that, for someone like me that was interested in
learning songs, there would be the chance of hearing a song I never
heard before, or picking up one that I wasn't quite sure of. Oh
yes, an arranged big night would be talked about for two or three
days previously. Two people would meet, and the first thing one
would say would be to tell the other that there was a big night
in such-and-such a house tomorrow night. And that person would
tell somebody else, and so on, with the result that the place would
be like sardines before nine o'clock. Many a time I thought it was
a pity we didn't have bigger houses. Mind you, the kitchens, especially the old ones where they pinned the table up to the roof,
could hold quite a few people.

People would start to gather at about half-past eight or so.
There were certain people that had their certain places, especially the older people who wouldn't be joining in the dancing all
that much; they would be around the fireplace. The fire would
be let die out — almost (because the fires never died out for maybe
a hundred years back home); it would be let go very low so that
it wouldn't be giving very much heat, otherwise in a small room
with a thatched roof the heat would be putting the dancers out
of the house. The people gathered around the fireplace would be
talking about crops, or the price of cattle, or horses, or something
and smoking pipes — mostly clay pipes that would be left over
from wakes.

The pipes would be passed around too. That was part of the
hospitality and part of the welcome, that when somebody came
in to our house, it didn't matter whether they were smokers or
not, my father offered his pipe to this person. I don't know where
that fashion started, but it was going strong up until I left home.

There would be also news stories circulated around the fire. If somebody's wife maybe away two or three valleys back had a baby, that was big news, and if somebody was thinking of getting married, that was big news, and if somebody was thinking about building a new house, that would be thrashed out and talked over for ages.

Very often when a stranger would come in that didn't know that people talked about their neighbours like that, and someone would say to my father, 'You know Barney so-and-so from ——?' (maybe fifteen miles away), the stranger would wonder, how on earth does he know somebody that far away. They would have no idea that my father probably met that bloke every fair day, and saw him at church every Sunday. Another thing that they had trouble with was the pipe going round. That was not very hygienic in their eyes. I remember a Scotch woman, Mrs Kyles, and her daughter being in our house — a lot of Scotch people used to come over to our area on holidays — and there was a bit of a hooley going on. Of course my father was giving people his pipe, and they couldn't believe this. They thought that was being really rough!

On a big night there would be refreshments for the dancers. There was tea. There might even be a few bottles of whiskey going around, there might even be poteen, and maybe Guinness, which in those days we called stout. The people who lived very near didn't really eat in the house the hooley was in, 'twould be only people who had a far journey to do, like five or six miles out over the mountain, well then they got some refreshment to carry them along.

The musicians, of course, were number one. They had to be treated properly, anyway. There were usually two chairs put up on the kitchen table, and they sat away out up there. For two reasons: one was, they were right above the dancers, and they could see the figures of the dance and they could enjoy themselves, and along with that they were out of the way, because some of the dances were a bit hectic, and they were all very proud of their fiddles; and if there was a hectic dance going on and four or five people collapsed on a fiddle, that was the end of it! So the fiddle player was away safe, away in a corner or up on a table somewhere. So, let the dancers kill each other, who cared, the fiddles were safe anyway.

A big night would be chiefly dancing. The people that weren't dancing would sit right around the wall, and the fiddler or the two fiddlers would be in their seat of honour parked up on the table, and there would be about eight couples on the floor. As they danced around, people would be taking out the time, beating out the rhythm of the dance with their feet. You would know when you would be drawing towards a house, and they were dancing in the hobnailed boots on a concrete or a flagged floor — you would know two hundred yards away from the door what dance they were doing, by the timing, because they were keeping perfect time with the music.

As the dance went on and on it got more and more excited. They almost worked themselves into a frenzy — the sweat was pouring off them. If a man had to sweat that much working on the land, he wouldn't do it: he'd sit down and wipe the sweat off himself. But he wouldn't sit down while the dance was going on if he was fit to carry on.

The most popular dance at the big nights when I was a kid would probably be the highland. It was originally a Scottish dance as far as I know: in Ireland you'd very seldom see a highland danced outside Donegal and Tyrone. It was a pity, because the highland could be a fantastic dance — a lot nicer to watch than to do, because it was a bit strenuous to dance it. There would be about twelve turns of the tune, it would go on and on, and in the end somebody would drop out, and gradually there would be maybe only one or two left — the toughest would survive!

The mazurka wasn't as popular as the highland in our area back home. One of the reasons was that to do it properly took four couples. The kitchen of the house was small, and all you could have would be one set of eight people. I remember the open-air dancing, like crossroads dancing, and there would be maybe four or five sets of eight people; but you couldn't have that in a kitchen.

The beat never stopped for the mazurka. Sometimes in the highland you could ease off a little, but the mazurka went all the time from beginning to end of the dance. The old four-couple mazurka would be four couples joining each other, dancing face to face. It didn't mean a damn what you were doing in the dance, you kept the timing going all the time. They reckoned that that was one of the reasons why they had tips on the heels of the shoes and little iron plates called toeplates on the soles. People reckoned that's why they were invented. 'Twasn't true of course, but it made a nice story.

But you didn't need any space at all for the highland, because you could dance it round all the time. The first half would be done in semicircles, the second in complete circles. It would be very awkward to dance a highland like you would a waltz, coming around the whole floor. You would be turning so fast that if you hit someone you'd send them into another wall! And the timing would be a bit awkward when you would be moving around — it was much easier doing the beat standing on the same spot all the time. 'Twas a bit more like tap dancing.

In later years the people started doing the dances, sort of in slow motion — in time with the music, but with no beat action, only just doing the bare steps and not the in-between things. They never sweated! Whereas the old people — I remember men of up to seventy, and women the same age, they would sit down from the dance and they would be huffing and puffing, breathing very hard, and the sweat dripping off them. There was one bloke in particular, and like myself he didn't shave every day; he used to have a nice little stubble of beard on, and you could see the shiny drops of sweat coming off the front of his beard! So he was giving himself some abuse, with the great big hobnailed boots on. And believe me, a pair of them boots were about as heavy as a packed suitcase!

Naturally enough, after a few dances the dancers would be in need of a break, so then there would be a bit of a lull, and somebody would say,

'Packie, give us a song!'

So if it was my turn I sang a song, and then some other body sang one, and somebody would tell a story or do their party piece. They never went to any particular part of the room — just wherever you were sitting or standing, that's where you stayed. Nowadays at folk festivals they have what they call 'singarounds': well they remind me very much of the big nights back home.

Then the dancing would start up again. And there used to even be rows about the girls, men used to fight about the women. Oh, it was all a very interesting commotion. And right enough, it sounds like blowing me own trumpet, but in our area back home I can remember, all the girls were beautiful. They were mostly red-faced, of course, and a lot of that came from getting so much outside air. In the hay time they would all be working, working like men in the fields, and they were so healthy-looking: they all had red cheeks, and in those days they all had long hair, and they looked smashing. They did. Looked really nice.

After the dance, at four or five in the morning, the people would go home. Especially if it was the summer time, when it would get light early. They would try to be home before day, before the sun would shine, anyway. Although it was nothing new for a hooley or a country-house dance to carry on to the next day, just like the weddings.

There were quite a lot of what you would call characters, back home. Well, it was very easy being a character simply because there was no distraction, there was nothing to take the people's minds off the character. I knew one fellow, and if he came into a rambling house it made the whole evening: that made the night for people, because he was going to be unsensible or come out with something that hadn't been heard before. It was a bit like the days of the old bards, when there would be a court jester and a bard invited to the palace to entertain the king. Well, these characters were just as important as the old bards and the old jesters and singers from away back centuries ago.

They were too numerous to mention, of course, but some of them had a very warped sense of humour. When I say warped, I don't mean nasty, but I mean, they could make jokes off the top of their heads while you wait. They would be fantastic jokes, but to an outsider they wouldn't mean a thing, because these jokes would be relating to the interior or the centre of the area, or to some particular person that was in the rambling house that night. If the same joke was told twenty miles away from home, the people wouldn't understand it 'cause they didn't know the place and they didn't know the people concerned.

That was the kind of jesters we had in the old days, really bright as buttons: quick thinkers, and more than half of them could neither read nor write. But they had this kind of an alert brain that as soon as they went into a room they took in the whole thing, and there and then they could stand in the doorway and come out with a big rhyme or a joke about somebody. There was one fellow in particular that no gathering was complete without. He was funny, witty and a lovely singer. He wrote some very nice local songs too, but he could walk into a room full of people, and he could start a song, and he could name maybe ten, twelve people around the room and include them all in the song. And the lines all rhymed. So, let's face it, if someone can do that, I think it's brilliance. It wasn't education as he wasn't an educated man. It was just a gift, I suppose.

There were a few people in our area who were known as storytellers; one was a grand little old man called John McGrath, and there was Thomas Sweeney, our nearest neighbour. There was a little man and his sister called Paddy and Biddy Haughey. Neither of them were married, and they lived together in the same house; to pass a night away they would visit the neighbours and tell stories. They would be invited to the big nights. They were lovely singers too, and they used to stare into each other's faces when they were singing.

A lot of the stories got a bit embroidered too. The right good storyteller, even when he was telling a true story, would mix in a few exaggerations here and there, to make it sound good of course, and then maybe when my father would retell it, he wasn't against adding on a few words here and there, and if it started as nothing by the end it became a big story, a serious story.

People would tell mostly the most ridiculous stories you ever heard in your life; they wouldn't be true ones anyway. There might be a joke or two attached to them, or it might be just a dead serious one about fairies or supernatural happenings. Here's one just to give you an idea of the kind of story you might have heard if you were at a hooley in our house:

There was a young couple lived in a shepherd's cottage way out in the Barnesmore mountains. 'Twas a very isolated spot. The nearest neighbour lived a long distance away and there was no road for miles and miles in any direction. They had only one child, a baby girl of four months, and she was very ill. Now it was firmly believed in them days that often the fairies took away a strong healthy baby and left a sickly non-thriving one called a changeling in its place, and this was supposed to be one such baby.

The first big snow of winter was just starting, and the shepherd had to go out to the mountain to bring the sheep in to lower lands where they would be safe from drifting snow and landslides, which do sometimes happen on mountain slopes. So off he went with his dogs and a bundle of food, leaving his wife and a sick baby warm in the cottage. The baby was in a rod cradle near the turf fire. She gave a little cry, so her mother heated some milk, hoping that she might take some as she hadn't taken any for two days. When she had the milk ready she lifted the baby from the cradle but it was dead.

At that moment there was a knock at the door and in came a young woman. She was poorly dressed and covered with snow and she had a baby in her arms. She said,

'Can I have some milk for my baby? She's dying of hunger!'

The shepherd's wife said, 'You can, and welcome. I had some ready for my own baby but she just died.'

So she gave the milk to the baby and food to its mother. The stranger woman seemed very interested in the dead baby and asked her age, how long since she first took ill, and if she was christened, and many other questions. Then she started humming a lullaby, picked up her own baby and walked out into the stormy night.

By this time the shepherd was coming back from the mountain, and he heard a female voice humming a lullaby. He couldn't see who it was, because it was already dark. He listened till the voice died away in the distance and then he went into the cottage, where his wife was crying for the loss of their baby. Try as he might he could not get the lullaby out of his mind: it kept haunting him till he couldn't stand it any longer, so he took down his fiddle that was hanging above the fire and started to play.

He never heard the lullaby before that but he played it note for note as he heard it from the woman's voice. It was getting more and more beautiful each time he played it, and he became completely obsessed with it and went into a trance and carried on playing it till his wife shouted his name. He looked to where she was sitting holding the dead child and he couldn't believe what he saw. The baby's eyes were open, her hands and feet were moving in time with the music, her cheeks were nice and red and she looked quite happy and healthy.

That baby grew up to be a very beautiful girl and very successful during her life. Legend has it that the strange woman was really a fairy mother who paid the shepherd's wife for her kindness by returning her baby and taking away the changeling.

Now if you want to believe that story I won't try to stop you. That's how my gran'uncle Big Pat Byrne used to tell it. He played the air too, a very nice air, and he called it 'The Firestone Lullaby'.

My Dad was a good ghost-story teller; but I never believed any of them when I was a kid, or when I grew up. There was supposed to be a ghost appearing at a bridge away back in the mountain, a bit further back than where we lived. When I was home on holiday one time Neil Boyle and me decided we would go and see this ghost. I remember it was a very cold night, and like two idiots we sat on that bridge from twelve o'clock till it cleared on a cold winter's morning, waiting for the ghost; but the ghost never turned up!

I could not bring myself to believe in signs or ghosts or ban-
shees or witches. Mind you, there were such things as coincidences
that really would lead you to believe that there was ghosts. Now,
you might sometime, you never know, be in the area I was brought
up in. Well, our house was about a quarter of a mile on a slope
from the river, and about two miles further away there was a
mound and a little cluster of houses, the townland of Meenagolin, where we used to go at night for the sake of getting away from
our own little area, where there wasn't much happening. What
I'm going to describe could be seen clearly from Meenagolin but
not from anywhere else.

Now on a certain breed of a night, when the breeze would
be blowing the clouds and there was a good, strong moon, rows
of lights used to start within a couple of hundred yards of my
house, and run right down the moors and disappeared in the river.
And when one lot would be about disappearing, another lot of
lights would start at the house and run down the hill. Little lights,
just like flashlamps, or the light of a candle, only they were all
sparking. Anyone would think that was what they called a will-
o'-the-wisp, a ghost. But it wasn't, in fact. We got so used to it
we never noticed it, but strangers were afraid of the area.

What was causing it was a kind of mineral in the land, and
when a cloud passed over the moon on a breezy night, a darkness would funnel down the cloud. And in that darkness, these
lights would show. When the moon was shining direct on the land,
it was too strong for the mineral in the land to glitter. So, as a
cloud came down, these lights kept with it, but before and behind the cloud there was no lights. Very often in September or
October we would get a breeze from the south-west, and if there
was a full moon you had a good chance of seeing these lights.
Several people claimed that it was ghosts, fairies, will-o'-the-wisps.
But it wasn't.

But the old ghost stories were so obviously lies you couldn't
believe them. My Dad and Big Pat and other people were probably making them up during the day to tell at the gathering that
night. They were good entertainment when we'd be sitting round
the fire. Now, mind you, although I never believed in ghosts for
one minute when I was young, a few years ago I had an experience
in Italy that kind of set me thinking. I'll tell you the story of that
later on. A lot of people listening would think, oh, that's another
of Packie's tall tales. Well, the snag about it is that it is the truth!

10

SUCH LIKEABLE MUSIC:
FIDDLES AND FIDDLE PLAYERS

Fiddles were as plentiful as stones in our area. There were fiddles all over the place — in nearly every house. That was part of the furniture! You went into a house and the first thing that struck your eyes was a fiddle, and the fiddle was always hung in one particular place, above the fireplace, on what they used to call the 'brace' of the house.

None of the fiddles had cases. The fiddle players, if they were going away to play somewhere, they wrapped a sack or an overcoat or a mac around the fiddle and put it under their arm and went away over the mountains, even in pouring rain; and the fiddles would all play, I don't know how. But nobody ever had a case for the fiddle, because they said that was the ruination of a fiddle, to put it in a case. If you left a fiddle in a case, it was never the same again. When they came home, that fiddle was hung on the brace.

Now the smoke from the fire went up behind the big flag, and the fiddle was hung on the outside of the flag, and it was always kiln dry. And a lot of them fiddles were probably a light colour when they were new. But they were all jet black; the turf smoke blackened them so much that in the dark you wouldn't see them! And the dust of the fire would settle on them. I remember Big Pat Byrne, my gran'uncle, when he would take down his fiddle, the first thing he'd do was blow the dust off it. But they were always against the cases.

There was a fellow called Jack Clark, who married a girl from our area — in fact, only a couple of houses from where I was born. And he had two beautiful fiddles, very valuable fiddles. He brought them from America with him, or his mother brought them from America. One of them was a smasher, it was a full-size. And then he had a three-quarter size fiddle, and the three-quarter size was always hung up where the smoke got behind it and that's the one that was mostly used, if it was lent out to anyone. But the other one was stored away, was left in the case and I'm afraid it went useless. Lost its tone completely. I remember when it was a lovely fiddle, and years and years after I enquired about it and discovered that it had lost its tone. They reckoned that was because it was left in the case.

People wouldn't believe in buying a new fiddle. They would wait and wait until somebody got really hard up for money and then sell their fiddle, which was in some cases the last thing that would leave the house. The kitchen chairs would go before the fiddle would go! But they had a thing about the new fiddle, that it took a long time to break it in — the older the fiddle, the sweeter the tune, they always reckoned.

There were fiddles bought down in the town. There were also families that used to come around selling fiddles. Some people used to make their own, and in fact, there used to be tin fiddles, that were made by the tinsmiths. I remember the Dohertys — that was a very well-known family of tinsmiths and fiddle players in our county — selling tin fiddles. And good little fiddles they were. There was only one snag about them: the Dohertys were great tinsmiths, but others found it very hard to put a tin fiddle together properly. When the pressure of the strings comes on it, it'll open, very often between the neck and the round of the body. That was the weakness. The gauge of the tin was so narrow, because they couldn't use the big thick tin, because that'd kill the sound, and they couldn't reinforce it, because that'd kill the sound again. So they used to pull apart with the stress of the tuning.

The last tin fiddle I remember belonged to a fellow called Hugh James Harkin, lived in a place called Croagh. Now he had one, and he used to play quite a bit on it. But he's dead now, and I suppose his family didn't play it no more, and then it would go useless. You see, tin fiddles had to be sort of mollycuddled and cared for, because tin will rust after a certain time, and it had to be kept cleaned and very very dry, because the tiniest little speck of moisture on tin and in a day or two you have a red spot.[1]

Now the Dohertys that I just mentioned: as far as music was concerned, they were reckoned to be the tops. But they weren't just 'musicians'. John Doherty used to get grossly offended if anyone called him a musician. They were fiddle experts, and that was

---

1 Some time after this conversation was recorded Packie came across a surviving example of a tin fiddle still in good working order, one made by Mickey Doherty (father of John, Mickey and Simey), in the possession of the fiddle player John Gallagher of Ardara.

a higher class altogether. John was a very popular man, and his brothers Mickey and Simon too. When I was a kid John Doherty was still tinsmithing, and a very very active man. You'd see him going along the road, like a pole, his back straight and his head high, and all his gear on his back — tools and all for making the tins. Tinsmiths would go anywhere, and ask the people what they wanted. And sometimes then they would come round selling the tins: when they had a lot made they would go away out with horses and carts through the country into the mountains, selling these tin cups and milking tins. They were useful things. They were great where there were kids, because if they fell they didn't smash, whereas if you gave the kids cups they would be smashing them as quick as you would hand them to them.

I knew John Doherty very well. In fact, it was through John Doherty in a kind of an indirect way that I got started on the folk scene in England in the 1960s. But that's a story for later on. When I would be about twelve years old I remember asking John to play specially for me once. He produced a tiny fiddle, less than half-size, and started to play. I thought I never heard anything like it. At the time I was considering being a fiddle player, and that kind of spurred me on. I couldn't get over this. I thought, well, if John Doherty can do that with a toy fiddle, what could he do with a real fiddle, and I thought I should be fit to do pretty well with an ordinary fiddle. But I knew in time, before I made a fool of myself, that I would never be a fiddle player — never one that was worth listening to anyway — so I packed it up completely.

Now, as I said before, winter was the principal time for the music. It fitted, because if you were inviting musicians to your house for a little session, they could be there at one or two o'clock in the afternoon, because wintertime wasn't the season for doing very much on the land, and they would have a few drinks and a meal and all before they would start the music. Then they would probably play for quite a while for the people of the house before the rakers or the ramblers would move in and the dancing would start. There was one old fiddle player called Paddy Boyle; he was a native of around Glencolumbkille, away in the west point of Donegal. If you invited him for an evening's music, he would be with you about eleven o'clock in the morning or twelve noon. And he would play and play all day, and all night, and sometimes he might maybe stay next day, and play and play on. And John Doherty too, he used to do the same. I've heard it said that John Doherty and Paddy Boyle and Big Pat Byrne, my gran'uncle, could play all day and all night — a twenty-four hour session — and never repeat a tune. And funny, I believe it. I've been told no end of stories in my youth that I don't believe: I did at the time, but I got away from them since, and when I thought them over I discovered they were impossible. But the three men I mentioned, that was not impossible for them, to play for twenty-four hours — that's with little breaks in between for meals and drinks and so on, and little rests, but never play the same tune twice.

Paddy Boyle could walk long distances to play, over the mountain with the fiddle under his arm. He lived in a place called Calhame: if you were going the straight road from Glenties to Bruckless you would pass by his place. Paddy would walk from there down almost to Glenties town, to Drimnacrosh, and played there, and walked back when the dance was over, and that would be fourteen miles or so: nearly thirty miles a night, with the fiddle in a rago bag or wrapped up in an old mac, and the rain wouldn't keep him in. And he walked from Calhame to a place called Largnaseeragh, and that's away back in the mountains between Ardara and Glencolumbkille.

The old players weren't educated people, but they had a way of getting out of all predicaments, you know. The other night I heard a story about Paddy Boyle from James Byrne, a fiddle player from Meenacross, when we were talking about some of the old characters from long ago, and you can be sure that it's true because I've been in buildings where Paddy done the very same trick. It appears that Paddy was playing one night at a dance in a hall down near Calhame, and there were a few very good fiddle players there, John Doherty, and Mickey and Francie Byrne — some of the very best Donegal fiddle players of years ago. It seems that the music was so good that after a while the people stopped dancing and just listened to the fiddle players. These boys started playing some very fancy stuff, in flat keys and all, that Paddy Boyle knew he could not in any way cope with. He couldn't compete with these fellows. But like all the old musicians, he kept one trick up his sleeve.

He started a tune up on the stage, hopped down off the stage and started dancing a reel to the tune he was playing, and done that all the way round the room! The other musicians couldn't do that, so they had to sit and watch him dancing all round the room and back up onto the stage again!

If old Paddy was still alive, he could tell some good old stories about nights out. I heard him tell stories about scraps and fights and trouble that he got into. But he'd always be careful, if he saw trouble brewing, to put the fiddle far enough away, so that nothing would touch it! There used to be some real funny times. There was jealousy amongst the musicians too, you know, and there was jealousy amongst the dancers and singers. Oh aye. There would be friendly arguments — well, start out friendly, and 'twould get heated then. Finally someone like my father would cool it down:

'Now, now, boys, there's no time for arguing. Play a couple of tunes!'

He had a great way with people; he could settle any argument with a minimum of fuss.

But there was many a row about tunes, you know, many a fight. There was one story told about two brothers who lived in the Carrick mountains about twelve miles from our place, oh, way back before my time. One played pipes and the other played fiddle, and they had a row one day about some particular tune. People reckoned it was 'The Floggin' Reel', and it might have been, but they fought until one of them — I don't know now was it the piper or the fiddler, it's so long ago and I heard it when I was so very small — he got such a beating from his brother that he was blind for the rest of his life. The brother beat his eyes out! because he reckoned he was playing bum notes. They way they would say it, of course, 'twould be in Gaelic. Now, if you lose your way, if you get lost in a fog, there's a *seachrán* on you. Well, he was putting a *seachrán* on the tune; the tune was lost, as far as the listeners were concerned. I suppose he deserved a chastisement, but beating his eyes out was a bit on the drastic side.

Now my gran'uncle Big Pat was very well known. He used to go away for days at a time with the fiddles and the gun, away shooting birds and hares and rabbits and playing the fiddle. Wouldn't come back for a couple of days maybe; and his relations never worried about him because they knew that he was in somebody's house, he was all right. Too drunk to come home, or whatever was the excuse!

He had a long white beard. He was about six feet three and built like a tea chest, square as could be. I was only something like fourteen or fifteen when he died. And he died with maybe a thousand old tunes. Not one of his family would bother about collecting them, because by the time Pat died we were getting interested in modern music, learning the waltz and the foxtrot! Mind you, I can still remember quite a few of Big Pat's tunes today.

Now I don't want to say this too loud, because I could get into trouble over it. They'll talk about the Byrnes and the Dohertys and the lot, but I think Big Pat was about the best fiddle player. He could play rings around Paddy Boyle, anyway. Yes, Big Pat was very good. And do you know, he had only three fingers on his left hand. He was cleaning a gun when it accidentally went off and blew off one of his fingers; I forget which finger it was, but it was one of the two middle ones anyway. Yes, he had only three fingers on his left hand, but he could play as good as anyone.

Big Pat had some strange sayings. He could be very scathing of other musicians — mostly fiddle players: he didn't think any other instrument was worth listening to. If someone wasn't playing well, and wasn't taking out all the notes and the long draws of the bow and all this, he used to say,

'Och, there's no venom in his music!'

If he saw some other fiddle player scraping away furiously, he would call that 'sawing the fiddle in half with the bow'. Or if the fiddle player's elbow was jumping up and down while he was playing, Pat would reckon that he was 'just scratching himself'! Because in Pat's idea, the elbow should hardly move anyway, except back and forward; it should not go up and down — I don't know if he's right or not, probably he was. There was a method to everything he said. Even though it was mad there was a method to it. Oh, they had their ways of saying things.

It's possible that Big Pat and Paddy Boyle might be considered a bit rough and ready beside some of the best today, but they played really nice music, and they played only the best tunes: if they picked up a new tune and found that it didn't seem to fit the fiddle music, they scrapped that one. John Doherty, till the day he died, had the same habit. If it wasn't a tune that he thought was reasonably suited to a fiddle, he didn't play it, he left it away. Pat would do the same, Paddy Boyle would do the same, and very likely if you mentioned a certain tune to one of them, he might say, I can't remember that'un. He knew it right well, but it wasn't a good fiddle tune, so he wouldn't play it. I think that habit is what kept the traditional music going.

Like a lot of the old players, Big Pat had a story for nearly every tune he played — where it came from and how it got its name and all this. I was telling you the story of 'The Firestone Lullaby': well, here's another of Pat's stories. I've told this story often enough, but it's possible that some people reading haven't heard it yet. I'll tell you the bare bones of it, but Pat used to drag it out. He told all his stories as if everything happened to himself.

Pat was coming home from playing at a hooley or a wedding late one night and it came on a big downpour of rain. It was a very dark night, so to shelter from the rain he went into a vacant house. Now there was supposed to be a ghost in this house, but Big Pat would not believe in ghosts. Oh no, he was too brave, and let's face it, now, he was a bit of a tough man, a good fiddle player and a great poteen drinker, and he could stand his own against a couple of men at one time. He really was an all-round man!

He groped about and found a chair and sat down till the rain would be over. When his eyes got accustomed to the darkness, he noticed the form of a man sitting on another chair opposite him. He waited a while, but the fellow said nothing, so finally he thought, 'Oh well, I'll have to find out who this is — it's some-one like meself coming in out of the rain.' So he said,

'Stormy night, isn't it?'

The bloke in the other chair answered, 'It is that.'

Pat said, 'What have you in the box?'

'A fiddle,' said the other one.

'I carry a fiddle meself.'

'Oh, is that so? Well, why don't we play a tune?'

So, good enough, they decided to play, and they both tuned up their fiddles. Pat said,

'You play something while I get a bit in my pipe.'

So Pat was caulking his pipe and your man started playing a tune . . . and suddenly Pat forgot all about the pipe. He could not shut his ears against the tune. It really seemed to haunt him. He said,

'Oh, play that one again.'

So the second time he picked up the fiddle and started to play along with the other fellow. They went on and on playing the same tune as the night wore on — a long winter's night. Pat found he couldn't stop. He tried a few times, but it was no good, the hands and the fingers would still go on and he was there stuck to the fiddle, playing this tune.

After a few hours, the bloke on the other chair said,

'Is that daylight I see through the windows?'

So Pat turned around to see if it was. 'Aye, sure enough, it is.'

When he turned back, the man in the chair was gone — vanished.

Pat swore that that was the first ghost he ever saw, and from that back he believed in ghosts. He remembered the tune, and he played it everywhere he went after that. He never could find a name for it, so he called it 'The Ghost's Welcome'. I put that tune down on a record a few years ago. I'm glad I did, because it's a tune that I've never heard anyone else play. Pat probably composed the tune himself and thought of the story around it.

Now, I was talking about Big Pat and Paddy Boyle and John Doherty being able to play for twenty-four hours and never repeat a tune: that reminds me of a story that was often told in our area, and Big Pat himself used to tell the story. There was a shoemaker that lived away, back over the hills from our place. And in those days you'd only one pair of shoes and you wore that Sunday, Monday, every day of the week, and every night of the week. There was one bloke in our area that really needed a pair of shoes. And the shoes were all handmade in those days (they called them 'shoemaker's shoes') and he went to this shoemaker away out over the hill — who was a pretty brilliant fiddle player. So of course, the man that wanted the shoes took his fiddle with him and away out over the hill. And to take the mickey out of him, the shoemaker said,

'I'll tell ye what, I'll give you a pair of shoes for nothing, if you can start playing when I start making the shoes, and play on and never repeat a tune till I have the shoes finished; and at that time, I'll give you the shoes for nothing.'

So the bloke said, 'Well fair enough.'

He hadn't very much money anyway and this was a great way of getting a pair of new shoes. So he started playing and the shoemaker started making the shoes, and they called halt when it was time to eat and smoke and all that. Then, right, off they went again, and the story goes that this fiddle player played one tune after another, and there was no such thing as faking it because the shoemaker himself was a pretty keen musician. He played on and on, all day and into the night, and the following morning, and was still playing when the shoes were finished and polished and dried and ready to put on the feet, and he never repeated a tune.

He would've played each tune a few times, of course, like you would for a dance, so that was a slight advantage on the musician's part, because the dances can last five or ten minutes. But the snag was to remember what tunes he had already played, and the shoemaker would know if he did as he was waiting for this. The whole collection of tunes got an Irish title, they were called

Luach na mBróg, which is Gaelic for 'The Price of the Shoes'. It's a pity those tunes weren't put into a book for him, because that would really be a valuable book now. No, they were never written down, but some of the older musicians back home picked up quite a lot of the tunes and sort of put them in a little formation and used them in marathon fiddle sessions. Big Pat himself must have had over a hundred of them tunes that he could just rattle off like that, and never repeat one. Oh yes, he could, just kind of automatically: one tune reminded him of another and so on. And there are still lots of those tunes played today. 'The Mason's Apron' was one, and 'Saddle the Pony', that was another. That's only two out of maybe a couple of hundred.

But your man got his shoes, anyway! And they would have been a good pair of shoes, right enough, even if the shoemaker was listening hard to make sure that the fellow didn't repeat a tune. They had great pride in their shoemaking, like the tinsmiths had making the tin fiddles and stuff like that. That was the one thing about getting an article made. If you went to some person's house, and asked them to make something for you, you might be damned sure that that was a genuine article because that was their reputation at stake. There wouldn't be much point in his losing interest and then making the shoes, and probably making them that the first time the man put them on, the heels fell off or something. No, the reputation had to be kept up.

There was great competition between the tinsmiths back home, the tinkers, who could make the best milking tins and tin cups and all that. There was one family, the Wards, they were really good, and the Collins and the Dohertys too. They were always looking for little improvements here and there; it was their living, but along with that, it was their pride. There was a bit of pride there. And the musicians were the same now. They would try to tell you,

'Ah, no, I just played it off.'

But they didn't. No such stuff. They spent a lot of time trying to improve the way they played a tune, trying to improve their fiddle ability. They were all seeking perfection. Let's face it, no musician ever tried to be worse than he is.

Strange enough, and this is something that never could be explained, but Donegal and Fermanagh and Tyrone had the same style of fiddle playing. And then Derry, which was just as near Donegal as any of the others, also a border county, was entirely different style — very Scottish style. Probably it is because it was nearer to Scotland than it was to south Tyrone or southwest Donegal. And then again, Sligo, which is the next county south of Donegal, has a completely different style of playing the fiddle altogether. But Donegal and Tyrone in particular, and Fermanagh, they had the same style of playing, the same tunes. And in fact the same dialogue. Reading that book there now of John MacGuire[2]: nearly every word he uttered was exactly as my parents would talk, call things the same.

---

2 *Come day, go day, God send Sunday:* John MacGuire, ed. R. Morton (Routledge & Kegan Paul 1973).

11

THE ART OF SURVIVAL

The times have changed so much you know that it's kind of un-
believable. The people in our area back home are about five
hundred per cent more enlightened in worldly things and happenings in foreign countries and all than they were in the old days,
but they're a bit behind in other ways. They are! There are things
that they know nothing about; like the art of survival. They have
no idea what to do if they haven't got something: they just either
sit moaning that they haven't got it, or if they have the money
they go out and buy it.

Well in the old days there wasn't any money, so there was
no point in going out to buy it. So you made it. You improvised
some way, but you got this article. I don't know really which is
the best kind of education, but I would still prefer living with nature and to be fit to say, well, I'm a survivor, rather than always
depending on something that's manufactured in God knows, Tai-
wan or somewhere, and waiting till you had the money to buy it.

There wasn't much buying and selling of anything in the old
days other than groceries, and livestock. Anything that possibly
could be made at home was made at home. A lot of the clothes,
for example: the wool came off the sheep, it was carded, spun
into thread, and the women knitted it. They used to make some
smashing pullovers, and cardigans — Jerseys and Ganseys. The
name came from the fishermen from Jersey and Guernsey. The
Jersey was open down to the chest, and you usually wore a shirt
inside it, and the Gansey had a collar up to the neck, with a row
of buttons down the shoulder, which you opened to get it off.
I remember when I was five or six years old I had one suit which
I was very proud of, green wool, all knitted — trousers, cardigan,
the lot. Even they used to knit braces for the trousers, and knitted ties! Some men back home could knit in the old days too, and
spin. I could spin, and card; I was a good carder. I used to card
the wool for me mother when she was spinning.

When I was a kid the old men used to wear what they called
a 'grey flannel' — the Irish name was *báinín brocach*. It was a

big shirt that would go down over all the clothes, some of them right down to the knees. Big Pat, my father's uncle, and several around his age wore the grey flannels, but not my father or any of his generation. It was not the fashion no more. But that flannel would probably be woven in the house in the old days, and the shirt made by one of the women. The women themselves used to wear shawls; they were nearly all black — dyed black, some of them: the women would buy them grey and dye them black.

They would buy them, because in our parish there was no weaving in my day. But in the Ardara parish, everyone was a weaver. We were at the very end of the parish of Killybegs. There was only a little stream between the two parishes, and you could step over that and you were in the weaving area. My brother-in-law Patrick Keeney, who married my sister Memie, was a very good weaver. My mother would make clothes from the homespun, but very often the cloth didn't have to be bought. If somebody made a web — that's a whole long bolt that'd go from here away down the road — there might be a damaged bit on the end of it. When they were getting it examined, that remnant would be cut off. Somebody would give my mother a remnant and she would make a man's waistcoat or a pair of trousers or something. Some of the remnants were so big and so good that there could be a suit length in them, and if you were to be shot you couldn't tell where the damage was! The blokes that examined the homespun, they knew their job.

Bedclothes were all made at home. The blankets were much warmer than any blanket you can buy now, because they would be made out of real soft wool. Probably the sheep would be clipped and the blanket would be turned out all at the same household. Start with the sheep on the mountain and finish up with a blanket round you in bed at night.

I remember women in our house doing what they called quilting; they had a frame the size of a double bed, or bigger of course, allowing for the part of the bedclothes that'd come down over the sides. There would be three or four women sitting round this frame, sewing the lining to the top with up and down stitching, singing an old traditional song in unison. One of them quilts would last for forty years, as warm as could be. You needed nothing else when you'd a good quilt. The nearest thing to the old-style bed quilt are the duvets that you get nowadays, only they're a bit artificial, but these were made all wool. They were so nice and warm, it was sad having to get out of bed on a cold morning!

The beds were handmade too. They weren't made any particular size or measurement, and very often they were bigger than
the average beds you see today, which was just as well, because
in a big family you could put as many as five kids into a double
bed! I've never slept in anything as comfortable as the bed I was
brought up in. They were all timber. The mattress was made at
home too, and it would be horsehair and wool mixed. There was
a reason for this: horsehair will not pack tight, the ribs are too
strong, and that kept the wool from packing tight, because wool
is dead material. And it'll pack, which meant that in a couple of
years you had what the old army 'biscuits' — the old flat mattresses
— were like. But a good horsehair-and-wool mattress would last
near a lifetime.

Yes, everything that you could possibly make, you made it.
We all made our own ropes, out of straw and hay. That's what
the song's about, Casadh an tSúgáin — 'The Twisting of the Hay-
rope'. That's how they got the undesirable out of the house, they
got him to twist a rope, right out of the door, and when he was
outside the house, banged the door and locked him out. One of
Séamus Ennis's stories, of course.

We had little things that is never heard of now, which is a
thing for making grass ropes, called treá-hooks. They're the sim-
plest things you ever saw, but they were such clever inventions
that you could make the nicest rope, make a rope as thin as your
little finger, and make it any length — miles long. Then they would
be used for tying down the thatch on cornstacks and houses and
other jobs.

My father used to make ropes for horse reins, out of what
we called rago bags, sugar bags. That two-hundredweight sack,
when it was ripped, thread after thread — and that was a slow
job, taking out one thread after the other and laying them all out
in nice skeins — that sack would make a fair piece of rope, enough
to use as reins for a horse. They were stronger than the grass ropes,
they were the nearest thing to hemp rope, and they were used
with a rock tied on each end, and this would be laid over the roof
of the house to stop it lifting off in the storm.

Them ropes were also used for burdin' — that's carrying
things in. They had them the right size and the right shape, made
in doubles; they called them 'hangers'. There was one long rope
which they doubled up and knotted at the end. On the loop end
there was a timber ring called the ged. They laid the rope down
on the floor and put the sack of flour or whatever it was down

about halfway between the ged and the knot. Then when you picked up the knot end and put it through the ring, it locked. You had it arranged so that it locked at the right distance to fit your shoulders. It was a very clever arrangement, but so simple and very comfortable. You would put that sack on your back then and wear it like a waistcoat, and walk for miles with it. They were very useful.

Some of the bigger stones for building — lintels and door-jamb stones — would be carried in burdin' ropes. The sheaves of corn and the loose hay would be carried that way too. A haystack longer than a house would be built by as high as ten men carrying these burdens on their back, same fashion. The hands were free. You'd see a bloke lighting his pipe and going along the road with this big load on!

The creels were all made by the men; I've never seen a woman build a creel. They were square baskets, stood about two foot high, about a foot wide and about eighteen inches in length. On a good day it was nice to watch a man sitting out in the field, with the standards stuck in the soil and working these rods around. They were so nimble-fingered. When they would come to leave holes in the side for picking up, they would have them holes all identical in size, no measurements.

They used to make them indoors too, in the winter when it would be too cold to work outside. The standards are supposed to be stuck down in the ground. Now how can you do that in a house? Well, they overcame that, because they cut a great big sod and took it in and left in on the floor, and they stuck the standards down in this sod of earth. It took two men to lift this big wet sod, but mostly it would be wheeled in on a barrow and put in the centre of the floor.

Probably the creel would be manufactured in the centre of the floor, and the women would be doing lace-making, and embroidery around a little lamp in another corner of the kitchen. Lace for cuffs and collars, and lace belts, and lace petticoats. The priests used to wear a lot of lace in the garments inside the vestments — lace up to the elbows. And the knitting would be going on. Probably a couple on the other side of the fire would be having a chat, or smokes out of a pipe.

Another interesting thing was dyeing the wool. Naturally when the garments would be knitted and finished they would be white, plain white. Well then if you preferred them brown you would take a knife to pluck and scrape this stuff called *crottle* off the rocks; it was a kind of lichen that grew mostly the north side of the rock that the sun wouldn't shine so much on, that'd be damp. The women would boil that in a pot with some alum to make the colour fast, and put the garment in and let it boil with the crottle, and it would make the nicest colours. You put in a certain amount if you wanted a light, yellowish colour, and the more you put in the darker the dye would be. The women had it off to a tee, they had it so well measured that they could lift a handful of crottle out of the basket, and they would know that that was enough to get a light yellow or a dark yellow or a tan or a light brown.

If they wanted a green dye, they used to use *scutch grass*, this grass that would grow between the ridges of potatoes, about two or three feet high. Like the crottle, it depended on the amount you put into the water how dark it would be. Now the crottle would not wash out, never! Till the last thread of that garment would be worn out, it was still the same colour. But the trouble with the scutch grass was, it would run, and after a while it would start getting paler and paler until it was a horrible colour, because there wasn't enough venom in the grass to hold a fast colour. Then they used other things for other colours — maybe blackberries for purple, and blackthorn for blue, and several other things.

Yes, the people had their own methods — there were lots of little tricks and customs like that. I count that as part of survival, to make something useful out of nothing. Like the sack that came containing meal or sugar and ended up as a rope. Old barrels were recycled too. In the old days the paraffin oil used to come to the shops in wooden barrels. I suppose some of the barrels would hold up to forty gallons. Then when that barrel would be empty, the shopkeeper would sell it to somebody. People made tubs out of the barrels by cutting them right around the middle. Then they cut one stave on each side about three inches out of line with all the other staves, which meant that you then had a grip, two stout staves on each side, and that's how you carried this tub — two people mostly, because they were very heavy. They used to use them for feeding cows, and for salting fish: throw a layer of salt in the barrel, then a layer of fish, then more salt on top of that, and so on. Then when the salt melted it came up like grease-thick water, rose up over the fish, and it would keep them for months and months. But believe me, them fish were salty!

Another thing the tubs were very useful for was washing bed-clothes and other large articles — working suits and that kind of thing. That was good fun. They used to be all washed outside. People would take their tubs away to the river, or to a stream, and build on a big turf fire, and you'd get the fire going well, boiling pots of water. There were big chunks of carbolic soap, disinfectant soap, with more of a stink than a scent. I also remember this stuff called 'Rinso' — it was a pink powder, and it would make froth. The articles — blankets in particular used to be lovely for washing — would all be put into one of these big tubs, and the boiling water poured on, and 'twould be let sit until that water would be cool enough for you to jump into with the bare feet and tramp the blankets!

There was a chap talking one time on the television about wine making, and how they jump into the tub of grapes in the bare feet, and it reminded me so much of washing blankets. When we came home from school and we saw washing, that was the greatest thing: it was so nice when two or three of you would get into this big tub of froth on top of these nice soft blankets and soft water and Rinso and carbolic soap, and dance and sing and jump about. The more we danced and jumped about the better the clothes were washing. They would be spread out then on the rocks or on the grass and be dry in a short time.

Almost every man in our area could do his own repairs and little bits of carpentry. If you wanted a door, or something, you would very often make it yourself, for two reasons. One was, you wouldn't give anyone the satisfaction that you couldn't do it, and two, you probably didn't have the money to give to a proper carpenter. So you made the door. Next time round you probably wanted to make a box, or wings, or a crib for your cart or your horse-drawn vehicle, and you thought, well, I made a door so now I'm going to make that. And you finished up kind of independent. I did a lot of things like that back home; well then in this country I done quite a bit of that kind of work on building sites, doing chippying and carpentry work. Nothing like cabinet-making, I never got that far, but I was a fair good strong, rough carpenter. No job ever collapsed till I got away from it anyway!

Now I'll tell you a funny thing about the way people used to make things. If you had a carpenter today to make a door, the first thing he'd do would be to measure the space; but they didn't do that back home! If we were there now, I could show you a door in the house where I was born, that was made about a mile and a half away. Another bloke made it in his living room. He was in our house quite a lot and he knew exactly the size of the door.

He didn't measure it, he just thought to himself, yes, now that would be about the size of it, he made the door, and it fitted perfectly. Now that sounds like a tall story, but the door is there yet.[1]

Mind you, in spite of all that, slip-ups did happen once in a while. A girl who lived a few miles from our place was getting married one time, and her uncle, who was a bit of a do-it-yourself fanatic, promised her a kitchen table as a wedding present. He worked day and night to have it finished before the wedding day. And it was a perfect article, would last her for her lifetime, and probably that of her children as well. On the evening before the wedding he got his horse and cart ready to deliver the table and he asked a neighbour man to help him carry it out of his living room where he made it. Well, they tried every way they could think of, upside down, sideways, endways; but it was no good, the table could not be got out of the room. They even removed the door and all the timber work from the doorway, but it was just that little bit too big to get through. He couldn't take it to pieces because he glued all the joints and fastened them with heavy nails, so the table stayed in his living room — it still is there as far as I know! The bride never got her present, and he was so embarrassed he didn't even go to the wedding.

---

1 Sadly, since this conversation was recorded the old house has been bulldozed to make way for a modern dwelling.

12

THE OLD THATCHED COTTAGES

When I was a kid the houses in our area were all almost identical. They were all one-storey thatched cottages, they all had fairly small windows, and they were all the same colour — white as snow, painted with lime wash. All the windows and nearly all the doors were on one side of the house, usually facing east or south. Thinking it over now, I can't remember ever seeing an old house in our area facing north or west.

The houses were all built on the green land, and very often surrounded by trees. Our house was built on the side of the hill, with a high ditch behind it to protect it from the storms that would come over the hill. I remember when I was very young my father got a bundle of young trees from the Department of Agriculture and planted them all around the house. Then he got heavy stones from the river and put them on the roots to stop them from getting blown away.

The reason for all the houses being only one storey was on account of them being thatched: it was much easier getting up one floor than going the height of two floors, and along with that an ordinary ladder could reach only one floor, whereas if you had a two-storey thatched house it took a very long ladder to get you up to the apex. The reason they were all white was because the lime was the cheapest way of painting. Mind you, if it got a heavy shower of rain on it before the lime dried on properly, the whole thing flooded off the wall and went away down the stream, and you had to do it all again.

Now there wouldn't be a lot of furniture in the house — the bare necessities. In the kitchen (which served as the living room, because the cooking, the sitting, the chatting, the music, everything all went on in one big room), the furniture would be one table, which was always against one wall, and if you had more than five or six people you pulled it out to the centre of the floor. There would be five or six chairs. Straight-backed chairs, that could be used at the dining table, and that would be the same chairs that you would sit on all the time. Probably made of bog timber, that was dug up, that lay there since the time of Noah's ark. Was that sound and solid — you wouldn't drive a nail in it. Bog fir, and bog oak.

When you would be cutting the turf, the peat, for fuel, you would come on this timber right away down on the bottom floor, six or seven or eight or maybe even ten feet deep. The land grew, they were so long lying there. They fell on the flat land first, then the land started growing and growing, till it grew about ten feet over them, so it gives you some idea of the number of years that them poles were lying down there. It was very hard work, sawing the bog timber. But, no matter, I've seen the chairs and the tables and all made of the bog oak and the bog fir, and all the roofings and doors was all dug up. No shop timber at all. The whole roof of the house I was brought up in was all dug up out of the land, and some of them poles would be up to twenty feet long, and as straight as could be. Just the way they fell, hundreds and thousands of years ago, and they're still there to this day — thousands of them, lying probably right under the house where I was born.

Did you ever see a two-legged table? Well I did, dozens of them, in our county and in Tyrone too. We called them side tables. They were permanent fixtures. Never could be moved around the house because they were hinged to one wall on iron loops which were placed in the wall when the house was first built. There were also loops on one side of the table with an iron rod running through. That meant you could fold it up against the wall and pin it to the roof when not in use. It could also fold down towards the floor. The legs were hinged to the other side and used to fold against the leaf so that when the table was folded you'd hardly notice it there. It was folded up out of the way for the big nights and merrymaking, because the ordinary table would be big enough for a family of maybe ten kids and a few adults, so taking up valuable dancing space. Probably like the wedding present I was telling you about it couldn't be got out of the room anyway!

There would be a fireplace in every room. That was essential. Big, open fireplace. What we called the brace, the big chimney flag, would be about six feet high from the floor. These fireplaces were about the width of a wardrobe or so, and you would think the smoke should come out through the room, but it didn't; it went straight up along the back wall and out the chimney on top, because this brace flag was sticking out about three feet from the wall and sloped right back to the roof. That created a suction draught up. You could light a paper and let it go, and whoosht! 'twould go way out the top of the chimney.

Up until I left school our house had an earthen floor, a mud floor packed. Talk about the timber coming out of the bog hard packed — you couldn't drive a nail in that floor! Later on the mud floors were painstakingly taken away bit by bit and concrete was put down in its place, and to this very day it's a concrete floor. No covering or carpet or anything. The mud floor was harder to keep clean, because you got, say, wet weather outside, and the people tramping in and out, and coming out of a cowshed with dirty shoes, and walking in on this mud floor, wetting it — it got really mucky and slippery, so they done away with them, and started laying concrete instead.

In the areas where they had good stone quarries, where they could quarry up these big flags the size of a bed, they made floors out of that like crazy paving. That was smashing for dancing on, with toe plates and tips on the hobnailed boots. I've seen the dancers with the boots dancing on the flagged floor, and they could leave a row of lights behind — knocking lights out of this hard blue whinstone.

When the houses were first built everything was taken into consideration. Very small windows so that it didn't cost much for glass, an iron bar built into the wall above the fireplace for hanging the cooking pots on, a hollow in the wall behind the hearth to make a home for the crickets; and sure enough that's where the house crickets used to live. This hollow was covered with a big stone to stop the coals from falling into the cricket's home. There was a superstition that if you annoyed them or harmed them they would take revenge by eating your socks. This big stone is mentioned as 'the cricket's singing stone' in the song 'My Lagan Love'.

If the house had an earthen floor, which all the old houses in our area did, there would be a flagstone laid in the floor right in front of the hearth. Now this stone served a few purposes. With so much movement close to the fire and so many feet wearing hobnailed boots the earthen floor would soon wear away, but not so the flagstone. All the cooking and boiling for people, cattle, pigs and poultry was done on the kitchen fire, so naturally there would be some water splashes, and a wet earthen floor can be slippery as ice and very dangerous for children running about in bare feet. They could easily slip and fall into the fire, but the stone could be wiped dry; with the heat from the fire it dried almost immediately anyway. Sometimes another big flat stone would be set in the centre of the floor and used for dancing on. This stone was hollow on the underside, which amplified the tapping. It used to make quite a racket.

In nearly every house there was a hole left in the wall near the fire. It would be about a foot square and went about halfway through the width of the wall. This was for storing pipes (the smoking kind) and spills — little slices of bog timber used for lighting pipes, paraffin lamps and candles. This hole in the wall was called a 'bole'.

Some of the old houses had what we called 'outshots'; that was a kind of an alcove a few feet wider that the rest of the house and long enough to hold a bed. This outshot was always in the back wall of the living room, possibly because with the window and door on the front side there wasn't room for it there. Some of the outshots had real beds built in, others had seats wide enough to sleep on. If it so happened that someone in a family became ill, that person was moved into the outshot, to be fit to see and hear what was happening and join in a conversation if they were fit enough. All the spinning, carding, sprigging, knitting and so on went on in the living room, so there was always someone on hand to attend to an old person or comfort a sick child. There was a fireplace in every bedroom, but keeping two fires going day and night in wintertime was a big consumption of turf, so having the patient in the living room was also a financial advantage. The outshot could also be partitioned off and used as a storing place for pots, pans and other kitchen utensils. Oh yes, it had a few uses to its credit.

The drinking water and all the water for washing churns and things like that came out of a spring well. There was a spring well at every house. It was just a hole in the ground about two feet deep, built around on the inside with stones, and probably a big flagstone over it to keep the sun from getting at the water, and that water was running summer and winter, a flow coming out of that. At some farms there would be five and six of them wells running. The biggest would be about two foot by one foot, and the smallest maybe a foot each way: you could only get an ordinary-sized can in, you wouldn't get a big bucket into it. And that water was cold, because it never saw sun or wind or rain, and a lot of it came out of the rocks. It would sting your teeth like icecream, even in the summertime.

We had no bathroom or toilet inside the house. In fact, no bathroom anywhere. When you wanted a bath, there was the river for you, and in you went. People hardly ever had a bath in the winter, because there was no need. The weather was so cold, and you weren't working very hard and you didn't sweat any. There were bath tubs — corrugated zinc tubs, like the miners' baths in the north of England — but people didn't like them. They would say, 'I'm not going to sit in that.' And there wasn't a room in the house where you could have privacy to get into one of these. In fact all these baths were ever used for that I remember was for storing foodstuffs for cattle and for washing big articles in like an overcoat or a pair of trousers, and apart from that they were pretty useless. You went away down the road and into the river, soap and all. Come out and waddle about naked until the air dried ye, and you put on your clothes and you were away.

All the houses were built convenient or as near as possible to a little stream. If you wanted to wash your face, you picked up the soap and you went to this little stream, and you washed your face and ran like hell back to the house and dried yourself. You brushed your teeth out there too. Shaving was the only thing would be done in the house because lots of people couldn't shave with cold water. But anyone who could shave with cold water took his razor and his little glass with him out to the stream. And you always had nice clean fresh water because it was running fast. They were cutthroat razors of course. To strop them a man would just take off his belt. There was a nail somewhere in the house drove specially for that; he put the buckle on the nail and done his razor.

That was something that wouldn't be tolerated at all, to have a toilet or a bathroom in the house. A lot of the little toilets were built over the running water, built over a stream, and everything was flushed away to the river. Anywhere you saw a little loo on its own, you may be sure there was a fast-running stream there. It would be built up on blocks, or up on ribs or something, so that there would be a little space from the floor down to the water. The idea of that was in case of a flood of water coming, that it wouldn't sweep away the loo. In later years they built septic tanks, and nowadays people have pull-chain loos right next door to the dining room. They wouldn't have that in the old days.

I remember lots of new houses built when I was a kid. You built your own house and the neighbours came and helped you. There are houses still standing in good shape back in our area that are up to four hundred years old, and not one stone ever became dislodged in them because they were really put together. And the stones were mostly all dug up out of the farmland and gathered here and there along the road, because the quarries weren't so good. There were some that were quite a distance away from us where you could get nice, square stones, which you wouldn't get in our area because there aren't any free-stone quarries — it's mostly all blue whinstone and that, which will not cut out square no matter what you do with it. And if you tried to dress it, you hit it with a hammer and you want it to cut one way, it'll split the opposite direction on ye.

The walls were built using lime and sand mortar. The limestone was quarried out of the land and burned in a kiln dug out of a turf bank. The fuel used for burning the lime was very likely dug out of the same bank. The sand was collected from the river or sometimes the sea shore. Cement wasn't used in any building simply because it had to be bought. A few things connected with building a house would have to be bought, but not many. Things like windowpanes, door hinges, wall pins and so on. Mind you, the pins and hinges didn't cost much; they would be made out of old horseshoes.

Somebody would consider building a new house, and he would dig and dig away at the peat soil, first, till he would get down to very hard soil — we called it 'till'. Well that was a sort of a mixture of congealed sand and mud and that was hard. You could hit that with a sledge and you wouldn't nick a flinch out of it. Now why this solid layer was there, was because the weight of the peat baked it down, and made it so solid it'd be almost like a concrete floor. So, he dug a trench out of the peat first, down to this solid bottom, and then his neighbours would come and they would roll in these great big stones into that trench. And pack more till soil in between them, and tramp them down. Then they would start to build the house on top of these big rocks. And that house couldn't move, do its best. The trenches were what we call nowadays the foundation. And nearly every house in our area is built on a row of huge big stones, that took maybe five or six men with crowbars to drop into this big trench.

They would build on and on — there was always some one or two in an area who understood the building of a house a bit better than the average man. And he would give the directions. Then when it came to putting on the roof, they went away out on to the moors and they could tell by looking at the top of the soil, if there were any what we call 'fir sticks' — especially in the early autumn and late summer, when the dew would be pretty heavy on the grass, before the sun would shine on it. Where there would be one of these great big logs — lying since the time of the Flood when they were beat down — they could tell, because the dew did not fall or collect on that particular spot. It was strange about that — you could always tell, you would see a dark shadow in the dew, which was all glinting and shining on this little keeby grass that grows on peat land, but not directly above one of these fir sticks.

Then the digging would start: dig up then a big trench, right on top of this log, lift it out, then split it and take what they called 'spills' off it, for watlings. First of all they made what they called 'couples', using two big heavy logs — maybe oak in fact, heaviest timber they could find — joined up at the top with the bottom ends resting on the outer walls; and with a few bars of good solid timber down a bit from the top, that's what held the roof up like purlins. Then they got poles, we called them ribs, also dug up out of the ground, that would run the full length of a room — well, most of them would — and put them from wall to wall; then they tacked these spills or watlings to the ribs.

Next came the trickiest job in house building, cutting what we called 'scraws'. They were sods of tough grassland, some of them twenty feet long, two feet wide and a few inches deep. These were laid on top of the watlings, one end touching the side wall and the other going over the top and a little ways down the other side. Cutting the scraws was an art in itself: you needed two men, one slicing the sod with a spade and the other rolling it up on a stick till it looked like a giant toilet roll! Laying the scraws on was also a painstaking job.

Now the idea of putting on these big sods of very tough grassland was so that the thatch would have something to bed on. If you put the thatch sitting on top of ordinary timber, it wouldn't stay there: first breeze of wind, and the whole damn thing would go over the mountains. But you could pin the thatch down to these scraws with forked rods. Ropes were put from gable to gable on top of the thatch, and they were called 'stretchers'. And the cross-ropes, which would go across the roof, would be interwoven into the stretchers so as to form a big net. That was known as 'bridling' or 'cormuggling'. When that net was tightened down, the thatch didn't have any room to move, 'cause as soon as the thatch

starts moving, the air gets it and away it goes. So that was to stop
the air from getting in.

Then there would be the 'slings'. That was a very good strong
rope made of plaited sprit or straw, mostly straw, and it would
be put over the whole roof then: three or four on the length of
a room with a big stone tied on each end. The storm from the
southwest in our area was pretty severe. We used to get some real
rough storms, blowing a gale for two or three days, and it would
tumble anything that wasn't tied down. So there would be no
point in driving a solid peg in a wall to tie this rope to, because
the pressure of the roof, with the wind getting into the thatch,
would break any rope, or break the peg that you put in the wall,
or probably tumble the side out of your house. So they put the
rope across, and they tied a big rock on each end: the rock would
be about two feet from the ground so that in the event of the roof
moving, it could move up a little, but when it came down the rocks
came down with it, and when the roof was down flat the rope
was still tight on it, holding the thatch in its place. It was quite
an art, keeping the house from blowing out into the tide maybe![1]

Oat straw was used for the thatch. The thatching was really
a trade in itself. It was called long-straw thatching, which was the
kind that was used all in our area — in fact, I never saw this 'scob-
bled' thatching, using reeds, until I came to England. I could do
a bit of thatching, but I wasn't good by any means. But my brother
Jim was a marvellous thatcher. He wouldn't let me work on an
important roof like a dwelling house. The art of thatching was to
overlap the straw so that the rain wouldn't go down through it.
If that happened you could wake up in the middle of the night
and you'd be surrounded by a pool of water. But if Jim thatched
a house, that house was as waterproof as a bottle — not a drop
would come through.

---

1 The following incident related by Packie gives a vivid illustration of the force
that storm winds could attain. Emerging from the house after one particularly
violent gale, Packie went to check on some shelters he had rigged up for the
sheep using sheets of corrugated galvanised iron. One sheet remained missing,
even after Packie had searched the entire property. Some days later he over-
heard the following conversation between two farmers in a pub in Ardara:
    'Did the storm do you any harm, Jim?'
    'No it didn't, but it must have been rough somewhere over the hill: there's
a sheet of zinc lying down in my meadow and I don't know the hell where
it came from!'
    Packie joined in the conversation and was able to ascertain that the sheet
in question was his. It had been blown a distance of some three miles over the
hills!

On a nice sunny day when you would look at a roof newly done with oat straw (corn straw, we used to call it), it was beautiful. The sun brought out the gold of the straw and if it had happened to rain a shower and the sun shined strong after it, that was the nicest thing you could look at. You could see a new roof for miles, see it shining.

The thatch had to be redone every couple of years. That was to have it stench all the time (stench means waterproof), because after two or three years it began to decay on the bottom. The weight of the straw started matting, so the only thing to save that was to put a new lot on top of it. You left on the old straw but the new stuff kept the water from getting through, and it didn't get any worse. I remember we were tumbling an old building near our house at home and there was well over three feet deep of old thatch on it! Started off as a couple of inches, and years and years went on . . . some of the houses yet, I suppose the roofs would be up to three feet thick. People still use that technique.

It wouldn't take very long to put on a new layer of thatch. My brother would do a couple of rooms in one day. And so could plenty others. They put on new ropes each time: the old ones were taken off because you would have undulating straw, kind of wavy, if you worked on top of the old ropes. Then they found out in later years that ordinary netting wire was just the very thing. And all the houses back home that still have the thatched roofs, and the outhouses and cowsheds and everything, have wire instead of ropes. There are not many people left now that can make these ropes.

The scene is changing entirely over there. They're all building bungalows now; they are not country houses no more — they're suburban dwellings in the middle of a mountain! And it looks out of place entirely. Well, all right, good luck to them, it's progress and they don't have to work on the roofs no more because they're all slated and that'll last while man liveth. But they are not as comfortable as the old thatched cottages.

13

LEAVING SCHOOL AND LEAVING HOME

In between the time when I left school at fourteen and came over to England for the first time at twenty I was living at home, helping out on the farm with my father and my brother Jim. I was never really into farm work in the way that Jim was, but my parents wanted me to stay home. I missed a couple of opportunities because of that, and the first one came right after I left school. I could have got into a store, get in as a clerk to the store manager, which I could have built myself up in. It was a place called the Egg Store, in Bridgetown, about seven miles south of Donegal Town. It dealt with a lot more than eggs. It was a kind of a wholesale place; the manager bought the eggs and the butter and the stuff like that from all the surrounding places, the shops and farmers and smallholdings around. He sold them in job lots and they were shipped to Scotland and England and to cities like Belfast. They were looking for somebody and the news spread. I had just left school, and was a likely enough character to work in a store like that. They approached me and my people. Both me father and mother thought, no, I would have to work on the land, have to give my brother Jim a hand, because they knew that Jim would never leave the land. They thought two heads were better than one and four hands were better than two.

So, for them six years I stayed at home anyway. I worked on the land with Jim. He was working Big Pat's old farm. He had it rented at that time — it was only after my second or third trip to England that we bought it together. He was working that land in conjunction with my father's land. The cattle and the sheep were all over the place. So my brother didn't say, that's my land and that's yours, because that wasn't heard of. They worked together, and I stayed home and helped both of them until I was twenty and got tired of it.

I cut turf, and cut hay with a scythe, and cut stooks of corn with a sickle (what we called a 'hook') and did everything that he did. I did a little bit of fish poaching, too, in between days on the land, like I was telling you earlier. That was mostly night work, but not all: I used to do a set net in the river, but fear made me stop that!

That was the time that the new music was coming in, dance-band music, and taking over from the traditional music and dancing. Around that time the dance halls were beginning to come into fashion, and there was people building new halls here and there. There was no dance band in our immediate area, but in the bigger towns like Donegal town and Ballyshannon, they had their own dance bands. These dance bands would be booked once in a while to play for the dancing in the new halls. Course, we would be there to hear the new bands. They weren't playing ceili music, they were playing the new music, and that music sunk in.

Every band had at least one saxophone, because they had no amplification and they had to make noise. The piano accordion and the saxophone were the likely instruments, because they could fill the whole hall. Then they would have somebody for doing the crooning — it wasn't called singing in those days! Everybody was a Bing Crosby at that time. A lot of it was American music. Around that time sheet music became popular, and several people around learned to read music. The bands could all read music in those days. I couldn't, but we were so sharp at music, at the uptake, that we had only to hear a tune twice or three times and we had it off as good as the bloke that learned it out of the book.

It wasn't long before I was learning to play the saxophone myself. Now, the first time I ever tried to play a saxophone I played a tune on it. There was a fellow by the name of Peter Ward, who had a shop and post office. He used to go to Dublin regular on business. So one time he was down there he bought a saxophone. We used to go to his house to swap stories and songs; he was a very nice character and full of music himself. So he was trying this saxophone one night when I was there, and he was making real weird sounds with it. I was laughing at him, so he said,

'You try the bloody thing then!'

So he gave it to me. I happened just to get a few notes out of it — well, that weren't as bad as the ones he was taking out of it. Before I left that night, I could play a tune on it. So I graduated from that to picking up tunes that were easy to play on a saxophone. Then when I got to England I bought one myself and ended up doing quite a lot in dance bands over there.

Long before I left home I was also taking an interest in girls — oh aye, we weren't old men when we started that caper! One reason why we started on the female trail early was because there wasn't all that much else to do. The country-house dancing was dying down, beginning to slack off at that time. We had free Sundays and free nights, so the only thing was, get out to the females! There was no cinema, and girls didn't go to pubs in those days. Things were a lot more out in the open in those days than they are today. Sunday evening was a great time for meeting the girls, because there were an abundance of them, and young men too! They'd all go for walks on Sunday evenings and we would be going about on our bicycles, and meet up with them, and walk with them for the evening, and probably only go and sit on the wall, or somewhere. Maybe if there was a girl you fancied she would take you to her house and you would have your supper and come home. Her father would think, well, if he's man enough to come in here, a stranger, he's man enough to be made welcome, and that was full stop.

I was I suppose as successful as any of the lads. There was one thing certain, that we never took anything too serious, and the girls never took us too serious either. It was different to nowadays: after three or four meetings they can see wedding bells hung above their heads. No word of that with us. You just went to a dance, and if you saw a girl you fancied you took her home from the dance and you arranged then that you would meet her again the following Sunday afternoon. We used to go to a place called The Warren, by the seaside, and there was miles and miles of big sandy dunes and ferns and scrubs of bushes — privacy supplied by Mother Nature. It was a good enough place to meet your girlfriend. Sometimes we would hide for a while behind a bunch of ferns! 'Twas harmless pastime.

We — the young lads — were more than half the time without a copper at all. We were all smoking, of course, and the trouble was to get twopence for the packet of fags. I used to get a few bob doing turns for people at fairs. No matter what you done for someone, it was called a 'turn'. I would drive cattle home from a fair, or help somebody into the fair with cattle. There were no pens at the fairs. There was one field fenced in, and the cattle were put in there. So you had to be with them all the time to keep them from mixing with other people's cattle. That would be my job. I'd get maybe two shillings for my day — 10p in today's money. It may sound like very poor wages, but the two shillings bought sixty cigarettes, and that made a good week's smoking for me.

The second opportunity I missed came when I would be eighteen or nineteen. My father had two brothers, Joe and James.

Joe went to Scotland and never came back. He got married and brought up a family near Glasgow, and died over there. But my Uncle James went to America, and he became the head of the Des Moines power and light company, in Iowa. He was managing director or chairman, or something; he did pretty well for himself, anyway. One time he wrote home that he would take me over there and get me into the power and light company to work under him. But my parents wouldn't let me go. I think my mother had the strange idea that she had to keep me where she could keep her eye on me.

It would have been a very different life if I had gone to America, indeed it would. But everything happens for the best. I had a much nicer life pleasing myself. If I had gone to work for my Uncle James I would be pleasing him until he would retire and I would be pleasing whoever came after him. It would be all, 'Yes sir!' and touching my hat, and no way would that work with me. I never met my Uncle James; he may have been a very nice man, but somehow I cannot see someone getting to the top of a national company by being nice or being good fun all the time. That may be harsh judgment on someone I didn't even know, but I don't think he was very much like my father, because if he was he wouldn't be at the top, neither would he be a millionaire. Fame and fortune was nothing in my father's mind. A good song, a chat with a neighbour and watching a crop growing was his idea of happiness.

Thinking back, I think that incident was probably the cause of me leaving home. I was very keen to go to America, and when I was barred from going there, I kind of kicked over the traces and thought, well I'll go away anyway, and England being the nearest place, I came over here.

I was cycling home from a dance in Dunkineely one Friday night with Phil Keeney, a fellow from next door, and he said he was going to England on the following Tuesday. I thought, well, if he's going, I'll go too. I forget what the fare was, but it wasn't all that much. Jim gave me the money anyway. It was 1937.

14

FIRST TIME OVER TO ENGLAND

About six or seven of us came over to England in a bunch: we were all at the dance in Dunkineely the previous week. We came over from Belfast to Heysham in North Lancashire and then got on a train to Kettering in Northamptonshire. Phil's brother Charlie was working in Corby and living in Kettering, and another bloke that was with us, Gallagher, had a brother living in Kettering. I'd been on Irish trains before, but they seemed to have square wheels. I couldn't believe it, how fast the train was going, and I couldn't stop looking out of the window at things passing.

We all went up to the steelworks at Corby, where we heard they were looking for men. I got a job all right, but it was down in what they called a soaking pit. Now that pit was about twenty feet deep, and there was drops of muddy water falling down on my head. You'd be wet to the skin before you'd be in there half an hour and you worked like that the whole day. So it wasn't long before I thought, there must be something different to this. So I got myself a job on the railway, with horses. Nowadays a lot of people don't believe that once upon a time there were horses on the railway. Well there were horses on the actual railway line, and that's where I was most of the time, shunting, with horses, at Kettering station.

Language was quite a problem at first. The English people and me — one of us didn't understand a word the other was speaking. It took a good while, but I worked hard on it. I listened to every word that was going. The other blokes who came over with me had a good enough chance, because they were going to work with Irish people, and predominantly people from their own area — their own neighbours in fact. When I got on the railway there was only one other Irishman on the railway from Kettering to Leicester, so I had to learn a lot of English words and phrases and gestures.

But even though I had a bit of difficulty with the language I always got on extremely well with English people, right from the start. I was a cheerful bugger, I suppose, and if I was going up or down stairs I was probably whistling or singing. People used to forgive me a lot.

The yard foreman was a man called Scarritt, a rough, grumpy old fellow but a real good man. He used to eff and blind and swear at me:

'Do I 'ave to write the effing thing down for you Paddy?'

After a while we got to understand each other. At that time I was very even-tempered, and he used to call me everything he could think of and it didn't light on me. Then he would laugh and give me a fag:

'Oi, come 'ere you silly blighter and sit down, and we'll 'ave a smoak!'

He used to give me a hard time about the horses too. He was careful of the horses. They weren't Shires, but they were better even: Clydesdales. They all came down from Scotland only semi-trained; they weren't accustomed to traffic or anything, but they were all bridled and led. They weren't completely wild, like mustangs. They were brought down in trainloads, and they were circulated around all the railway yards. There were men appointed at each yard to do the breaking. I had a hand at the breaking, but I wasn't really long enough at it to be a master horsebreaker; but I was very fond of them, and funny, if you really like something you can get along with it. I was well used to working with horses, of course. My brother Jim was very good with horses, much better than I was. I was probably better with cattle and sheep, but I could get along with horses all right. I loved the Clydesdales. I like the Shires too, but the Shires just go at the same rate all the time. You can't hurry them up, they're going to go at their own padding way. But the Clydesdales were good horses, really good.

So there I was in Kettering, shunting wagons with horses. I was drawing wagons into the yard, where there was a permanent crane. It would take two men to work an engine, one to drive and the other to do what we called the rope-running, the shunter bloke; he had to change the points and all. But when you got a horse well practised to working on a railway line, she'll stay between the two irons, and you can go ahead and leave her and she'll plod along. I could run away ahead and change points and the horse still kept coming on.

I always loved watching the Co-op horses delivering milk. The man would fill the basket with bottles of milk, and the horse would probably be going down the other side, and when he got to the bottom of the street he would turn right around and come back up again to meet the man. Horses are marvellous animals when you train them, they'll do anything for you.

There was one horse in the yard at Kettering that I really liked, a big grey mare called Jess. She was about the biggest in there, but she was lovely. She was kind of given to me, well to keep me quiet. I was always complaining and grumbling about something. They gave me this mare to work anyway, and she was great. But I made one bloomer with her, and only she was a good one she wouldn't be alive the day after, and neither would I. There was a big cinema in Kettering that was burned down, the Empire, and the railway company got the job of drawing all the scrap iron from the cinema down to the station and load it in wagons — I don't know where it was going. On this particular day it appears there was a rush to get a few wagons filled, and I was sent up with a four-wheeled dray to the cinema for a load of scrap iron.

Now I had no sense for the weight of scrap iron, and there was two or three blokes there that had less sense than I had. So we started loading and loading and loading, I suppose forgetting what we were doing, and I started away from the cinema. I knew by the way she started there must be a lot of weight on, because the ground was pretty level, and she made a couple of efforts before she got the dray started. It was level then till we got to the top of Market Street, but Market Street was pretty steep going down. I started her down this street, just sitting on, and of course she wasn't really fit to keep the load back. I hadn't the brains to pull her into the side and let the wheel run along the kerb and use it as a brake — the old drays didn't have brakes, the horse had to do it all with the breeching, with the harness. She started slipping on the street — it was cobbles, of course — and from about halfway down Market Street till the very bottom she never lifted her back feet. They slid on all the time and she kept the vehicle from running over her till we got down to the bottom. Now that was then Montague Street, so far as I remember, which was a very busy road in Kettering, and I started to get really worried that if she dives out and there's a vehicle coming — a lorry or a car or another horse and dray — it would be a bad smash of course. I don't know why, she probably must have sensed something, that there was an accident about to happen, but Jess made a drive for the footpath and she got the wheel stuck in the kerbstone — I didn't rein her in — and just at that very time a doubledecker bus passed by. If she had a' go ahead the bus was right through us, because he hadn't a hope of stopping: he was also on a slope.

We got back down to the yard, and I was shaking. The mare was wringing with sweat, and old Scarritt said to me,

'What the 'ell Paddy, 'ave you been gallopin' this mare again?'

'No,' I said. 'She can't be feeling very well — she's very warm.'

'You can't be feeling so well yourself, yer bugger, you're pouring sweat too!'

And we were, both of us were sweating. The scrap was all weighed before it went on, and there was a little short of three ton on her. If any time you're in Kettering you'll see that Market Street is pretty steep now, and in those days it was cobbled.

There was one horse in the yard nobody wanted to work. He was a light horse, very active, and so unruly he had to be always muzzled because he would bite, and we couldn't take him up the street because he would eat the arm off somebody. It finished that he was sold to a farmer. He was the only Irish horse in the whole yard! They wanted to put him on me, but I would have nothing to do with him. I wasn't a good enough horseman to handle him, to start with. I preferred this Jess; she was a cross between a Clydesdale and a Shire. Oh she was lovely, the best horse I ever handled. She was young too, only five years old at the time, but she saved my life, her own life and the dray, and probably maybe some people on the bus.

I had another crash while I was working for the railway. This was at Leicester. I was still based in Kettering but they sent me out to Leicester, on loan. At the time I wasn't very used to reversing a four-wheeled vehicle because I didn't have to do any reversing shunting; working about the yard all I had to do was hook my horse and pull a four-wheeled vehicle probably from the weighbridge to the wagon. I was stupid anyway; I should have learned to do it before I attempted it, but I went away to Leicester as a carter. On this particular day I had to go to the city with a crate of china for Marks and Spencer's.

I would have no trouble if they had've given me my own mare, Jess, the grey one that I was using in Kettering. But they gave me an animal that could hardly stand on his feet, and he would go the wrong way anyway. If you tried to rein him he would go in the opposite direction. He was the nearest thing to a pig. He would be the worst horse I ever met in my life — and that's why they gave him to me! Anyway, I pulled up outside Marks and Spencer's. Now there was a slight incline in behind the store, where I had to go to leave this crate, so I thought it would be wise if I went forward and reversed back to get a straight go at the entrance, because it was only a little wider than the dray I had on. So I did. But instead of reversing back into the upper side of the street, I pulled the horse the wrong way and the dray came around and got on the fall of the street, and the kerbstone was only about two inches high of course, and up the back of the dray goes on the pavement and straight through Curry's window, the bicycle store! The crate of china went bang! down on the bed of the van and probably it was all smashed, I can't say, I was too much afraid to ask.

The railway company paid for the damage, because it was an accident. But they sent me back to Kettering. Well in Kettering it wasn't long before they decided that they had enough of me. I didn't mind the yard, but I didn't have very much company. Old Scarritt was there day in day out, and there was one other bloke who used to do all the weighing — the weighmaster. But apart from that I didn't have a lot of company, unless there was something to be taken away out through the town. Then I was never in a hurry back, and maybe there'd be something waiting for the dray to come back, and of course I would get a telling off about that. When you get careless in a job, everybody knows that your heart's not in it, and anyway they decided to get shot of me. So I was transferred to Corby and Weldon to do odd jobs. I was porter, platelayer, carter, messenger, window cleaner, luggage handler, sweeper and tea maker.

At that time, do you know it was easy to find work. There were plenty of jobs going, but for a lot of them you had to be willing to muck in. There were lots of dirty jobs such as digging trenches or working in Corby steelworks, which was really rough work — working in furnaces and places like that where the heat would be dreadful. The big steelworks at Corby was Stewart and Lloyd's, and it always frightened the life out of me. After I left there, when I worked on the railway I used to have to go in there sometimes to look for tarpaulins and things to go on wagons, pick them up and get them loaded and take them out to the yard. But it always scared me. There was something frightening about it. It was so weird, all that noise and hissing, and there was steam coming out of every pipe that you looked at. I never went back to work there no more, although I could have got a good job there when I was on the railway. This Scotsman called Burns was the head patrolman, the head security guard, for Stewart and Lloyd's, and I got to know him through playing darts in pubs. He told me he would get me on the patrolmen, and that was a pretty good job. 'Twould be free uniform, and free quarters. I was asked for an interview, but there was something about working there that was making me shake so I never went.

But I was never out of work. Working on the railways was all right, and I stayed there until war broke out. I lived in digs all the time. That was one thing I always tried to get — what I called a respectable place to live. In those days it was live with a family; there was no such things as bedsitters. You went to somebody, and you lived with them as one of the family.

Now when we first arrived in Kettering, three of us got digs in a funny house, Mr and Mrs Goode's. One of my first memories of England, something that stuck in my mind ever since, was a clock that was on the mantlepiece of the living room of that house. It had the most beautiful 'Big Ben' chime. I'll never forget that sound, and being musical it meant a lot more to me than to the others. There were three Irish lads already there, so that made six of us. Most of them were working nights, because that's where the big money was, but Phil Keeney was on days, and I was doing all day work on the railway. When I would come home, the others wouldn't be away to the night shift, because they used to work from ten to eight, and they would still be probably asleep. Two of them would get out of the bed and Phil and me would get into the bed. Four of us used the same bed. It hardly ever cooled! Eleven shillings a week it cost.

After a while I got a wee bit browned off and went to a family that lived straight across the street, the Robinsons, from Gateshead. They were marvellous. I stayed there all the time I was in Kettering — a year and a half or so. They had three little girls. I remember eighteen shillings a week I was paying for full board. I got a room to myself, the best of food, washing done, socks darned, trousers pressed and shirts starched, and the little girls used to fight with each other who would polish my shoes for Sunday. One day Mrs Robinson came to me and I knew there was something wrong, whatever it was. I can still picture her face as she said,

'Packie, I'm afraid I have bad news for you.'

I thought, oh no, somebody's dead, or she has some bad disease or one of them's going to die. But she said,

'I have to put up your rent two shillings.'

That was a pound a week. She was really in a bad way, she didn't know how to tell me. About a week before this I got on as a permanent railwayman (I was on trial up to that), so I got an extra three bob a week. So I was earning then three pound three. Two pound seventeen or two pound eighteen was the usual run of wages. A pound was a fair bit out of the wages, but I got everything I needed, and I still had two pound all to myself.

My mates and I used to come down to London at the weekends. You could have a whole weekend in London and a train ride from Kettering there and back, and you would be back home and you might only have ten or twelve bob spent. Six and sixpence was the return fare from Kettering to St Pancras. We used to come all the way to Kilburn High Road, just half a mile from where I live now, where at that time there was an Irish dancehall called the Banba. We all had girlfriends around London. We would meet the girlfriends, take them to the Banba. Sixpence each was the admission for the dance. You got ten cigarettes for fourpence, and we could take the girls for a meal after. We would stay with friends, and when we would be back in Kettering if we were any more than a pound out we were really spending.

It was while I was in Kettering and still working on the railway that I first started in showbusiness — playing saxophone in dance bands. When I first came over I could play a bit, but only to amuse myself and annoy others. I bought a saxophone from the Salvation Army, and I was at it for a year or two when Norrie Paramor gave me the idea first of joining a band. He used to run a show called 'Beat the Band', and if you could play any tune, on any instrument, that his band couldn't play, you won a pound. So I went in for this, and played a tune on an old saxophone that he gave me, and it was a tune that his band couldn't play. So I won a pound, and like the half-crown that I won for singing when I was five years of age, I thought, well that's made me now, I'm in the money! Norrie Paramor advised me that I should get into some outfit, so I started work with a band called Charlie Walker's, playing in the evenings and at weekends. Charlie was a rum character himself: what a man! It was a really nice little band though.

I mentioned earlier that I never learned to read music. So I played the saxophone completely by ear. Well, all the musicians in the dance bands in those days could read music. But there was always somebody in a band kind enough to play off the new tunes for me, and I was very quick on the uptake in those days. I would listen to it once; the second time around, I would play it with him, and the third time, I was fit to carry on, note for note.

So, everyone in the band had a sheet of music up before him. I had one sheet of music for years, 'Red Sails in the Sunset'. It didn't mean a bit what dance was going on, I was pretending to be playing off that sheet of music. One night when I was in Charlie Walker's band we were playing at the old Market Hall at Market Harborough. This hall was a round building with about eight or nine or ten rows of seats, and then there was a space in the centre for the dancers. It was the first carpeted singing lounge that I was ever in. It looked really pretty respectable, and a lot of older people used to come for a night out.

I used to do a solo here and there, between dances. On this particular night I was going to do a song with the girl that was singing. I played the melody first straight on the saxophone, and she sang a verse, and we split it up like that. The song was 'In My Little Red Book', which was a very popular song at the time. So, I played it off, pretending to read the music on my stand. One of the band members had gone out for the solo and came back in from the car park. As he opened the door the draft sent everything flying — whisht! away goes my sheet of music. It hovered a while first and then finally it decided it would go down to the audience. It landed right between this man and woman that were sitting in the second row. He picked it up and looked up and there was nothing left on my stand. I suppose he didn't mean to say it so loud, but he said to his wife,

'He wasn't playing "Red Sails in the Sunset", was he?'

There was one very red face in the band!

I done quite a while with Charlie Walker, and then I got into a bigger outfit called Jack White's. Now Jack White's was the very first band to play the signature tune for 'Music While You Work' on the BBC, and I was always so very proud that I belonged to the outfit that played that.

Later on, and after the war, I used to freelance. Anyone that wanted me, I would go and do an evening with them. I done an evening with Jack Payne, and that really put a feather in me hat. I thought, I can't go wrong now! Didn't do me a bit of good, but it satisfied me. I even done a session with Max Jaffa. So I happened to move occasionally into higher circles.

It was sometime in 1939 that I left the railway. Well, the railway left me! The Robinsons went to Australia, and I moved to Market Harborough. That's where I was when the Nazis invaded

Poland. I was intending to make my life in Market Harborough, because I was doing very well there. I had very nice digs with a quiet respectable family, Bill Fellowes and his wife, and his son young Bill. I was working as a salesman for Betterware products during the day and as a barman in the Cherry Tree pub at night, and still doing gigs with the dancebands now and then.

Selling door-to-door for Betterware was all right; it was interesting. The only trouble was, you had to keep yourself fairly well dressed, and I used to forget to shave an occasional time, or maybe forget for three or four days. There was no money worth anything in it, but I was getting enough to pay the landlady. Then I worked for a short while in the cattle market at Market Harborough, which at that time was a very big cattle market. I was a ringman — I used to show the animals in the ring, turn them in the right direction.

Old Bill, my landlord, was a foreman in the rubber works: they used to make rubber buttons and washers. Old Bill, his brother Sam, and young Bill played in the works darts team, and I became the first person who wasn't an employee to join the team. We were good. Sam and young Bill could hit anything you mentioned, and I wasn't too bad either. We won everywhere we went and got our names on the Leicestershire cup.

So that's the life I was leading when the war started. The compulsory call-up didn't come until later. After a while I decided it was time to take a trip back to see my family, because it was already a few years since I left.

15

THE MAKINGS OF AN ACTOR

At the beginning of the war I stayed back home for quite a while. I helped Jim and my father out on the land, cutting turf and saving hay and doing all the other jobs there was to be done. I also done a bit of droving cattle and horses at that time, which I'll tell you about in the next chapter. And something else I done quite a bit of was acting in little local drama productions and appearing in local concerts. In fact I very nearly became a professional actor down in Dublin.

I appeared in quite a few plays when I was at school and then, in later years, bigger plays. James McDyer, the schoolmaster, produced quite a lot of plays, and I was in mostly all of them. They were put on in the local halls; the idea was to gather up money for repairing the school — keeping the broken panes replaced. They were mostly comedies — sort of ad-lib plays. We didn't worry too much about learning all the words, because we could always think of something to fit. There were some really good little plays that I never saw before or since. McDyer wrote one or two short plays — sketches, he used to call them. They were very funny. I wrote one or two which I produced myself and had a few of the neighbour lads and lasses acting with me, and they were a bit of fun too.

I remember one sketch that I wrote. It was called *Signing On* — it was the time that the dole was getting quite popular. There was these two blokes and me. One of the chaps and me was coming in to sign on, and the other bloke was a real toffee-nosed character in the Labour Exchange, and he was giving us all kinds of troublesome questions to answer. It took a lot of thinking out really. We had to answer each question that he threw at us in a very roundabout way — which the Irish understood immediately — and also in a way that didn't incriminate ourselves and didn't give him any satisfaction, and he'd have to ask the same question maybe two or three times. When all was said and done anyway neither of us got the dole, we had to carry on working. I remember old McDyer used to laugh his heart out every time we done that one. He gave us a bit of help with things.

The next play that I wrote was a full-length one called *The Rolling Stone*. That was four acts, and each act would be over a half-hour or so. McDyer gave me a good hand with that. He had a little hall beside the school, and we used to practise in there, and we gave it the first run there. I wrote it out word by word. The others copied out their parts. In fact they copied it out from beginning to end, because I made it a rule that everyone had to know every other one's part, so there was to be no confusion as to who should say what or when should somebody talk, because we had no prompters, no stage managers, no nothing like that.

The story was about two brothers who lived with the father and the mother. One of the brothers was a good horseman, but he had one horse that was very difficult to work. Somehow or other the younger brother had a way with horses that he could work this horse. Then the older brother took a notion to sell this particular horse, and he sold it to a horse dealer. On the way home the dealer had an accident and the horse jumped off the road with him and hurt him badly. He lay in hospital for quite a while, and anyway he died. Now in between the accident and the dealer dying, the younger brother, who was me, came over here to England and got on radio! This radio in the play was about the first radio that was ever heard in our area other than the one that McDyer had. But we didn't have a radio: what happened was that I went into the wings and sang, and one of the girls pretended she was switching on the radio. Honest to God, there were no end of people in the hall that believed that it was a real radio. They did, because they knew nothing about radios. Some of them had heard the one that McDyer had, but plenty of them had never seen or heard one.

What I sang in the play 'on the radio' was just the songs of that day, which were the ballads. The ballads of Stephen Foster's were pretty well known in those days. My mother had a world of Stephen Foster's songs, and lots of the people around had. Not just 'Swanee River' and soft stuff like that, but other ones like 'My Old Kentucky Home' and 'Goodnight'. So anyway, the younger brother returned home, and the older brother took ill and was in hospital. The younger brother was really a bit of a useless bum. He was over and back to England, and he wasn't really making any money, and he wouldn't settle anywhere, and he wouldn't help on the farm. He was forever talking big — he would have to build a new house, and he would have to do this. In the end he made good. He met up with a girl back home — they were babies together — and he married this girl and he done all right for himself after that. The brother married another girl and they all lived happily ever after.

We took the play around a bit, and performed it in local halls around the county. It got very good write-ups, too. Now at that time the character of the younger brother wasn't a bit like me, because that was before I started the wandering. But it's a funny thing, and many's the time I've thought of it since, but I became exactly like that character. When I left home in 1937 I was the makings of a very sensible, well-together bloke, and I got exactly like that character nearly in every way, about singing and telling stories — lies and truth, it was all the same — and away at night instead of coming home at a reasonable time, not fit to get up next day to go to work and all this caper. Just the same as I was doing in real life, only a few years later.

Besides the plays, at that time I used to appear in local concerts with a mate of mine the name of Eddie Keeney. We used to do two-man acts, and one of us would be the comedian and the other would be the side man — probably time about, because we were both on the same way of thinking, as daft as brushes. We done some right good little sketches at that time and shortly after. We used to write songs and do them as duets. He was about the same height and build as me, and we would try to dress as much alike as possible, well, everything to drive the fool further. I suppose the stuff we were doing wouldn't be either looked at or listened to nowadays, but in them times we were a bit of fun. People could laugh at us along with laughing with us.

Eddie went to America and got into showbusiness over there. He's still in New York, as far as I know; many a time I thought I would like to go to America and visit him for old time's sake, but it never happened. He was a clown — very nice fiddle player, and played the accordion. We used to travel quite a distance on bicycles for little concerts, and schools where there would be gatherings. We would cycle up to fifteen miles each way, maybe in the pouring rain and get wet to the skin. We never got paid, but we would get a good meal.

Some time after *The Rolling Stone* McDyer decided I had the makings of a professional actor and that he would try and get me into the Abbey Theatre in Dublin. He was impressed, not so much by that play, but by the things I was doing and the way I could carry on in some of his plays. I always got a fairly prominent part in his productions. Also, if I never acted, I had the gift of talking myself out of nearly any predicament, which he said would be a good asset for the stage. I could ad-lib like hell, and at that time I could talk like a motorbike, just 'brrrrrr....' straight through, no stopping for ages.

He went ahead with the plan anyway, and at that time I had every intention of joining the Abbey players. The theatre paid my way to go to Dublin for an audition, and stay overnight. I had a talk with the director — I can't remember his name now. I was offered the job; it even got so far that they got the size of my hat, gloves, shoes, suit and everything. Anyway, I turned it over in my mind and I thought, it would be great to be a player, but it would mean being tied down, that when somebody wanted me I would have to hop to it. I just couldn't do that. So I ducked the whole thing, and soon after that I returned to England, while the war was still on.

McDyer was very disappointed, indeed he was. It was all so wrong of me to not make up me mind in good time before he went to all this trouble. He was a good man, McDyer, a good old stick indeed. He was retired at that time, and in fact his son was teaching in the school. Later on his son got moved on, got a better school somewhere. Our school wasn't really what you would call an attractive school for a young master to move into. As I mentioned before, it was a dingy, cold place, with the snow coming in the crick in the wall But McDyer stuck it, and he was hardly ever ill.

Still, if I turned my back on being an actor, it wasn't the end of my career in the entertainment business: there was plenty more in that line to come.

16

DROVING DAYS AND
THE COUNTRY FAIRS

Of all the occupations I have had in my time, the one thing that I always went back to when I had the chance was working with cattle and horses — droving, and buying and selling animals. This was when I would be back in Ireland: between the time I came back from England the first time and when I finally sold the farm Jim and me had after he died in 1964, I was back and forth between England and Ireland no end of times — and whenever I was back home I would be on the lookout for a bit of droving work.

I was always fond of cattle, always had a way with them — and horses too, although I think I was much better handling cattle than I was horses, because I made a few slip-ups with horses, but I never remember doing anything completely wrong with cattle. Droving was a very nice life — 'twas a wandering life, and you were always meeting so many people.

I started droving pretty young, in fact: 'twould be before I was fourteen, because while I was still at school, I would take a couple of animals somewhere maybe for my father or some neighbour. One time I delivered a cow that a chap had bought off me father, and I had to take her out to St John's Point. I remember this very clearly, because I got there about two o'clock in the afternoon, and the herring fishers were just about to go out. I remember this fellow saying,

'We won't go too far today, there's a storm coming.'

And there wasn't a breeze. They'd only rowboats in those days, and they hadn't much hope if a storm came on on a rugged coastline with a little rowboat. In fact they didn't go out at all that day. I looked at the sea, and it was as calm as could be, but this fellow knew by some tilt of the waves or the colour of the water that there was a storm coming, and sure enough one did come. And the storms on the coast of Donegal could be rough! There were a lot of fishermen lost over the years at St John's Point and

Inver and right around the coast to Aranmore. I think there were six lost from one boat — nearly forty years ago, I suppose — and the husband of the girl who lived beside me was drowned. They would get caught in freak storms that would come on them too suddenly, and ground seas, where the storm would be under the surface of the water, the water would be churning and tip the little rowboat over.

During the war years, after I came back from my first spell in England, I used to do a lot of droving and walking in Counties Tyrone and Fermanagh and Derry. The army were a proper nuisance, because they would have up to twenty lorries coming along the road at a time, and me on me own trying to keep twenty or maybe thirty cattle together with these lorries coming through them was not easy! During this time there was another occasion that I will never forget.

I had to walk a couple of horses from Ballysadare to Ballybofey, and if you ever look on a map you'll find that is a heck of a distance. They were untrained horses, and I had to walk every inch of the way. Took me a couple of days. I broke the journey outside Ballyshannon, and why I broke the journey was, there were tinkers camped on the side of the road, and I was feeling a little bit tired at the time, and very thirsty, and I could smell tea. It was the Collins family, and they were horse dealers, so they all came out into the road to look at the horses I had with me. I tied the horses to a gate and sat down and had tea with them.

The tinkers used to make their tea in an open pail on an open fire. They set up a tripod, they hung this pail over the fire, and they made the tea like that. It was strong tea too. We started swapping songs and tunes. Old Collins, the father, was a fair good melodeon player — old three-stopper melodeon — and his daughter Kathleen, who was about fifteen, was a beautiful singer, and her brother Ned, who was a couple of years younger, was a great mouth-organ player, and I had a whistle with me, of course. I should be on the road, but I couldn't leave — the crack was good.

I got a very nice song from Kathleen. She was very shy — so shy she wouldn't look at me, and she sang staring into the side of the caravan. The song was called 'Young Alvin', and I don't know where it came from, but it was one of the best and the most obscure stories that I ever heard. After she sang it I asked for the words and scribbled them down on a bit of paper. It wasn't so easy trying to get the words down because there were about four of them all singing it at the same time and all talking at once. Mrs

Collins could not shut up. She would be telling me one line of the song while I would be writing another, and it was most confusing. Little Kathleen wouldn't say a word at all. I would ask her something and she would look at her mother! They were never in England, the kids, but they could name the places so well that appeared in the song, like 'Woostershire', and 'Airl's Coort'. Probably I didn't pick up the song exactly as Kathleen sang it, but I did pick it up well enough to add in my own bits where I didn't catch it. I put it on an LP about thirty years later (*Songs of a Donegal Man*).

Kathleen sang another song, in Gaelic, it was called *An Cúileann Súl Glas* — the green-eyed girl. The air to that was one of the nicest things I ever heard. It was a beautiful evening towards the end of September and we were just sitting on the grass. She had a very high-pitched, plaintive voice, and listening to that was marvellous. The sound seemed to get into the trees and stayed there. I have the air to that song yet.

The father had some really good tunes. We done about two solid hours playing the same tune — I got so carried away with it I wouldn't let him stop. It was one that he called 'McShane's Rambles', a jig. So it finished that I stayed on all the evening and all through the night. When day dawned I should be at least as far as Donegal town, but I wasn't, I was still back outside Ballyshannon, at Finner. I had to belt on for Ballybofey. I was nearly a day late arriving with the two horses, but it didn't matter, I had some nice tunes with me.

I always carried a whistle or a mouth organ when I was droving. Say now if I left a fair at Dunkineely or Ardara and was heading for Donegal, you never know, there might be a little music session in some place in Donegal when I would get there. It was a great way of passing the remainder of the night, and it's nice to be fit to sit down and play a tune here and there. Oh aye, and I used to get bottles of Guinness and threepenny loaves and things for playing bits of music.

Indeed I would play on the road when there was nobody around. People will tell you that cattle are fond of music. Well, I don't know. Maybe I wasn't the greatest musician in the world, but I never could see that it made one bit difference to them. They could be awkward buggers no matter how many instruments were playing! They'll listen to music — you'll see their ears moving, but it doesn't mean that they're going to be well behaved. Although mind ye, here's a strange thing: some cows, if they get accustomed to singing while they're being milked, they won't give the milk if there isn't a song going on. I know that for a fact, because my mother had that habit of singing away when she would be milking, and my brother Jim used to sing away or whistle. The cow would be quite patient while the song was going on, and if you stopped singing, or if a stranger started milking, she would get very fidgety and keep looking around and moving her feet, wondering where was the song. Cows can be pretty intelligent. They look stupid, but they're not near as stupid as they look.

It would be during those years, the early war years, that I first started working for some cattle dealers called the Leonards. They were two brothers from Pettigo — two very nice blokes indeed, and great characters to work for. I started droving cattle for them; I was also looking after cattle on the farms, but mostly going to fairs and driving the cattle. In fact it finished up that I worked for them over many years. Whenever I was back in Ireland I would do little jobs for them, up until the week before I left in 1965.

These lads were cattle dealers and cattle exporters. They used to ship the cattle from Derry over here to England. So they would go away to a fair and they would buy maybe twenty or thirty cattle. Then there would be other people, smaller dealers, from that area would buy cattle, and the lot would be put on the road and I would be put after them with a stick.

I got the offer from the Leonards to work chiefly for them, but freelance too, and I was a sheep drover too for other people. I went to live in the Leonards' house and on their farms, in Pettigo. Right on the edge of the border of Northern Ireland, very near the border of Tyrone and Fermanagh.

There were a few lorries, in fact, but for a long time after the war the petrol wasn't all that easy got, so in those days I was a lot cheaper than run a big lorry! I would have to drive the cattle long distances. From Ardara to Donegal is fourteen miles, from Donegal to Pettigo is nineteen, and 'twould be over another twenty miles to Omagh. Well, I walked cattle from Ardara to Omagh, from one end of Donegal right down well into Tyrone.

With cattle I would put as high as eighty animals in front of me. It was not difficult driving cattle, really. It would be difficult until you got them away from the towns where they were bought and away from their own surroundings. Once you got them out on a mountain road, and they got tired and their feet got a little bit sore, they got stupid, and they plodded on straight and never tried to give any trouble.

There was one time I had a right set-to. At the time there were very few cars on the road. It was night-time and I was coming from Ballintra fair, and this character came along with a little van. He never pulled up at all, he just drove in through them, and he hit a heifer and knocked her down. When he came out of the van I tackled him with a stick, but he was a pretty active young fellow and got out of my way. I cracked the glass in the door of the van. There was a law case about that, and he was charged for reckless driving. Funny enough I didn't have to go to court, but I was charged for not having a light.

Often two of us would start away with the cattle. One day a bloke called John McLaughlin was with me, a crazy character, but a good-natured chap. It was very hot, it was about the beginning of August. After we left Ardara a big black cloud appeared. It started a thunderstorm and a big downpour of rain came. Now McLaughlin was going to a dance that night on his way home. He always carried a mac under his arm. So he took off his trousers and his jacket and rolled them up, and put the mac on top of his shirt, and put the jacket and trousers under the mac, and that's the way we walked through Donegal town; he had nothing on only a mac and a shirt.

Mind you, the people probably wouldn't have realised anything. They might think he had his trousers rolled up to his knees. In those days the trousers had thirty or thirty-two inch bottoms, and when your trousers got wet, they spun round your leg each step you took. So we used to roll them right up to our knees and pin them up with safety pins. We had to be ready to make a quick dash somewhere, and if your shoes stuck in the leg of your trousers, you were hip head over heels. You had to be always on the alert to save an animal from breaking away on a byroad or going through a fence. When you get accustomed to cattle you'll know if one's going to do something out of the way. You can almost see them planning!

I did sometimes take a dog when I would have sheep on the road, but not for cattle. The trouble with cattle, they get frightened of dogs, and if the dog nips one, that one'll get very nervous, and that one'll cause trouble in the whole group, because fear and nervousness is very catching amongst animals — as we used to say, it's 'smiting': they can sense if one is afraid, and the whole lot starts giving you trouble then, running off the road and all that. I never reckoned that dogs were much of an asset with cattle, but with sheep, yes, they were useful. Because sheep can be crafty buggers you know. They'll lie down on the roadside when they get tired, and then you're stuck with them. But if you had a dog that would bark, that kept the sheep going. I could bark just like a dog at the time, and that sometimes came in handy!

Droving was a lovely life. We were very respected people, because we were doing a good job and we were peaceful. We were a bit of fun; it would be a giggle to walk along the road with us for a while, and we had the news from everywhere. Newspapers weren't all that popular in those days, and we were sort of news spreaders as we went along. The music was part of it all, too. We used to have little sessions here and there, like nights before fairs and horse markets. If we went to Ballyshannon, we would go down to Gallagher's Bar, and one of the Gallagher girls would get on the piano and we'd have a nice little sing-song. About Pettigo we'd go to Paddy Flood's and have a few songs and a few drinks. Around Pettigo at that time, and down the Donegal end of Tyrone, was a smashing place for country-house dancing. There were a few dancehalls, too, but the country-house dancing was really what we delighted in. It was very much like the dances and the big nights in my home area, which had pretty much died down by that time. Donegal, Tyrone and Fermanagh always seemed to have the same music, the same dances, the same culture, the same way of pronouncing things, the same obscure names for articles on a farm. Then you had Derry and Sligo and Leitrim, which were as near to Donegal, and 'twas an entirely different way of living.

Yes, it really was a grand life. I wish I was young and strong and that was going now, I'd be at it again. But there's no cattle droving now. They're put up in a lorry and that's the end of them. There's no fun in the fairs nowadays, because the auctioneer does all the talking. The people just stand around the sale-ring looking like they lost a pound and found a penny. I was at a mart in Donegal the last time I was home and I never understood one word that the auctioneer was saying. I didn't know who was buying cattle. I was looking all round, I couldn't see anyone buying, but somebody did buy them, because they were put down.

In the old days everybody knew who was buying cattle and horses because you would hear them shouting, calling each other all the names you ever heard. The horse dealers especially, they always appeared they were going to kill each other — sticks up to each other's faces, and telling the other what he could do with his so-and-so horses, and the other could do the same with his so-and-so money. And the language would be blue. But that was all fake, that was good business. If you didn't know that you would be scared stiff or think they were all fighting mad. I was so used to it, if that wasn't going on I would think, oh that's not much of a fair.

You carried on dividing down to the very last pound. But that was only the start of the argument. Then it came to what they called the luckspenny, that was, when you'd slapped hands and made the bargain to sell your animals, you gave the man back a little, to show that you wished him good luck of the animals. I remember when 'twas sixpence to the pound. Then it came to just whatever you wanted to give him. But he would always be looking for more. If he bought an animal off you and you gave him three or four bob, oh he'd be looking for more. And there would be an argument about that too. But it was all good fun. It was dead serious while it was going on, but it always finished at the bar. Didn't mean a thing what the row was, it always finished that one bought the other a drink. I used to be a go-between — the bloke that sort of tried to cut the cord at two ends: work for the buyer and the seller at the same time. I used to get a drink or a few bob from each of them that way!

At that time I could talk like hell, and I knew the cattle trade from end to end, because I was in it day and night. I would always finish the bargain, and divide to the very last, and I could always make the seller believe I was doing him a favour, and the buyer, who was probably my boss at the time, knew very well that I was working on his behalf. There was a lot of Irish spoken at the fairs — all the bargaining was done in Irish. That was probably the last time I spoke any Irish myself, at the old fairs forty years ago.

I used to show horses at the horse fairs too. I was pretty good at keeping a horse on his feet and jumping about in the right direction, but some of the dealers were up to some pretty low-down tricks. Somebody would bring a three-quarters dead old horse into a fair to sell him, and the lads that were showing the horse had this method of a nail in their elbow. They got a strap of leather and put the nail through it, a nail with a fairly big head and a very short stem, and tied the strap tight around at their right elbow, underneath their overcoat of course. The sleeve of the overcoat would be so wide that it would be outside the nail, until they would bend their arm, and then the nail came out through the cloth of the overcoat. They stood on the left-hand side of the horse, and held his head good and tight towards them, with their elbow bent so the nail was sticking into his neck. He would jump suddenly, trying to get away from this pain, and he didn't know where it was coming from, and his eyes would light up and his ears would move about and he would get all lively and excited. They would hold him as best they could, and tell him, 'Quiet, now,' and explain to the poor gullible farmer who was looking on,

'It's all right, it's only when he sees another horse; he'll settle down, he's very quiet really.'

Then they would give him another jab with the elbow. The farmer, if he wasn't up to this, would think,

'Oh, that's a good lively horse!'

Maybe the poor old horse was about to die, but he would be quite active-looking, and the unsuspecting farmer would buy him.

Another thing they used to do was to put a whin — a very sharp pointed needle that grows on a gorse bush — under the horse's tail, and he would always imagine that there was somebody behind, and he would be trying to get away from this, and you could hardly hold him. And another trick was to put ginger sticks up in the horse's bottom. Yes, there was many a farmer bought a horse and spent his money unwisely.

Now I showed horses in my time, but I never stooped as low as any of them tricks. I wouldn't inflict cruelty, because I think that was a low-down thing to do. But I could use a plant on them, tickling them, so that the tail would be going and they would be prancing about. A 'plant' is a young ash stick, about three to four feet long. They're dangerous things, because they cut instead of bruising. If you were hit on the head with an ash plant it would probably cut you like a knife. They are very thin — no use for leaning on: they were only for use on animals, but even then you had to be careful that you didn't cut an animal. To tickle a horse when you were showing him was harmless enough: you walked beside the horse, as near to him as possible, and you had the plant under your arm with the thin end of it backwards. With the undulation of your steps and the horse's steps, there was no notice of you keeping your arm moving, and the small end of the ash plant was tickling the horse right in the flank. That kept him on the go too.

Everything about fairs was good fun in those days. We used to have lots of street singers and performers of every kind. People like the Collins family that I was telling you about, and Margaret Barry was doing the fairs at that time. In my very early days there were the ballad sellers too, selling the penny sheets, but by the time I came back from England at the start of the war they were all gone.

There was one performer in particular who sticks in my memory, a fellow called Paddy McCarthy. He would come into a fair, and he would borrow a cart wheel. Pigs and sheep were taken into the fairs by horse and cart, and there would be lots of carts around the town, mostly at a place called the diamond. Nearly every town had a diamond in those days. Now Paddy would borrow a cart wheel from somebody, and a cart wheel can be a heavy thing, shod with iron, and from a real farm cart — a solid cart, not a spring cart. It could be anything up to a couple of hundredweight. He caught that wheel and wheeled it up his leg, spoke after spoke, till he would get it to his stomach, and he would stagger about under the weight of it there for a while. Then he would get it as high as his shoulder, and he would stagger around with it on his shoulder. All of a sudden, he heaved it up, he put it on his chin and spread his arms out and walked around the fair with the cartwheel on his chin. I've seen him do it.

Paddy was making a good living as a performer at the fairs. People would throw money and all kinds of stuff. He had no fixed abode — he went from town to town, anywhere there was a fair or anything in the line of entertainment. I think he had done a fair bit of circus work, and he would have been over fifty at this time. He wasn't a big man — about five feet nine or ten, but built real solid and square, up to about sixteen stone. I've seen him pull a lorry with a ton of potatoes on it by his teeth, with a rope tied to the front of the lorry, and he wouldn't even let the driver come out of the lorry.

He never had any gear of his own, he had to borrow every-thing. He would borrow a ladder. I've never seen him do this trick with a ladder longer than about ten or eleven feet. He would plant this ladder in the middle of the street, and he would go up it! Not leaning to anything, not gripping on anything: it was an act of balance. He would go on up and get to the top, and he would be swaying, and he would turn over on the top and he'd come down the other side; he would pick the ladder up, put it on his shoulder and walk away to another part of the town where there would be a bunch of people and do the same.

The old fairs carried on as long as they could — up until I sold the land in 1965 it was all the old-fashioned fairs. But then the cattle auctions and the marts put them out of commission. The marts are mostly a cooperative thing: so many farmers in an area would club up together and build a mart, a cattle ring and sheds and weighing machine and all that. I think the sales are held every week or two weeks. I often wonder if the people who remember the old-style fairs really get any thrill out of going to the marts. I'm afraid I wouldn't if I was back home and I don't think I'd be very anxious to go to one. I know I'd miss the bargain making, dividing, hand slapping and the arguments that were so much part of the old fairs. They were as much a place of entertainment as of business.

17

WARTIME

After a spell back home, doing odd bits of droving work, helping Jim out on the farm, and almost becoming a professional actor, I came back over to England, in maybe forty-two or forty-three. I can't remember exactly what I did when I first came back — probably working on a building site, or something like that. But after a while, when I was living in Northampton, the call came to join up. There was no conscription in Ireland — the war hardly touched Ireland. But if you were living in this country there was no distinction made. I wasn't doing work of national importance like some of the blokes who came over with me who were still working at Stewart and Lloyd's steelworks in Corby. So, I got notice to report.

I failed the medical because of my lungs. I remember the x-ray machines, which were about the first body-scan x-rays; they were about the size of a wall of a house. It scared the life out of me when I went in! Now, during the war anything was accepted: you could get in the police, you could get in the army or any part of the services — providing you were physically fit. The one thing that was going to stop you was being unfit, and the slightest little thing — even if you had only a slightly bent arm or fingers, or anything like that, it would be against you, even to the end of the war. I knew a bloke who caught his finger in the chain of a hoist, and it had to be amputated — only just down about as far as the first joint. Well, he was turned down for the army, because that was his trigger finger. So, because of my lungs, they didn't put me into the army and send me away to the front: they put me instead into the Home Guard — 'Dad's army'.

Now this is a time of my life which I don't really like to recall, and over the years I have hardly mentioned it to anybody, because I'm not very proud of the job that I had to do. I was drafted in to what they called Internal Security work — or Insecs for short. And really, we were insects; it was a low-down kind of service.

There were very few of us in the Insecs. It was all so secret; you could be in it, and your best friend wouldn't know. I wasn't going to let anyone know what I was, in case they weren't 'all right' — on the level. Like it could mean that I would get my throat slit maybe. In Northern Ireland they had the B-specials, but we were known as G-specials, government specials.

I didn't have to wear uniform, and I didn't have to do any square-bashing. I had one job to do, and that was to keep my ears and eyes open, and also be sort of plausible — be the kind of a fellow that could gain somebody's confidence without making it noticeable that I was trying to do it.

We didn't have to live in barracks or anything; we just lived at home and carried on a normal life. They didn't really give us any training, but they advised us how to be an easy-going con man. I don't know why, but they reckoned I was fit to do that. They also trained us to poke someone's eyes out! If you saw somebody going for their pocket, there might be a gun in it, you just let him have it in the eyes with two outstretched fingers, and stooped at the same time, so that if he did get the gun out and tried to shoot even though he was blinded he would miss you. I never had to do that, thank God, and I usually had two blokes with me, and they never had to do it either.

I had a tin hat, a gas mask, and a pair of studded gloves that were too small for me. I was also given a dud service revolver. Many a time I used to see these blokes with big heavy rifles and packs on their backs and think, oh you poor silly buggers! There was Packie, dodging about with a little toy gun that you could put up your sleeve. I felt rather important, in spite of the fact that I had the lousiest job in the world! Mind you, the gun was only for appearances, because it would never fire: the pin had been filed down, we weren't given any ammunition, and neither were we trained how to use and handle it! I was never asked for that gun when the war finished. I had it for ages, and one time after the war when I moved to Market Harborough a second time I took it with me. I thought, hell, what am I carrying that thing for, and I handed it in at the police station.

I was based in Bedford, but wandering. Like, I might have to spend a couple of nights in Cambridge, or down in Farnham. They would tell me where to go. Very near Bedford there was a place called Thurleigh, where there was a big American base. There was another big one at Lakenheath. It was a very likely place for the 'floomers' to be. That was the word for someone who was a bit doubtful. A floomer could be either an informer, a spy, or working in some way for the other side. There was plenty of people doing that — for money of course. A few pounds went a long way during the war, and it was very tempting when the opportunity was there to take the money.

So a few of us used to do the pubs around them areas and keep the eyes and the ears open. There were also American servicemen looking for the floomers. We knew there were, but we didn't know them, because they were dressed in ordinary uniform, and we were English civilians as far as they were concerned. We used to have many chats with them, and we used to have friendly little disagreements with them over women, because they could get the girls and we couldn't. They had the money to hand out, and we had very little. And they had the gift of the gab, for chatting up the 'dames', and we were a bit behind the wall when that was handed out.

In the Home Guard they could call on you for several jobs besides the Insec work, but they never asked me to do all that much, because I was kind of useful in the pubs. I was a very fast talker, and I could talk myself into someone's confidence. If there was somebody that the authorities would be a wee bit worried about, they would ask me to befriend him. A policeman would be too noticeable, but I could always get into a casual conversation with somebody. You stood as near to them as possible, and you turned round one time and you accidentally put a tiny splash of beer on his arm, and you apologised and you wiped down his sleeve and you got into a chat with him.

Very often the pub landlord would be a go-between: he would know about the suspected person and would let you know who he was, or he would give you a hint that it would be wise to go to such-and-such another pub. During the war landlords and police were like twin brothers: that helped Britain to survive, and many a little drink would go out to the copper on the beat.

If you discovered anything suspicious you had to report it to the police. Or anybody destroying something useful. The only thing I had to report, and I wasn't a bit proud of it, it was something that the police never knew about. Two Scottish girls that were down doing Land Army work: I discovered through the landlord of a pub in Market Harborough that one of them was carrying a radio transmitter or receiver. What was she carrying that for? Carrying an ordinary wireless was an offence in those days. I don't know what happened to her — my job was done when I reported it.

I was sent down to Southampton at one time. I was in a camp about ten or twelve miles out of the city, and when I was there, the whole centre of the city was tumbled down by bombs. So we were sent in to dig for bodies and survivors, but I never found so much as one finger! I went to Coventry, and the same thing happened. Coventry was almost flattened, and I never found a person dead or alive in the rubble. And the same in Plymouth. I was there digging away all right, but I was the only one that didn't find anything. There was one bloke in particular who found a lot of people: he used to dig out youngsters, little kids, some of them still alive.

It was all voluntary work in the Home Guard. I made a living doing building-site work — little bits of carpentry, and concreting, and I used to drive a dumper. I worked for Betterware products too, selling door to door. I still had my saxophone, but I did very little with it during the war. There weren't all that many dances. To start with, there was the black-out: the street lights weren't showing, and if you had any light inside your house you had to have a black cloth on the window. It would be a chancey thing to open a dancehall in a street where there would be no lights, and hardly any lights on in the hall. A lot of the musicians were conscripted, too: out of an average little dance band of six, four of the members might be away in the forces. So a lot of the bands disbanded. There was still an occasional dance here and there, like at St Philip's Hall in Kettering, where I used to go on Saturday nights. But there wasn't all that much happening in the entertainment business.

But, as I said before, the wartime is the one bundle of years I don't like to mention. People will tell you about the great years of the war, but 'twasn't a bit great as far as I am concerned. The one redeeming thing that happened during the war was the friendship among people. Like if you had a cigarette, you took a few pulls out of it and you saw that somebody was staring at you, and you knew that that poor fellow didn't have a smoke for a couple of days; you never saw him in your life, but you offered him a smoke, and maybe that cigarette would go right round a bus stop.

It got so bad that we had to take our own glasses to the pub for drinking out of because the publicans wouldn't provide them. Now a lot of that was caused by the Irish, I blush t'admit, because when they would get very drunk they would smash the glasses. During the war the publicans couldn't get glasses. So if you had no glass, you got no drink. There was no point in taking in glasses because they would be stolen in the pub, so we used to use jamjars to drink the beer out of! It was funny to see a girl drinking out of a jamjar — her fingers wouldn't be long enough to get round it, and she would have to hold it with both hands.

I was back in Bedford when the celebrations were on VE day. It was just go crazy. Bedford was quiet by the side of other places where they really went mad — I believe Trafalgar Square was out of this world. But in Bedford there was a chap so excited that he threw himself in the river just opposite the Swan Hotel and drowned himself. He was probably mad drunk, I don't know, but he jumped yelling off the riverbank and drowned himself.

18

BOOSTING!

The war years were a bit of a lapse as far as I was concerned. But I have to admit the years after the war, when rationing was still going on, did create a few opportunities for making a living, that is if you weren't above doing a bit of smuggling what — we used to call 'boosting'. It was harmless enough really, and it was something that appealed to my sense of adventure, I suppose.

I still giggle at the way I used to smuggle nylon stockings. They were like gold dust in England, and there were plenty of them to be got back home for about four bob a pair. You could get just whatever money you would ask from the Americans to give to the girlfriends. The Americans, to give them their dues, when they have money they're not bad about it, and they nearly always did have it, so they were good customers. I used to smuggle lots and lots of nylons. I carried an old mandolin with me over and back to Ireland, one of the old-style mandolins with a big hole in the centre with a grille. I cut the grille around so that I could get me hand in, and five or six inches of the neck was hollow. So I used to pack the nylons up in there.

I remember one time I was coming back from Dublin to Liverpool. I had a girl with me, Mary Duffy from Monaghan, one of the craziest people I ever met. Now at that time the Irish authorities were very strict about what passengers could take out of the country, so every piece of luggage would be thoroughly examined, and God help anyone found to be carrying an illegal commodity. Nylons being a very condemned item I could have been locked up for it. There was about four hundred passengers in the customs queue and we were almost at the back end, so on pretence of passing the time Mary started singing a popular song, 'Somewhere in France with You', which was made famous by Vera Lynn. I joined in singing and playing my mandolin as loud as possible. Mary wasn't a great singer, in fact she was a horrible singer, with a sharp screeching voice. Add to that my deliberate bad singing and out-of-tune mandolin playing and it wasn't first-rate entertainment. The customs men were looking at us and putting their fingers in their ears.

Besides the customs men there was a few *Gardaí* on duty making sure no-one slipped by before examination. One of them couldn't bear to listen to us — maybe he was fond of singing and didn't reckon much to our contribution, or it might be that we were singing a patriotic English war song, but whatever the reason he asked us to shut up, which we didn't do. After a few minutes he repeated his request and I gave him a bit of back-chat. He just grabbed me by the shoulders, almost lifting me off the ground, and marched me straight out the exit door towards the boat. After a while Mary appeared staggering with my case and her own luggage. We got on the boat, me carrying my mandolin stuffed almost full of ladies' nylons and feeling quite pleased with myself. They didn't give Mary a rough time owing to her having extra luggage, which was just as well, because she had about a dozen pairs packed into her knickers!

We had another racket for the Americans when I was back home after the war finished. I was living in Pettigo, which is right on the edge of the border between Northern Ireland and the Free State — in fact the Termon River runs right through the centre of Pettigo town, and one side is in Fermanagh and one side is in Donegal. The Americans stayed on in Northern Ireland for quite a while after the end of the war. They would come down to the border edge on an almost deserted road, but they would not come across into the Free State, into Donegal. There was a bloke the name of Paddy Gallagher and me; we used to do a roaring trade, carrying the booze across for them — it wasn't so very far from the bridge to the pubs.

They had to pay us in advance, 'cause we hadn't the money to buy what they wanted. They were very trusting really:

'Say, Mac, how about a couple of boddles of whiskey. How much will that be?'

You made a quick calculation but took a long time out of it, pretended that you couldn't count very well!

'Three bottles . . . ah, that'll be about nine pounds.'

'Nine, huh? How much is that in dollars?'

But of course, we knew nothing about dollars! So, down the street and get a few bottles of whiskey, or a can of Guinness or whatever it would be that they wanted. The whiskey was better, 'cause we could drive a bottle in each pocket of our jacket, stick our hands in our trouser pockets and go away whistling here or there and we weren't noticeable. The Guinness we used to carry over the bridge in a milk can, and that was a wee bit of a dodgy business; it worked for a while, but one night we had a mishap that put an end to that little trade.

When we went to the centre of the bridge each time, we used to fill the lid of the can and drink it! We were on no man's land. On this particular bridge — it wasn't a main road, let's face it — there was hardly ever a custom man or a policeman on either end. It was one bridge that was mostly always clear, and very few people used it for smuggling. We used to fill the lid of the can, which held about two pints or so, and drink it, each of us, then start away. Well, they were paying us for the full amount, so we were getting a couple of pints for nothing you see, not to mention the profit from the sale.

On this particular night — I don't know why I remember it, because I was often soberer and forgot things — we were having our usual mid-way sit-down. There was a slope up to the bridge and a slope down the other side, and we were sitting on the top there drinking away, course we were drunk I suppose: picked up the can and stumbled. The can fell on its side and it had the fall of the road, away it went, and the lid came off. The Guinness was pouring out of this can down the bridge, and it rolled and rolled, and we just sat there laughing, and let it go — what more could we do. I'll never forget that can going down the road. It was making the damndest noise you ever heard, because at that time the road wasn't even tarred, and it wasn't a level surface, there was rocks on it, and there the can was ripping away down the road. We retrieved it later on, but there wasn't much left in it when we got it. We drank what was left and tough luck on the Americans, we didn't see them no more. We lost good customers. I was scared of going into the North for quite a long time after that in case they should recognise me.

Why I was living in Pettigo at that time is because I was back working for the Leonard brothers, the cattle dealers. My memory is no good on dates as a rule, but I do know that I was back there working for them late in 1945. I left England when the war finished and I was out of the Home Guard, and I went back home and got into the cattle business again. I was a very good seller of cattle, and I could judge cattle all right to buy them — I wouldn't do anything wrong.

I used to do other jobs for the Leonards besides going out on the road driving the animals — like working in the fields and carting. They used to go away and travel all over Ireland to find cattle, and I would stay back on the farm and get the cattle ready for shipping that they brought back, which was rather an important job. They depended a lot on me, because there used to be wagonloads of cattle coming home to me, and I used to handle the lot. I had a free hand, and if I wanted help I could employ someone while he was away.

Supposing there was forty cattle, and there was twenty-three of them to be shipped on a certain day, I could pick out the ones that I thought would suit — roughly about the same size, age and appearance, and near enough the same condition. If you did that it meant that when you came to making up the price of them it wouldn't be so difficult. All you had to do was average them, and you wouldn't be more than a pound or two out. And I could hit them pretty sharp. There was several things I couldn't do, but I could look after cattle all right.

Then I would take them to what we called the punching pens. A vet would come along and examine them one by one and put a brand in their ear so the police, the customs and the shipping agents would know that they were tarriffed cattle, that they weren't smuggled into the North. Pettigo and Belleek were the two punching pens that we used. It was great because you could buy the cattle in the Free State, drive them to the border edge, get them punched there, drive them across then into the North, and you could take them anywhere through the North and no-one troubled you. I used to gather them up, bring them up to Pettigo punching pen on foot, then drive them on foot to Kesh in County Fermanagh, where I would load them onto a train; they were away then by train and by boat and that was the last of them.

I was a good loader; I could load wagons of cattle as good as anyone, which is important really, to load them properly, otherwise if one goes down you could have a right mess. That was railway wagons, heading for the ships, before the lorries became popular.

Then the lorries came in. They were handier because they could go at any time, they could always wait for an hour or so, but the train went at one particular time, and if you didn't have your cattle there, you missed out, so it was always a rush to get your cattle away.

In between working for the Leonards I used to do spells for other people. This is where the smuggling comes back into the picture. Now, if you got the animals ear-punched at the border like you were supposed to, you would lose a few pounds that way, because if they were punched they were a bit down in the market. The home-bred animal was always supposed to be more valuable than the driven one, and if they were punched they were supposed to be driven cattle, and they came from God knows where. Whereas if you bought cattle from your own area, you knew that these cattle were a good stock.

So that was the principal reason we used to smuggle them through what we called 'free of the ear' — not punched. We would take them through and they would be sold as local cattle. You got someone in the Northern side to stand for them, to sponsor them for you: someone that probably had sold some cattle a week or two before to some shipping man and they were way out of the country. So if you arrived with five or six cattle and they were put on this man's land, and of course, they were all his cattle, as far as the authorities were concerned. That way then when it came to the fair, he would sell them for you. Of course, he got a backhander out of it, or you done him a favour some other way. They all joined together to fool the government — although it didn't always work I regret to say.

We didn't restrict ourselves to cattle, either. Rationing was still going on for ages after the war was finished, and when you were constantly crossing the border with cattle as I was, well someone would ask you to do a bit of smuggling on your way back — carry some tea or tobaccay back into the South, the Free State. You would be well enough paid for doing that, and it was very tempting. I have to admit that I did my share of smuggling.

Tea was so rationed in the Free State that you could have about two cups of tea a week. But in the Free State there was lots of sugar, so that used to go the other way. But the sugar wasn't capturing the same return of money, because it's bulky. You couldn't carry much more than half a hundreweight across the mountain. Now a half-hundredweight of tea, that was worth something, but the same weight of sugar wasn't worth all that much. There was also Free-State butter going out into the North, and tobaccay was coming in. Tobaccay was like tea, you could carry a lot of it.

Of course, we used to get into some scrapes. One time there was four of us smuggling tea into Donegal from Tyrone. We kept off the road, we went through the mountains all the time. We heard this noise away at a distance, coming the opposite direction to us, but the thing was, it could be some other poor fellow

BOOSTING! 143

doing a bit of smuggling, so we didn't take a lot of notice. But suddenly the big men appeared, and there we were, each of us had four stone weight of tea in rago bags on our back. Threw down the tea and run for it, of course. I sprained my leg. I thought it was broke because it cracked. I rolled down a bank, and the policemen, two of them, they passed as near as ten to twelve yards, and they never saw me. The other three blokes got away, because they knew the mountain. The police didn't know the mountain, and they couldn't run as fast on land that they didn't know.

I lay there for quite a long time, and when I got up I wasn't fit to walk. One bloke just put me on his shoulder, and we came back, picked up all the tea. One bloke carried two bags of tea, and the other carried me and a bag of tea, and we landed the lot safe. Me with a bad leg. I was on crutches for quite a while.

There's still a bit of smuggling going on. There's one thing I do know: in those days you couldn't drop a couple of pounds to some policemen and say, 'Close your eyes.' That didn't wash. Backhanders can do a lot of . . . let it be damage or good, I don't know which, but they can really work in most walks of life. But no, you didn't approach a policeman, or a custom man neither, even on the Free-State side. You kept clear of them all as long as you could. Indeed, there was policemen beaten up with sticks, and there was horrible things happening, although I never happened to be in any fights with them, because I was always more dependent on me feet than me hands. Let me legs take me out of the danger, because I wasn't all that trained to deal with policemen.

No, it's better to run, and if you had cattle you ran. That's the first thing you would be told: 'Save yourself, lad.' You were going to lose the cattle anyway — they were taken away and auctioned — but you saved yourself. The penalty would be jail, and the man that sent you lost you then for other jobs. If the police approached ye you could be sure that the cattle were going, so the only hope you had is hide or be a good runner.

As I was telling you, in those days, smuggling was called 'boosting'. Whatever you were carrying or driving, that would be called the 'prog'. I don't think that anyone outside the smuggling fraternity knew that such words existed. 'Do the skip': that was to hop it. If someone was beaten up, it was 'laid' — which means a different thing nowadays!

19

KING'S LYNN YEARS:
FACTORY, FARM AND CIRCUS HAND

From the end of the war in forty-five I didn't really settle down to any particular job or profession. I was just a bit of a drifter — having lots and lots of trips back home. I never done myself very much good, either at home or over here — well not in fact until I got into the folk singing. That was the first thing that really tied me down a bit. I knew that I had to be reasonably successful at something, and I found that the folk singing was the only thing that was fit to cool me down.

I was back in England before very long. I worked on the railway again for a while, but not with horses this time. This was up at Gretton in Northamptonshire. I worked out on the line as a platelayer, putting in new sidings. I was a lengthman. I liked that job, and I done quite a term at that; although when I first started, being new, they put me into the tunnels to get all the smoke into my lungs that they could, which wasn't the greatest thing for my health.

Then I spent the best part of several years up in Norfolk, in King's Lynn. During the winters I worked in the sugar factory. I done three winters there: that would have been 1946, 1947 and 1948. I was two winters outside driving a dumper, and a loading engine, but the first one I was inside, working on the carbonating tanks: I was telling you about that earlier, because that was the year I was sent over to Dublin to meet the Gaelic-speaking lads from Connemara and bring them over to work in the factory. But in the end I couldn't stand the heat; it was getting too much for me, and I used to have very severe pains in my chest. That in fact was probably the beginning of my TB, which put me into hospital for a number of years in the fifties. So they put me outside the next two seasons. I remember the general foreman saying,

'You were a good man on the tanks, but I think for your own sake we'll have to put you out in the yard. Are you a driver?'

'Well,' I said, 'I do drive.'

'Right, have a practice on that loading engine, and there's a dumper there that you can haul in coke with.'

So I done two winters at that. It was cold — 1947 was a very bad winter — but it was good fun. And it was healthy. Before, when I was inside I was on three eight-hour shifts, but I was on steady days when I was in the yard, which was nice for me. I could go to the pub or wherever I wanted to at night.

During the summers I done quite a variety of jobs. I worked on a farm near King's Lynn for a fellow, believe it or not, his name was Ephraim Gotobed. A good lad he was too — quite a young fellow, he was only married a couple of years. He advertised for a contracting firm to dig a lot of big open dykes through this common land belonging to about five or six farmers, and he was appointed the head man of the common land. At that time I was working for a very small drainage contracting company called McCarthy's, and McCarthy got the job. One day there were a load of pipes to be taken from the main road down to where we were working. The tractor driver broke his leg the previous day, so Mr Gotobed came down and asked,

'Can anyone drive a tractor?'

So I said, 'I'm a kind of a driver.'

'Right,' he said, 'Come on up Paddy and bring down the pipes.'

So I did. Of course, we started yapping about horses and breeds of cattle, and all this caper, so when we got back he went to McCarthy and said,

'I would like to keep that man here on the farm.'

McCarthy said, 'Oh, fair enough. If you want him you can have him.'

So I stayed with Gotobed. I done quite a bit of tractor driving for him, and some horse work too, hauling things here and there, and looked after the cattle for him. The only thing I never had to do was use the milking machine. There were blokes specially for that.

We used to have great fun. There was one girl worked on Gotobed's farm: she was looking after the poultry. She was a very good-natured character, but quite honestly now she wasn't the prettiest thing in the world. She had great big buck teeth, and kind of squinty eyes. I used to take her to the pictures once in a while to get free eggs. Crikey, I used to come home with canfuls of eggs. There was then another girl that looked after the dairy, where they used to get the milk done up specially to send into hospitals and hotels — they were a very rich concern this Gotobed lot — so my mate Ted got friendly with her, and we used to come home with our cans full of milk and eggs.

Rose, my girlfriend, didn't mind me taking the poultry maid to the pictures, because eggs were rationed at the time and very valuable, but Ted's wife was the jealous type. They had a fight about it and she knocked out two of his teeth!

I remember one day as we were leaving the farm. It was pouring rain. Ted had the old van down on the roadside, and we were running down the laneway from the cattle sheds to the road. Gotobed's foreman — I think his name was Macklin, but we called him Curly because he was as bald as an egg — he came out and he called, 'Hey!'

So we stopped, of course — 'twas manners to stop.

'Now look!' he said, 'If I catch you coming round here again with that can, you and I'll be in trouble. You'll be in trouble for carrying it, and I'll get into trouble for kicking it over the hedge. If you're going to bring a can, bring one that'll hold something!'

Ted had only a tiny little can. So he said, 'Right, I'll bring a decent one!'

So we thought we would take Curly at his word. They had these huge big churns, eighteen gallons I think they hold, to take the milk away to the creamery. There were four or five brand new ones just arriving, and Ted said to me,

'Wouldn't it be a good one to put one away and carry it up some time when Curly would be about to see us?'

Oh we timed it nicely. About ten o'clock in the morning we both arrived up at the yard, carrying this huge can between us! Ted said,

'Right then, I've brought the kind of a can you said.'

'Oh, you,' he said, '—— off!'

They were smashing people on that farm. The Gotobeds's farm was at West Wynch, just a few miles outside King's Lynn.

Rose used to play the piano and I used to sing in a pub called 'The Chequers'. The landlord didn't pay us, but he always sent us home in a taxi with a parcel of food and beer. We had a small but comfortable flat out at North Lynn; nine shillings a week unfurnished, which suited us fine, because I used to scrounge bits of unwanted furniture, do some repairs and paint work and in a short time we had a nice little place.

After a while one summer I got tired of the farm work and took a job with a circus. I left Rose behind in our flat in King's

Lynn. The circus was called Grapellio's, and I was a wagon man — making sure that everything like harness, swivels, linchpins, traces, and stuff like that was all in working order. I was responsible for the road only — nothing to do with the ring or the performing animals. I had an open dray which carried the seating and most of the timberwork, pulled by two horses. There was a pug horse for helping out on steep hills. Everything was hauled by horses, and the performers helped with erecting, striking, loading, driving horses — everything in the show. There was one engine which supplied the lighting, and one car which belonged to Mr and Mrs Grapellio. That may give you some idea of the kind of a bum outfit it was.

The Grapellio family were the leftovers from a well-known international circus and as low-down as they come. They had one son, a useless brat of eighteen who thought he was only one step down from God because he could walk on a tightrope. I never could remember his name, maybe because I didn't want to, so I called him 'Puke'.

I travelled with that show for three months, getting more fed up day by day. We each had our place when on the move. The ringmaster always went in front with his animals — four dogs, two liberty horses, two parrots, a goat, and two draught horses pulling his wagon. He also had a performing skunk that could do very clever tricks with an umbrella and beach balls, but he had to be kept well away from the other performing animals owing to his bad temper and stink, which cannot be described in any language. He was kept in a little box car and hooked to the back end of my dray. I was second in the line. Behind me came Mitsi, a sixteen-year-old bareback equestrian. She had two horses, a mare and a stallion, and she used them for both road and ring. A very nice kid, and we all loved her.

One morning we were leaving Gainsborough. It was pouring rain. When we came to a fairly steep incline I hooked the pug horse to help mine over the hill. When we were about halfway up I could see that it was a sharper pull than I thought, so I shouted at the pug horse. All three got speeded up and as the dray lurched forward the linchpin in the towbar jumped out and away down the road went the box car with the skunk.

By this time Mitsi was just starting from the bottom of the hill, and when her horses saw the box car ripping towards them they went crazy, especially the stallion. Nobody knew exactly how it happened but the mare fell on the centrepole and broke it. The ringmaster saw what happened and came back to take over from me. I ran down to help if I could. Mitsi was screaming and her mother was cursing and swearing in French. Others were cutting traces to free the horse, and there was Puke, not doing a thing to help, calling Mitsi dirty names in broken Italian and getting in everyone's way. When he used one very nasty word towards her I couldn't take any more, and as I might never have the opportunity again I clobbered him. He fell on his back, and as he was getting up one of the clowns kicked him in the face. He ran down the road with blood pouring from him.

A few of us went up the road to where the box car was on its side in the ditch, expecting to be sick any moment when the stink would reach us. But when we got to the box, there was the skunk, as happy as could be, grooming himself and making tiny snoring sounds. He was the instigation of all the trouble and enjoying every minute.

I got the sack that very day, of course. I came back to King's Lynn by train and went out to the flat to find the front door open and not a stick of furniture in the place. I ran all the way to the shipping office where Rose worked, but they told me that she hadn't been to work for two weeks: her cards and a week's pay were still there. I went back to the flat, hoping there might be a note or something to say what was going on. There was a few plates and cups and all my clothes and gear, but no note. A woman that lived in the back part of the house said she saw a blue van taking away the furniture. As soon as the pubs opened I went to The Chequers. No-one there saw her for over a week, and by this time I was getting really worried. I stayed in The Chequers overnight.

We had a joint savings account in the Post Office, so in the morning I went there, thinking surely the money was gone; but it wasn't touched, which put me in a state of panic. I went to the police. They examined the flat but found no trace of forced entry, nothing broken, so that ruled out burglary. Then I remembered a space behind the door in the broom cupboard where she kept our few private papers. There I found the rent book, Post Office book, and other things of mine. But all her articles were gone. That relieved my anxiety considerably — at least she left of her own free will. I drew out all our money from the Post Office, left King's Lynn the next day and had a long, pleasant holiday in Ireland. I went back to King's Lynn later but I never did find out what became of Rose. I hope she is still alive and happy. I respect and forgive her for doing me wrong, because I deserved it.

I was working back in King's Lynn when my father died. It was January 1949, and the telegram was waiting for me when I got home from work. The landlady didn't think to send word to me that this telegram had been there all day. I couldn't get back for the burial. There was a rail strike, and I could not get to Liverpool from King's Lynn. I could by coming into London, but then the funeral would be over by the time I got to home. So I waited till the strike was settled; it only lasted a couple of days.

It never dawned on me properly that I wouldn't see my Dad no more until I went into the house. I just couldn't imagine that he wasn't there. I missed him very much, indeed, because he was a good man and a good father. May he rest in peace.

20

EARLY 1950S:
SHOWMAN AND STEEPLEJACK

After my father died I only stayed back home for a short holiday
before returning to England again. I can't really remember exactly what happened then. I can recall now plenty of things that must
have happened in those years, but I'm no good on what happened
after what. (Probably I would never remember any of this, only
I was prodded into it!) No, it is around that time that I cannot put
my thumb on anything, because everything was going wrong for
me. And 'twas me own fault, I was putting them wrong myself.

That was the time when I went on the wander. I know this
because I still have my I.D. card from those days. In them years,
if you didn't have a permanent address and a job, you were what
they called a 'displaced person', you were an itinerant, a wanderer.
And because I didn't have a permanent address and I didn't have
steady employment, I had to carry this card stating that I was a
'D.P.', and I had to be able to produce it if asked by a policeman
or a serviceman in uniform. If I was picked up anywhere, there
was an address on this card where I could be always sent to —
two in fact. There was one in Bedford, and one in Smethwick in
Birmingham. They were my two addresses, although I was hardly ever there.

I would go into some town and get digs for a week or two,
and work on a building site maybe — wheel concrete and do
rough carpentry and so on. Then I would move on somewhere
else and start selling something door to door: envelopes and
notepaper, or first-aid outfits.

I never drew dole, I always found something or other to keep
me going or pay my fare back home to Ireland. Sometimes I would
go busking: two of us used to come down from Bedford to North
London and do the cinema queues. My partner was Joe Kennedy
from Newcastle upon Tyne. He lost a leg in the war, and he used
to carry a big heavy piano accordion and two crutches. We used
to walk from Bedford to London and do the busk on the way

down. We kept alive, but perhaps we were wrong, because we were as proud as could be, and we wouldn't give anyone the satisfaction that we would just go on the dole. We thought we were worth more than that, so we decided to earn it, or do without it. After a while doing without you find you can't do without any longer, so we went busking.

We came as far south as Finsbury Park, and over east, Walthamstow and Dalston, we done the cinemas round there. We done quite a bit then away out, towards Ponders End and down there. There would be a queue outside a cinema, waiting for the door to open, and that's when we would perform. We played popular music, the kind of music you would hear in the dance hall, which was chiefly waltz and foxtrot and quickstep. I played a saxophone. I also played a huge big mouth organ, 'twas about a foot long. It was the nicest thing, it was the most like a piano accordion you ever heard, and with the accordion it sounded great.

Kennedy died just a few years after I parted with him. The remaining part of his amputated leg developed an infection which spread to his body and took his life. He was a really nice bloke, very even-tempered; he liked a smoke and a pint and the company of a girl. He was only thirty-two when he died.

I continued on in my restless life. I was restless in digs and I was restless in towns. There's hardly a town in England that I haven't lived in for a short while. I don't regret being such a wanderer, because it's worth it to meet so many different people. If you're stuck in the same job, you're meeting the same people day after day, and it gets monotonous. If you're moving around, you're always meeting new people. You meet a few you could do without, but the majority of them are really nice, and you're picking up what's happening to them, and swapping stories with them, and it can be a really interesting life. People in my station, the working class, sometimes they look down their noses at the middle class. But most of the middle class are all right if you know how to get on with them.

In the early fifties I lived in a lot of the towns around Northamptonshire — Kettering, Northampton, Market Harborough. I would maybe have a daytime job for a while. I would work on a building site, or build walls and cut hedges, you name it. Then I would go back into show business. Singing in pubs and cabaret, and playing the saxophone. That was something that went on and on for quite a time after the war. It was something that I never really knuckled down into or thought of it as a profession. But I would take a turn at it out of the blue, and do a while with the bands. Oh, a bad life. No life for man or beast!

In those years I done quite a bit of work with company road-shows. Munn & Felton's was one — they were shoe manufacturers, with factories in Kettering and Northampton — another one was Barrett's, and another bloke from Leicester — I can't remember his name now. I would do mostly singing for them, solo singing, and talking. I used to do compering for them, and also play a little bit here and there. At that time I was picking up well playing the whistle: I was a fairly good whistle player, and the fingers were working okay in those days. I used to do kind of little comedy acts with playing the whistle; anything that wasn't being done, I used to try it. If something is new, let it be good or bad, if it's new it's different, and different is good. So I used to get away with it anyway.

Munn & Felton's had their own roadshow, and one of the best brass bands maybe ever played in England. They used to tour. Nearly all the people would be working in the factory, although I wasn't. There's one good story from that time that I'll never forget. I was working in the roadshow, and at the same time I was also doing little bits of gardening and hedgecutting, digging up plots and all this caper, to supplement the little bit that I would get out of the band.

There was this yearly dividend to be handed out at the Co-op — what they called the 'divi'. Everyone that traded in the Co-op was a member; if you only bought tuppence worth you became a member of the Co-op, and you were eligible for a fraction of the divi that was going. And during the divi handing-out they always put on a fairly respectable concert, mostly for parents and children.

They booked a fellow, or at least this was what they told me, called Pat O'Brien, who was (according to them, although I never heard of him), a very well-known Irish tenor. The day of the concert news came to me through the Co-op, where I was a member, that Pat O'Brien couldn't make it, he had a bad throat or something. Would I stand in for him? So I thought, oh, it's me big chance! Away I went and I hired a monkey suit: clawhammer coat, propeller in me collar, hanky in me top pocket, flattened my hair — oh I was a real toff. The landlord gave me a ring: put on the ring and away to the Co-op hall. I was anounced as 'Pat O'Brien, the great Irish tenor'. I thought, there's one thing about it that

I don't mind, nobody knows me. And as there is no second chance to make a first impression I was looking my best and acting prim and proper.

Now they had a rule in those days: to keep them quiet, I suppose, the kids were all put into the first and second row, and the parents then were back from that. So there was two or three rows of little kids staring up, waiting to see this great Pat O'Brien. I appeared and of course started talking with me best Irish accent, making believe I was Pat O'Brien before I would start my song. This little girl, she wouldn't be more than about seven or eight, stood up in the second row and shouted:

'Mammy, that's the man what dug our garden!'

It appears that I did some gardening for her mother some time before. Oh crikey! I always enjoy telling myself that story. It cut the feet from under me anyway, and I was as posh as could be, the way a real Irish tenor would stand on the stage. How she knew me in my get-up I don't know, but she did anyway. I carried on — I said something like,

'You're right, darling, and you're a very bright girl, because I bet your mammy didn't know that, did she?'

And her mother said, 'No!'

You will put your foot in it sometimes, and there's no place in the world it happens as often as it does in showbusiness.

Another time we were doing the Ukrainian Hall in Leicester. I was doing my spot on my own. There were a lot of others on the bill but I didn't know any of them. There was an Irishman who was a flute player and doing a bit of singing. He was only a little bloke, about five foot six or seven, with a very strong Cork accent. I was going to play two whistles as part of my act, one in each hand, and I was practising in the dressing room. This character was hanging around and making a nuisance of himself, slugging out of a bottle and humming to himself. Me being the only other Irishman there, he was all over me of course. He came over to talk to me, and he was nodding about in front of me; finally he staggered forward, his forehead hit one of the whistles and pushed it right down me throat! Worse than all, it was a 'Clarke's' whistle with a tin mouthpiece.

I was about to go on to do a song, all dressed up in my stage gear, and there was my accompanists, a guitar player and piano player waiting for me, and I couldn't talk, never mind sing. There was a bit of quick thinking then on the part of the stage manager: he went out and told the musicians not to strike up the signature tune for me coming in. I was fit to play the two whistles though, so eventually I went on and I think that went better than if I sang a song.

But I couldn't sing any that night, and for about a month after I could hardly talk. The whistle cut the whole skin off the roof of my mouth on the way in. I made a kick at him, but he got out of the way in time. He wasn't seen no more, and he didn't appear. If he did I would've clobbered him, nothing surer.

Around this time I was friendly with a very nice girl in Northampton called Vera. I was living up in a place that I don't think exists now, called Far Cotton. I was in a house in a green field, and there's no green fields within miles of the spot now. Vera was the Queen of the Carnival in Northampton that year, whatever year it was.

I remember the Carnival well, because I had a horse and dray, with a little girl dressed up as Little Miss Muffet sitting on a tuffet in the middle of the dray. The sky opened, and for more than half the day the rain never left off. Everyone was drenched wet, including me; the horse that I had was not accustomed to traffic and I had to stay at his head all the time, patting him and talking to him, and I can remember me swearing too. Poor little girl, she was only about nine or ten — and there was another girl with her, letting a big spider down on a string. The first thing I had to do was to try and get the girls dried. Then I had to go all the way out to the north of Northampton. I had to leave the horse out there at the stable, and rub him down and give him a meal and all, and by that time it was ten o'clock at night and I had on wet clothes from about one in the afternoon. So I'll never forget that. Poor Muffet, I've never seen her since.

But Vera was chosen Queen of the Carnival that day. I had noticed her and thought that she was very nice-looking. And she was: twenty-two, and a tall, slim, beautiful girl. The following Saturday there was the crowning of the Carnival Queen, a ceremony in the old Corn Exchange, and a dance. I met Vera there and got friendly with her. She was a smashing dancer. I took her home that night and we went on from there.

We were meeting pretty regular, twice a week or maybe sometimes more, and one evening Vera plucked up courage and she said, 'Packie, why don't you come home and have a meal with us?' So I put on my best gear — at that time I used to dress up and look as good as I could — and I went to have this meal.

They had a beautiful house, very well kept, and there was a kind of a colour of money around. Vera's father was an all-right bloke — well, as all right as he could be, having to live with his wife, because she was a dragon. But at first she seemed quite pleasant to me. We were sitting in the front room, and I was given this very tiny little cup of undernourished tea that you get in these places, and I was trying to sip it and hating the sight of it. Eventually her mother asked,

'And what does Mr O'Brien work as, Vera?'

Vera said, 'He plays in dance bands.'

'*What? A showman!*'

And that ended the meal. She told her husband to remove me.

'Get him out of here, Richard!'

Richard didn't bother his head, he stayed out of the room. He wasn't silly, and he could see that something like this was going to happen. So Vera and me went out to a cafe.

We remained friends for quite a while. But 18 months or so after that poor Vera got TB, and she died in Rushden hospital.

Soon after Vera died I went back home for a while. Stayed at home and helped Jim with the haycutting and so on, and probably done a bit of work for the Leonard brothers. After I was there a short while my mother fell sick and was a term in hospital. They sent her home from hospital and they made us believe she was feeling fine. She was only home a week or two when she took bad again and died of peritonitis, an infection inside. That was November 1952. She was seventy-four. She was a couple of years older than my father, but up until he died you would think that he was fifteen, twenty years older than she was. He got very pale, his cheeks hollowed in, and his legs weren't so good. He had a touch of arthritis too. But she was as straight as your finger, a tiny little woman who could walk like anything and whip through a bit of housework. When she came back from hospital she was up and about — not doing very much, but on the move. There was myself and my brother Jim at home with her. My sister Memie used to come and visit us; she lived only about two miles or so away. In fact she spent most of the time with us.

The next time I went to England after my mother died I stopped in Birmingham as far as I remember. I got a job with a steeplejacking firm called Griffiths, a Welsh firm. The work was all right, but it was cold! Damn cold. If you pass through Bath on the train look out of the train window: in one particular place you'll see a row of churches, and they're in a straight line. The second church from the railway has a pretty high spire, and I helped to build the dome of that. I was up there on scaffolding.

I never was what you could call a mason, because I never practised, I didn't have cards to show that I was a mason, but I could do a nice little job with a trowel and mortar. I wasn't all that big, but I was fairly strong, and I was a good man for lifting. When you stand on the street and look up at the cross of a church, you think it's only a few feet high. But when you're up beside it, it might be anything up to twelve or fourteen feet high, and made of solid iron, and that would be taken up on a winch. In fact we winched every single thing in the old days, we never erected cranes. And I was a good man on a rope. I could winch a fair weight — three or four times me own weight anyway. I would do the pulling, and another man would be beside me, he would be the anchor man, the rope was tied around him.

I worked on and off at Griffiths for quite a while. Any time I went back there they started me on immediately. Then when things got a bit slack there, I was gone to Lord knows where — way up north or down south. I worked for them at Rubery Owens outside Birmingham, that was an iron foundry, and I worked quite a bit around Birmingham. I worked at what was the Old Trafford Engineering Company in Manchester, a heavy-engineering works; I helped to put in a big dust extraction unit that ran the whole length of the building. Then I worked for quite a long time up on the water towers, until they were finished in fact, at Brandon in Suffolk. I worked on the aerodrome at Lakenheath, pile-driving, and I also worked in Liverpool.

At that time I wasn't afraid of heights at all. But doing one job for Griffiths I had a bit of a fall. We were working on the roof of Ford's factory at Dagenham, putting a cowl on a chimney. Now a cowl is a thing that comes around with the wind that no matter what way the wind is blowing, the cowl stays in the opposite direction so the wind doesn't blow down the chimney and blow the smoke into the factory. We were on the very top. We were never supposed to bind the scaffold to the actual job we were doing, in case of the job collapsing. We were supposed to put up an independent scaffold, but that meant you had to put another scaffold outside it to strengthen it. Well that was maybe two days' work, having to haul up these iron bars. It was a lot easier putting one bar behind the chimney and two back into our own scaffold. So of course that's what we did.

Then the flaming top came off and away we went. There was
only two of us up there at the time, myself and a bloke called Jimmy Welsh, a very nice kid. There was a slope of a roof, well over
a hundred feet long. We both fell on that, but I kept slipping on
towards the edge of the roof in the middle, away from the corner
of the building. Jimmy slipped towards the very corner of the roof,
where the two walls and the roof joined. There was a loading bay,
and a place where they dumped sand and gravel and all that down
below us, and there was lots of old irons that used to be lifted
off lorries. It appears that one time a big item was being lifted off
a lorry, it hit the corner of the corrugated-iron roof and bent up
one corner of a sheet. Jimmy slid onto that, and the iron went
into his leg at the hip and ripped him right to the knee. He didn't
fall off the roof, because there was a heavy stone quoin at the corner, and the iron levelled out there. If he had fallen he would have
been killed for certain. I think he had to have the leg amputated.

Getting back to myself, I slid on down to the centre of the
roof and over the edge. The drop was about the height of a third-
floor window onto a concrete floor covered in bits of old iron
and stones and rubbish. I would be smashed only for one thing.
About ten minutes before the accident a lorry came in and tipped
a load of sand right in the middle of all this rubbish and iron and
gravel. I fell into the sand. And luck was with me several ways,
because there were some blokes moving some gear out of the way,
and they saw me come down, and they ran and got me out of
the sand before I was smothered. They got the ambulance: Ford's
had their own ambulance, and they came rushing — as far as I
know; I don't remember a whole lot about it, because I was chok-
ing. They took me away to hospital to get the sand cleaned out
of my mouth, my nose, ears, eyes, and all over. Within three or
four days I was back at work again. I didn't find out what happened to Jimmy until I came back, nobody would tell me. That
was one time my life was charmed. There wasn't a bit pity for
us, it was all our own fault. I suppose we never really understood
the danger we were in building the scaffold that way, but we did
after. I wasn't so keen on working heights after that.

When I got out of hospital I went back to Griffiths and I done
quite a while then in the machine shop in Birmingham, and I was
living in a part of Birmingham called Soho. Then I decided to move
on to Manchester. It wasn't long after that when luck came my
way and I had a marvellous holiday. There was a girl that I was
very fond of and I wanted to take her away for a holiday, for a

weekend. I had a mind to take her home, but that was going to cost too much and I hadn't very much money at the time. We decided to go over to Jersey. It was the time of the flower plucking, and I promised her a weekend over there. But as the time got nearer I only had a few pounds — not enough for the train fare even. Then — I think it might have been the Thursday before we were supposed to go — didn't some money arrive for me from Griffiths that I didn't know about! When I left there I lifted what was due to me, but I forgot about my bonuses and holiday money. This money arrived, and it came to me through I don't know how many places. It was forwarded on to my old address in Birmingham, and then to Liverpool, and everywhere I had been in digs when I was working for Griffiths. It was £16, and in those days you could go a long way with that kind of money. Did we have a good time! In fact we finished up in Paris after we'd been to Jersey.

21

SINGING TO CURE SICKNESS

I don't know when I first developed TB. I was probably suffering from it for years before I had any treatment. People nowadays tend to forget that TB was a real scourge before the new drugs were invented. My sister Anna died of TB in 1944 leaving five children behind, and so did plenty of other people, young and old. It was in the air, like the music and everything else. My girlfriend Vera died of it some time around 1953. And it wasn't all that long after that I had to go into the hospitals myself.

I first went into the same big sanatorium that Vera died in, in Rushden, Northamptonshire. In fact I was in the same ward that she was, because the hospital had been modernised in the meantime and what used to be the female section became the male section. I was only in there about a month or so, until they would get sending me back home, because at that time they had the belief that if you went back to your childhood surroundings, it would help.

I was over three years in hospitals with TB, going from one hospital to another. I was in six different hospitals in Ireland. My left lung was very bad, and in the first hospital I went to, which was in Glenties — not so far from my own home town — they built me up for this big operation to have it removed, what they called a pneumonectomy. When they examined me some time before I was to have the operation, they found that the right lung wouldn't stand it because it was bad, it was beginning to cave in too. So all they could do was squeeze the left one, put it completely out of action, and let the right one get all the exercise it could, do all the breathing with the one side, and I've been doing that ever since and I've never looked back! I've still got my left lung, and it's about the size of my fist.

It was sore work having the lung squeezed. It lasted for about a year in different hospitals. They put a silver rod through my side and set a machine going to pump air in, just like blowing up a motor tyre. It blew up and filled the space under the lung, and squeezed the lung up against my shoulder blade. Honestly the pain of that was pretty nasty, a couple of hours at a time over about a twelvemonth, but it was worth it.

I kind of enjoyed those years in hospital. It's not right to say that, but I did. We had our own little band in Glenties. We used to have great fun. The doctor there was very keen on musical therapy. He thought so long as we were playing music we were improving, and he was right you know. They may talk about complete rest, and medicine, and injections, but if you're not happy you'll never mend, no matter what treatment you get. We were as happy as could be, playing music like good ones and singing and swapping songs. And I was suffering from tuberculosis at the time — we were playing the music even before I got to the convalescent stage!

After Glenties they sent me here and there to see what place would agree with me. I went then to Killybegs, which is by the sea, which they thought might be a help. Well, it didn't do me any harm — at least I didn't die there. In that hospital with me was a man who ever since has been a very good friend of mine, Packie McGinley. His memory is a bit sharper than mine, and he tells me that was in June 1954. Then I went on to Castlereagh. That's where the squeezing stopped and they put me on the new 'Diapacic' tablets. Then I went to Merlin Park, then Galway, then Tohermore. In Tohermore I was feeling better than ever, and they gave me a donkey and cart to go into the town and do the shopping.

After three years continuous in hospitals I came out and went home for a while. I used to have to go back in once in a while. I went into Donegal hospital where I was supposed to have tubercular meningitis — but in fact it was only the aftereffects of all the tablets, medicines and drugs that was shoved down me.

Around this time, about 1957 or maybe 1958, I started to get a longing to hear the old traditional songs again. I'd been off traditional music for a long time, and into other kinds of music, but the old music had always remained number one for me, so I started going to *fleá cheoil*s — traditional-music festivals. This was while I was still not in the best of health, because when I went back into Killybegs hospital a second time, I remember telling the doctor I wanted to go to a *fleá* in Sligo. Dr Clarke was a Sligo man himself, and he said, right, and gave me all I was fit to grip in my fist of painkillers and tablets to keep me going, and told me,

'Away you go to the festival, for the whole weekend!'

But in the end I didn't go — I suffered a slight lung collapse or something, and he was as disappointed as I was.

I started entering singing competitions here and there. Needless to say, I didn't win them all, but I won a few. In fact there was one *fleá* that I won without even knowing that I was entered for the competition. Now this is true. It was in Sligo. I can't remember what year it was, but anyway, this is what happened.

It was a very nice warm day, and there were two tin-whistle players sitting on the bridge and playing away like two good ones, so I went over and sat beside them and that made three tin whistles. After a while a fellow came out of the pub, and I had seen him before, but never took a lot of notice of him. He said,

'Will you come in and give us a song?'

'Aye, well, fair enough.' I said to the lads playing whistle, 'I'll be back again.'

I went into the hotel. There was no microphone, of course; I just stood inside the door and sang some funny fast thing anyway. Ciarán Mac Mathúna, who I knew at the time, was sitting about. He was a producer for Radio Éireann. He still is, in fact. There was a good clap, and I came out, rushing with me whistle to join the two blokes on the bridge.

We went away down the street then and we had a couple of drinks and a meal. I wasn't too interested in the competitions, I was more interested in the whistle players, and I'll give them their due, they could play whistle. I hung around with them the whole day. In the evening there was a concert of prizewinners. My name was down to appear, but I never knew a thing about it until the MC said,

'Well now, for the surprise of the evening we have a man that I don't think you have ever seen before, but he happens to be the outright winner of the traditional singing in English.'

I wondered who this was, but he went on,

'I don't know whether his address is Ireland, England, or where, I've never seen him before, but his name is Packie Manus Byrne.'

I had to go out and do another song, and I was the winner.

I won a couple of other competitions at *fleás* in the late fifties, including one at Ballyshannon in 1959, but I think the one I was proudest of was in 1962-63, and that was the All-Ireland *Fleá Cheoil an Raidió*.

Seán Ó Riada, Seán Ó Síocháin and Ciarán Mac Mathúna were the three judges, but Seán Ó Riada was the chief adjudicator. It finished up with one song, but I had over thirty sung by that time: the way they worked it was that if you were won at A, you sang at B, and so on. I won a local *fleá*, I think it was held in Glenties. Then I won another one in Gorey or somewhere away down south, and then I was automatically entitled to sing in the final *Fleá Cheoil an Raidió* — that was the clear-up of all the *fleá*s for sixty-two and sixty-three.

And who put the toughest on me in that competition was a young fellow called Tim Lyons. I think it came down to only one point, and I think it was 97 and 98 out of a hundred. 'Twas a decent score anyway, and it was very near a draw between Tim and myself. Marie Butler came third. Tim and me spent all the money we had before we got out of Dublin. Tim was living here in Kilburn shortly after, and when I would come over I would visit him and his wife, who was a nice singer and a great spoons player.

The songs I sang in the *fleá*s were the old songs I got from my parents and neighbours, the ones that were doing the rounds before I was born, or maybe songs that I picked up from people on the road like the Collins family. The one I sang in the final on the radio was 'Molly Bawn', and I think it also got first place at a *fleá* in Sligo. It was a version I got from my friend Charlie Waters that time we were marooned in my sister's place in the snow. A lot of people back home associate that song with me. That came round through Ciarán Mac Mathúna, who recorded me singing it years before. He was out with a field-recording unit for Radio Éireann collecting traditional songs, oh, a long time ago, back around about 1946. Wireless sets were not all that plentiful at the time, but my brother had bought one. Ciarán gave that recording a lot of airtime on his traditional-music programme. He would include this song, and tell it both in English and in Gaelic how he found this particular version of that song that no-one else was singing. I know it must have been on for several programmes in succession, because I can remember my father hearing the announcement and saying,

'Oh God, not that one again!'

He got a wee bit browned off listening to it! But that song is still remembered: the last time I was back home, in 1985, we were doing a gig at the Green Isle in Dunkineely, and some bloke shouted,

'Will you do a request, Packie?'

'I will,' I said, 'What is it?'

And about four shouted at the same time, 'Molly Bawn!' There was no hope of getting out of it. I hadn't sung it for years, but I started out and I sang it from end to end and remembered it all, which I was rather proud of, because it is a long song.

There's a lot of versions of 'Molly Bawn'. John MacGuire sings a version of it, he calls it 'Molly Bawn Lowry', and there's a version of it in England called 'Polly Vaughan', and there's one in Scotland called 'Lovely Molly Vaughan', which is a wee bit faster. The version I had from Charlie was about the slowest of them.

I never entered no more *fleás* after I won the *Fleá Cheoil an Raidió*, but I've been back to adjudicate on a number of occasions. I was adjudicating in Sligo one time. A very mean-looking character came up to me, naming one of the competitors, and said,

'That's the one's going to win.'

I said, 'Sure enough, if she's the best singer, she'll win.'

He said, 'Bad or good, she's going to win.'

But it was no good, I wouldn't be influenced by a threat. All right, I was scared stiff! But that didn't mean I was going to give somebody a credit that they weren't entitled to. Paddy Tunney was there adjudicating too; as far as I remember, he was doing one half of the session, and I was doing the other, or some way like that. I remember Paddy saying to me after,

'It doesn't matter who says one thing or the other to you, if you think someone is the best, give them the verdict.'

Ever since then I have had the greatest respect for Paddy, because he had no favourites. This girl didn't win, anyway; another girl, called Irene Heaney from County Mayo, won and rightly so, because Irene could sing rings round this other one. With the result that I had to be smuggled out of town in the back of a van, 'cause of how I was going to be killed! Oh, they took it dead serious at the time. I heard they were looking for me. I was hid away in a spare room in the hotel, until a bloke got me out the back way and into his van. I lay down on the floor of the van until we got out of town. They weren't taking any chances on missing me either, because there were a couple of them hanging around on the bridge all the time!

There used to be other funny things happening at *fleás* too. I'll never forget one session at a *fleá* in Clones. There were about twenty musicians playing in a pub yard, and there were over two hundred people in the yard listening. I was sitting on the edge of a stone trough that was used to collect rainwater from the roof. There wasn't any rain for weeks so the trough was completely dry. A fiddle player came over and very carefully put his fiddle and bow into the trough right behind me to keep it safe, and then went into the pub. 'Twas a very warm sunny afternoon, but suddenly it clouded over and a very severe thunderstorm started, accompanied by a heavy downpour of rain. Everyone crowded into the pub, which was so full of people it was uncomfortable.

The downpour lasted for over an hour, and the moment it left off we went back to the yard to continue our session. Everywhere was soaking wet, the trough was almost full, and there was your man's fiddle floating around like a little boat! No sign of the bow — it might be on the bottom. I wouldn't think that fiddle played for a while, because it was still swimming when we left the yard three hours later. I didn't see its owner no more: he maybe got hopelessly drunk trying to drown his sorrows. I don't know if he did, but I do know that he succeeded in drowning his fiddle!

22

SELLING UP THE OLD FARM

After I recovered from TB I carried on more or less the same way as before. Over to England when the fancy would take me, doing every kind of work and living all over the place.

Looking back over all the years I spent wandering about England in the forties and fifties I am happy to have led the life I led. If I had to do it all again, I would probably do the same thing, only maybe I would do it better a second time. I never settled down. Well, everyone was settled, and it was nice to be different. There was lots of jobs, and there was lots of work, and there weren't so many unemployed. In the like of Manchester, if I had a few pound I could come down to Birmingham, or go to Liverpool, or somewhere, and see what was going on there, and find me a job of some kind. I wasn't a bit fussy what kind of a job it was. If it was clean, I dressed up and I went out and done it, and you found that nearly every town in England had a job for you of some kind. It was different to now; you didn't have big, vast areas of unemployment like in the northeast or Liverpool.

Finding somewhere to rest your head was never a problem either. There were plenty of boarding houses in those days. When you arrived in a town, you would go into any newsagents, or the post office, and ask for digs, and you would be given a list: Mrs This and Mrs That, a long list of places to stay. There might be one or two occasions when I didn't have enough money to chance getting digs, and if it was the summertime, well, I would kip down somewhere. There was one chap I knew that done quite a bit of wandering in his time, summer and winter; he never had digs, because he had nothing, only what he wore. If you met him you would ask,

'Where are you living now?'

'Oh, I'm lodging at Mrs Greenfield's.'

That was his way of saying that he was sleeping out, of course!

Building sites were a good place to earn your living for a while. Putting it all together, I've done quite a few years at that. If I was young again, I would be on a building site still. You go along the road and you see blokes on a building site and you think, look at them poor fellows, covered with dust and muck: but they're getting better paid than blokes whizzing about in maybe Ford Cortinas. Some of the work is a bit dangerous, but if you kept your head screwed on and didn't take any rash chances, you could knock in a good time. And another thing, it kept you physically fit. Funny enough, in the days before TB I was as fit as a fiddle and still had bad lungs. That's the nature of TB, of course: you can have it for years and years and you won't know it. We would be unloading cement, and I could put a hundredweight bag of cement under each arm off the lorry. And tinier blokes than me could do that — it's practice, not strength. You balanced them, kept them as high as possible, sat on your hip bones.

Another good standby for me was selling. Door to door, a lot of the time, although I done a few spells in furniture stores too. I was a good salesman. I think my accent was a kind of an incentive for people to stand and listen to me. Say now in East London, if you were selling with a Cockney accent: if people didn't want the article, they didn't want you. But the like of me, with a very unusual accent: rap on somebody's door and as soon as I start talking they get interested! And in the middle of their interest you can always sell them something.

The selling was a very useful thing to be fit to do: the experience I got in England as a salesman was very useful to me when I was back in the cattle business in Ireland. I was a good seller of cattle. And I knew how to buy as cheap as possible, and how to sell for as much as possible, because that's something you learn out on the road. Even door to door — if you were selling an article that was worth two bob, well it would start as two and fourpence. So you could say, oh all right then, two shillings to you. And you still had the correct price for it. And if you got the two and fourpence, you were fourpence up on the deal. So that's how selling and buying cattle works.

The Indians are prime at that! The Jews are pretty good, but they can't hold a candle to the Indians. The Indians and the Irish! In those days there were quite a few Indian salesmen going round with their suitcases, selling shirts and socks. Anywhere there was a big project going on, like Thurleigh or Lakenheath airbase, you nearly always got a few Indians coming in on the site selling socks to the workers. A man working from eight in the morning to six in the evening hasn't a lot of time for shopping, so you were very glad to buy the gear on the job from these salesmen.

I never was ambitious. That takes a lot of the fun out of life. Supposing I was selling, and I got promotion to being a supervisor: I would be in one office all the time, and I would have responsibility for other people, and that wouldn't go down very well with me. I would far rather get up in the morning and get away out and meet the people. If you met nice people, sit down and have a cup of tea with them; if you met nasty people you could laugh at them. Get as much crammed into life as possible.

I never worried about money. To this day I don't worry very much about money. I never had any, and I never wanted more than would keep me going. But I could always manage to keep myself going. With money comes responsibility. If you're earning big money, you're not getting it for enjoying yourself! You're getting it because you're browned off to the hilt about something, and you're at war with the whole world. If you're greedy and trying to make money, you're making enemies too. When I wasn't in England I would be at home. My brother Jim and me always worked together, whenever I was back. And they're past counting, the number of times I went over and back between 1937 and when Jim died in 1964. Come hay time of the year I would go back home and do a bit of work, and cutting the turf time I would very often be home and do a bit with him. Whatever was his was mine, and the land belonged to us both, and there was no dispute about that.

Jim never married, so there were only two of us lived there. Memie was long married at the time, and both my parents were dead. We had a nice going-on; we weren't badly off, you know. We weren't rich, but we could meet the times, and we were comfortable. He was happy for me to go away to England whenever I felt like it, and if he wanted to go away, which he never did, I wouldn't say no. That's how we worked.

We were both heavy smokers. At that time I could smoke like a chimney. I never had to say to him, 'Bring home cigarettes', or anything, and he never said it to me. If we were away down in the town, or if I was at a fair, the cigarettes were bought anyway. That was an understood thing, like the tea and the sugar and everything else, the cigarettes had to be bought. They were left in the house, and if he wanted a packet, he went and took one, and I went and took one, it didn't matter who paid for them. We lived like that all the time.

During one of my spells over in England in 1963 or thereabout I got a job as a salesman in a furniture store in London. It was Sidney Smith's store in Bayswater. It was a cushy sort of job. It consisted mainly of just talking to the customers and standing there waiting till they made up their minds to sign up the hire-purchase agreement, and I was doing all right at that. I was sorry to leave there, indeed. Why I left was that I got news from home, from my sister Memie, that Jim had had a heart attack and was in very bad health, and that I should go back to look after him. So I went.

I was expecting to find Jim lying in bed at death's door, but when I arrived at the house he was nowhere to be seen. He was out on the hillside looking about the sheep and cattle. He had picked up great and was active again, although he had to take very expensive drugs, he didn't need me to look after him. But anyway, there I was, so I stayed at home and we carried on working together and living together just as we always had done.

After a time Jim had a second heart attack. We were out in the fields building haystacks. Now a couple of days before that I was in a fair and I bought a few heifers. At that time of year heifers get very unruly, because they come in season, and of course they broke out through a fence, or climbed out over a ditch, and got away on the road. We always had the motorbike in the field, for getting places, so Jim said to me,

'You'd better get away after them. I'll go in and have the tea ready when you're back.'

So he went off to the house and I went away on the motorbike and took back the cattle. When I came in he was sitting in the chair, his favourite seat, and the kettle was steaming right up the chimney, the cigarette was lying on the floor beside him, and he was dead. And we were out building hay until about twenty minutes before that. He was fifty-three.

Now I'll tell you a strange thing that didn't dawn on me at that time. If you were going after cattle from our house, you might be very sure that this big red bitch would be with you. She had a sense for it. You could go away to church, you could go anywhere else, and she wouldn't bother following you, but if you went after animals, she would be with you. And that very day she didn't go. She was sitting in the centre of the kitchen floor when I got back, and the thought struck me, there's something wrong. I never thought about it while I was out after the cattle; I thought maybe it was because I had the autocycle with me that she just didn't bother, because she used to have to run like hell and she was big and fat. No, she stayed with him to the end. He put on the kettle and sat down and lit a cigarette, and he must have died instantly, because the cigarette was on the floor.

Then of course the land all fell to me. But I didn't want it, because by that time, after TB and all, I wasn't really fit to work on it. You need good health to work on a mountain farm. Apart from that, I wanted to get back to England, because I had an intention of going into showbusiness of some kind. I hadn't even made me mind up what kind of show it would be, but I was going to get into music and showbusiness some way or the other; which of course I did.

So I started trying to sell everything — land and all. It was no use to me. I suppose I spent about a year after Jim's death, which was in July 1964, trying to get everything sorted out, and that was a big problem.

I had some sheep which I was trying to get rid of, and at that time you couldn't get money for sheep, they were a very bad trade. I was at a fair in Glenties, and I had these sheep tied along in front of the house of a cousin of mine, Dr McCloskey, who at that time was very prominent in traditional-music circles. On this particular day he came out to have a chat with me. He said,

'You know what you should do: get rid of the lot! Give it all up come over with me to England, to Camden Town. There's a folk festival on there, so come over and give a couple of songs at the festival.'

So I thought, why not, it's a good excuse. I couldn't sell the sheep, and I had only three or four days till this festival would be starting, and I was thinking of leaving them on someone's land and forget I ever owned them. In the end I got a fellow to buy them. Willie Leonard bought a lorryload of cattle off me: he sent a truck around and loaded fourteen animals on and gave me the market price for them. The neighbours took the rest. So then I came over to England and I'm treading about ever since.

That festival was held at Cecil Sharp House, in Camden Town, the first one ever held there. Now John Doherty was supposed to come over with Dr McCloskey, but when he found out where Camden Town was — over the sea — he got cold feet. John was a traveller, and he moved all over County Donegal, but he didn't like the idea of foreign travel, and he would not go in a boat. So I came over in his place, and done a few spots at the festival and got a few bookings out of it. So that introduced me to the folk scene.

The other things that I had — farm implements and lots of other stuff — anything that the neighbours wanted I sold to them cheap, and some things I gave away. I didn't offer the property for sale. The forestry, the tree-planting commission, would have bought it from me, but they would plant trees on the whole thing and it would be useless for all time. So I talked it over with the neighbours, and I decided I wouldn't sell it until John Boyle, the lad next door, would have the first chance on it. His father and mother were always very pally with us: we were always in and out to each other's houses, swapping this and that, and if I was short of food I could go in and have a meal with them, and they would come to our place, and so on.

I had the land for two or three years, and I was paying rates all that time and getting no return at all out of it. So in the end John bought it off me. He was struggling to build himself up, but he really is successful now, and I'm so glad to think that maybe the land and the houses that he bought from me were one part of his success. He's an auctioneer, sheep breeder, land owner, insurance broker. He has a more efficient method of working the land than we had when we were young. There's sheep all over it now, and he has one of these huge big turf-cutting machines where we cut them one by one with a spade.

23

EARLY DAYS ON THE FOLK SCENE

At the time of the festival at Cecil Sharp House, around 1965, there were a few folk clubs going in London. A fellow called Ernie Groom was running one at The Fox in Islington, and he saw me at the festival and booked me to do an evening there the following Thursday. So I went and done it, and intended getting a full-time job somewhere after, but the bookings started coming in, and by some mistake or miracle I got into the precarious profession of a folk singer.

At first I was doing other work too, and got a job as a carpenter on a building site in Highbury, where they were building a new school. But the gigs started mushrooming and it got too much. Folk singing is not the lazy kind of a life that people seem to think. There's always a lot of travelling, and if I was away doing a club in Southampton or somewhere it was about two or three o'clock before I could get to bed, and then I had to be on the go again about half-six or seven in the morning. I just couldn't stick it, so I packed up the daytime job and went full-time.

I was happy to be back in the business of entertaining people, and especially on the folk scene. The dance bands and cabaret were all right, they kept body and soul together, but I could never have a chat with the audience like I could in a folk club. I think it's the nicest satisfaction in the world to do something for folk or traditional people, because they came to that club for one purpose, to hear you and to pick up stories and songs and tunes that they never heard before. In the pop world, or any other kind of music, they're probably talking amongst themselves and they couldn't care less — your music is only a background. But in a folk club you get a hearing, and people'll come at the interval and at the end of the evening, and they'll talk to you about the songs and tunes and all that.

In the old days when the folk scene first started, it was different to today. There was such comradeship. People had the idea that, if you help me, it's my duty to help you, with the result that the whole thing became a kind of endless chain. That is not happening today. There are maybe better performers today, and nicer premises for running folk clubs, but you have not got the same comradeship, the same loyalty, as you did.

I hate to say this, but as the years went on I became disillusioned to a great extent with the folk movement. It wasn't so commercial in the early days. I've nothing against commercialism, because you can't live on fresh air, but people didn't consider that money was the principal thing. I like to get paid, but when I first started, if I could get just what paid the landlady and kept me in a couple of pints, I would never think of refusing to sing in a club because they had no money. I did no end of them for nothing. I even went to South Wales, to Port Talbot and Neath, and done floor spots all the way from London, when I would have the money to spare on the railway. Mind ye, no end of times those very clubs happened to progress to being good thriving clubs, and they always got me back when they were fit to give me a good fee. I would go somewhere like South Wales and maybe do a couple of gigs when I would be down, and live with somebody connected with the club, and eat to the best and have drinks at night and all. So that's why I say that in the old days there was more companionship. Of course, it was a smaller scene. You could count in your mind and picture every club in Britain.

In the sixties there was a lot of clubs started up in London, especially around the Soho area. Charlie McDevett of 'Freight Train' fame was running a club somewhere around Regent Street, Karl Dallas was running one in Goodge Street, and Martin Winsor and Red Sullivan had a combined effort somewhere in Soho called The Student Prince. Curly Goss ran one called the New Prince, and I done them all, with several different people and sometimes on my own. There was a pub on Cambridge Circus which at that time was called the Roundhouse. Paul Simon was over here doing the clubs before he teamed up with Garfunkel, and I met him there.

A lot of the clubs in Soho used to operate on a Saturday night, and right smoky little places they were. Several of them were down in cellars below the street. People would be jammed into them like sardines, and very often the only way out was up a ladder! More than one of those places was a strip club during the week and a folk club on a Saturday night — you would stand and sing in front of the velvet curtain where the girls used to change.

I would go from one club to the other. There was one called the Wheelhouse that started strictly eight o'clock. I used to leave there about ten o'clock when I would do my gig, and go down to the Troubador in Earl's Court and do a floor spot there, and probably finish up in one of Curly Goss's clubs or somewhere that went through to six in the morning. I would get no money for that. I would get cups of coffee — they were none of them licensed premises. You would very often meet other people going from club to club, doing a little spot at three different places.

I remember one night a long time ago when Bunjie's used to be folk from eight to eleven before they would start some other caper, and Noel Murphy and myself met. Noel said,

'I suppose you haven't any money?'

I hadn't, and Noel had none.

'We'll go over to Bunjie's,' he said, 'and I know a way we'll get coffee and doughnuts.'

There was a pop group playing. Noel got his guitar, and I got a whistle of course. Believe it or not, the group packed up, and me and Noel done the evening, and got all the coffee we were fit to drink and three or four doughnuts each!

If you got involved in the folk scene and got your toe in the door of the folk clubs, you couldn't be dragged away from it, because the friendship and fun was great. I remember a club over in East London, and Bert Lloyd happened to be there. A girl saw me talking to Bert, and later she said to me that she wanted to meet him, just to say hello, because Bert was a god in her eyes — as he was in quite a few more eyes than hers. So we went over and I said,

'Jeanie, I would like you to meet an old friend of mine, but you needn't stay and talk to him if you don't like him. I think they call him Bert Lloyd or something.'

By this time Bert had on his big smile, and he asked her to sit down next to him. She sat down very gingerly and quietly, and Bert asked her about a song she had sung earlier. She was telling him, and Bert started outlining the song to her, the origin of it and other songs, and singing wee bits of songs, and so on. The evening went on, and there was Bert Lloyd and this girl, one of them singing to the other. She never got over that. I met her several times after and she always mentioned that occasion. That's what the folk scene used to be like in the old days.

I always liked the friendliness of the folk clubs. I would have great fun sometimes with young whistle players. They might be too shy to play on stage while I was in the audience, but out in the car park they would come to talk to me and they'd play there.

Once they got outside and away from the audience they'd play like hell. I liked that because, I don't know everything about whistle playing but I know a little, and if there was anything I could tell them I could afford to spend a little time with him or her, and I would hear them again a year or so after and be quite pleased that I was the instigation of putting them on the straight and narrow path!

Doing folk-club gigs, if I was working on my own, to tell you the truth I never rehearsed, or wrote down what I was going to do. I would get up on the stage and never had the foggiest idea what I would do, but I started something and built it up from there. If I found that straight traditional songs wasn't working, naturally I would cut down and do with about two or so for the rest of the evening, and carry on with comedy or doing daft things, like tripping myself up and trying to explain something to the audience in a way that I didn't even know myself what I was talking about.

If you're not a master performer, or you haven't the name of doing some particular thing very well, it's a great asset to have a lot of tiny little irons in the fire, lots of little things lying about in your mind here and there that you can pull on; if you have enough things to shove to an audience, at least they'll accept some of it. Bit of comedy, and maybe one or two stories, and something straight, and play a fast tune, and then do something daft with a whistle. Like Taffy Thomas used to say, if you cannot blind them with science, baffle them with bullshit. He had a good point there.

Gradually the folk festivals started proliferating, and they became a big asset to the performer. One of the first was at Towersey, a little village in Oxfordshire. I was booked for the very first one there. I went over to Ireland for a holiday, and it was to be that immediately I would come back I'd go to Towersey for the festival. But we had a real good party in a pub the night before I was to come back. Oh, we were well drunk. There was a bloke in the pub who was taking the mickey out of a poor old fellow. Now I'm quite peaceful, I'm not a troublemaker by any means, but the one thing I cannot stand is somebody taking the mickey out of a disabled person or someone slightly mentally retarded, or taking advantage of a young girl. I think there's nothing lower than that. So I clobbered this bloke in the pub, and he ran, and like a fool I ran after him.

He started along the pavement and I could see that he was a fair good runner. There was a girl's bicycle in the gutter with the pedal on the kerbstone, and as I was passing I picked it up and threw it. I thought that was the only chance I had of stopping him. But I missed, and the bike went through a shop window. Of course I was taken to the Garda station. I didn't get out for two days, and when I did Towersey festival was over. Eric Winter stood in for me. That was over twenty years ago, when I was a lot stronger and more active than I am now!

There was always the odd disastrous booking, of course, just like in every branch of the entertainment business; and in spite of all the loyalty and people helping each other out on the folk scene, well, there was the odd character that didn't have the same ideas of comradeship as most of the club organisers. In the late sixties I spent a few years living up in Manchester, and one night I was playing somewhere around there and a fellow came up to me and invited me to open his new club in a town near Stoke-on-Trent. He offered eight pound. I later discovered that he was released from prison a few months before, and he was evidently doing his best to go crooked again.

I arrived in good time and asked the landlord where the club room was. He didn't seem to understand what I wanted, or at least that's what he tried to make me believe. I heard after that Irishmen were not very welcome in that pub. So I sat down having me pint and two or three people came in, and one of the girls knew me from a club in Buxton that I used to do pretty regular. She had heard that I was on and had come down to see me. After a while this character that had booked me, Phil his name was, came in.

'Oh hullo, Packie, nice to see you. Come on up.'

We went into a room with no seats. One girl lit two candles and put one on a table near the door and the other on a window ledge at the other end of the room. A second girl welcomed all six of us and declared the new club open. People started to trickle in. There was no compere, no-one to say what was going to happen next, and nobody took a blind bit of notice of me. However, when all the floor singers, most of whom couldn't sing at all, had given us their two songs each, Miss Welcome tried to introduce me, but couldn't remember my name, so she settled for 'this Scotsman that hasn't been heard before'. I started my set and every eye in the room stared straight at me, wondering what planet I fell from. After a half-hour of no response, the silence was broken by a loud whisper: 'Police in the bar!'

To my amazement, within about six seconds I was the only one left in the room, so I collected my gear and ran like all the others. When I got to the street, the last of them was disappearing round a corner. I heard a car refusing to start in the car park. It was Miss Two-Candles, who also took the money at the door. So I went over to her and said,

'I understand you're the treasurer of this club.'

'Well, not really. I'm just giving Phil a hand.'

She made no sign that she was going to pay me or anything.

'Well,' I said, 'I'm expecting to get some money.'

'Oh, you'll have to see Phil.'

And no, she did not know of any place I could stay. Phil was gone and I could see that I was going to get no money out of it, and no place to spend the night. It was a beautiful mild September night, so I headed out of town. I thought I would walk the eight or nine miles to Stoke and get a train up to Manchester. I dodged along the road, and there was a field with a shed near the gate. I thought, ah, there's digs. I went in and curled up in the hay and fell asleep.

Being brought up on a farm, I should know better than to lie down in seasoning first-meadow hay, because when it is withering it casts off its seeds, and when they get in on your skin they're worse than any vermin you ever felt in your life. I woke up at daybreak and I was in a right bad way, scratching and itching in all areas. There was only one thing for it. I went out to the road, looked both ways, then got out of all me clothes, including me socks, and started bashing them against the gate post to get the hayseeds out.

I was so intent on what I was doing that I didn't notice two girls coming along the road on bicycles, probably going to work on an early shift. They didn't see me till they were almost level with the gateway. The one in front screamed and pedalled past as fast as she could. The other one got off her bike, turned round and made her best speed in the direction they came. They must have thought I was out of my mind, a naked man belting a gate post with his shirt at five o'clock in the morning! I'll bet they had trouble making their workmates believe that story.

Anyway, I'm sure I broke all records for getting dressed in a hurry and leaving the spot, in case they got the police. I walked to Stoke-on-Trent and got an early train to Manchester. It was the morning rush hour, and the train was packed to the doors, but I had two seats all to myself. I was performing such contortions trying to scratch four places at once that nobody would sit beside me. Lucky for me I lived near Piccadilly Station. I ran all the way home, got out of all my clothes again and rolled on the floor like a horse. What a blessed relief!

Now I didn't just sing and work in folk clubs. In fact one of the most enjoyable places I ever worked was in a synagogue! It was in East London. I got the bookings through a fellow that I met one night in Karl Dallas's folk club in Goodge Street: his name was Peter Sivico, and he was Chairman of the Jewish Entertainments Committee. He used to run these evenings (mid-week of course, I think it was Wednesdays), in this very nice, rich-looking hall of a synagogue in Walthamstow. So he invited me over some night. I went and I liked the atmosphere; they were making tea and telling Jewish stories that were really worth listening to. And of course I swapped a few Irish stories with them and we became the best of friends, and they started booking me.

I sang Scottish songs and Irish songs and modern songs for them. I always remember them, because they were such a lovely bunch of people to know, and they could spend lots of money too. When it comes to hospitality, there's no race or nationality in the world that are as generous as the Jews. They treated me like I fell from heaven. Fees weren't so big at the time, something like £6 (which was still quite a bit, because at that time I would do a gig for fifty bob). But they would always insist on giving me ten shillings extra or enough for my train fare home. I've worked in halls and places for most every nationality, but if I was a young man again, I would definitely like to work for the Jewish people.

Another unusual booking that I got through Peter was on a boat party in Hastings. 'Twas a mighty posh do, with lots of important people like politicians, clergymen, church leaders, and the Mayor was there, chains and all. It was all organised by Battle Town Council to celebrate Lady de Vere White's retirement from something or other, I don't remember what. I was to be a kind of mobile host, moving about and talking to everyone an putting on a friendly atmosphere. Her Ladyship was a very charming little woman of sixty or thereabout who got a great kick out of listening to me talking. I'll admit to embroidering my dialect a bit just for her benefit. Well, when you're trying too hard to make an impression or be on your best behaviour, that's often when embarrassing things seem to happen.

The boat where the party was was anchored out in the bay and we were taken out to it by a small motorboat. I saw a woman struggling with an armful of books and papers. She may have been one of the organisers. So, trying to be the attentive gentleman that I'm not, I offered to carry something. She thanked me in an accent that could only be produced by having three tongues and nodded towards a big, heavy-looking hardback book on top of the pile. I smiled my best, put the book under my arm and her Ladyship came along, grabbed my free hand and steered me towards two empty seats on the motorboat. But another woman had an eye on my seat, so grasping my second opportunity to be a gentleman, I let her sit down.

By this time the little boat was fairly full, so I stood in front of her Ladyship talking thirteen to a dozen, hoping I was living up to my reputation as an entertainer. Where he came from I don't know, but suddenly a wasp appeared near my face. Now if there's anything I'm more afraid of than wasps, it's more wasps. The boat was just starting away when I lashed out at the wasp. The book slipped from under my arm and landed edge down across her Ladyship's toes — she was wearing open sandals. She gasped, and as I apologised and stooped to retrieve the book the boat came to a lurch, and I lost my balance and butted her in the stomach with my head. She gasped much louder that time, and I made my second apology as I was getting to my feet and skidaddling to the other end of the boat. I could see that her and me weren't meant for each other. We arrived at the party boat. I tried to keep out of her way as much as possible but I couldn't help seeing that she was limping as she left the small boat. (How her stomach felt I have no idea.)

I thanked God when I got off the small boat, feeling sure that no more misfortunes lay in wait for me. The boat was beautiful; it belonged to a very rich German. They all referred to it as a yacht. After drinks and introductions we had tea and a selection of sandwiches and pastries of every shape and colour, as many as could sit around a table. They parked me at one end in the company of a bishop and his wife, giving me V.I.P. treatment of course. The bishop's wife was at least fifteen stone in weight and sat so close I could hardly lift my arm. After a few attempts I managed to pick up my cup, but just as I had it almost at my mouth the handle broke off: the cup hit the edge of the table and deposited its hot contents right on the bishop's wife's leg. She tried to stand up, but the chairs were so close together, and her being so fat, she couldn't manage it. But she did succeed in moving the table, causing tea to splash in all directions. Her Ladyship was at the other end of the table and said to me, with a twinkle in her eye, and in a not-bad-at-all Irish accent,

'Are you sure that wasn't meant for me?'

24

MANCHESTER YEARS:
SOME MEMORABLE CHARACTERS

I was quite a few years based up around Manchester, before I moved down to London in about 1971. I was doing the usual things: spells on building sites, trench digging, and everything that was going — built walls and dug gardens. And, of course, plenty of work on the folk scene.

Some of my best memories of that time were of working with Felix Doran. Felix was a great character. He and his brother Johnny Doran, and the Cashes, were travellers. They were horse dealers to start with. Then they broke into the lorry and transport business, and also scrap iron and horsehair — you name it, the Dorans could do it. But there was one thing they were masters at, and that was playing pipes. They were the richer travellers. They always had a fair bit of money to spend: if they saw something valuable, like a very good horse, they could just pull out the money and pay for it. Then in later years when Felix came over to live in England, he had his own big thirty-foot trailer and his own house.

But they were the good pipers. I still think that Johnny was a better piper than Felix was, but Felix was better known. It was like the Doherty brothers: in my opinion Mickey Doherty was a better fiddle player than John, and that's saying something! But John was the well-known one, because John done all the wandering about. And Felix did all the moving about. But Johnny Doran was some piper. I used to see him at fairs in the west of Ireland and in the midlands when I was a young fellow.

Working with Felix was good fun. He was a nice character, and a non-drinker. He had an old van, and 'twould be almost half full of scrap iron, and we would pile in there as happy as could be and do gigs here and there. We would go quite a distance. We both lived in Manchester, and we used to go as far as Leeds and down to Birmingham and Wolverhampton, and way over to Sheffield. They were English folk clubs — I could count on one hand the number of Irish clubs I done in twenty years. They don't know about me, and maybe they don't want to! I found that I could always get more gigs than I was fit to do, or at least enough to live on, doing the folk clubs.

Felix would play the pipes, and I would sing and play the whistle. We would do duets, and I would do solo singing, and tell a few stories, and Felix would tell a story or two in his dry humour, and he would explain about all the tunes, tell people where they originated. He was a big attraction in the clubs, because he was different. There was no-one else doing this kind of thing, and being a piper and a very nice talker, he made a big hit.

I remember one night we were doing a club in Wolverhampton at a place called The Gifford. Now there was some kind of horse trials or something to do with horses that Felix was at a few days before this gig, and met with a lot of travellers, the Humberside lot and the Birmingham lot, they were all at this event. He circulated the news that we were playing at The Gifford in Wolverhampton on the Thursday night. So, of course, the people running the club were expecting an ordinary night, but it was no ordinary night. Now Felix was a stickler for time. If he was due on stage in a club at eight o'clock, he was there at half-seven. He was a smasher like that, he would never let you down. We arrived at The Gifford at about seven o'clock, and the place was packed!

The woman that was running the club said to me,

'Do you know any of these people?'

'Well,' I said, 'I have an idea who they are.'

The club started. There was one of the travellers, he was about twenty stone and six feet six. If anyone coughed, he went 'Shhh!' And that person got smaller and smaller. In fact if someone only moved in their chair, he would stare. The evening went on and the interval came, and the barman was beginning to get very shaky because his Guinness was getting very low. They were drinking him out, women and men. After a while, the husband of the woman that ran the club came to me and said,

'Oh Packie, I'm a bit frightened. The Guinness is getting very scarce.'

'Well,' I said, 'you know what'll happen if it runs out.'

The landlord himself came in and was looking worried. He was waiting for the counter to go out through the roof. I went over to him and said,

'I tell you what, if there's anywhere at all you can get a consignment of Guinness, for God's sake go away and get it.'

He said, 'Aye, I was thinking of doing that.'

So he got a big van, and he went away himself with the van and came back just in time to save the situation. They drank that vanful. Then they wanted a carry-out to take away and he had to go out again, and knock up some pub that was shut, and take all the bottles of Guinness that they had back to the yard of his own pub and load it into their vans, about forty cases. Then away we all went out on a big council tip between Birmingham and Wolverhampton, I suppose about a hundred of us, and we drank there all night till clear daylight in the morning.

It was a good night for the folk club! There wasn't a wrong word or act the whole evening. They all paid at the door, and this big fellow was running the show! They were smashing singers, and we didn't have a thing to do in the second half. They wouldn't go up on stage; they just sat where they were, and they sang duets and they sang solos. There was one bloke with one eye who was a smashing good tin-whistle player, really good, and one girl was a lovely traditional singer. It was the best night ever at The Gifford club, and the woman that ran the club still talks about it anywhere I meet her. She told me that that night made the club, because the people that were there other than the travellers circulated the news that the like of this wasn't seen ever in Wolverhampton before. I enjoyed it so much that I went away to the tip with them.

Another night Felix and me were playing at a place in Stockport. It wasn't a folk club, but a kind of a nondescript club where everything went. You could be a pop singer or a classical singer, and no-one knew really what you were doing, because they didn't go there to listen anyway. We were booked to do it. The fellow that booked us was a bit of a shark, but I suppose he fancied getting us for smaller money than he would have to pay a big group. We went ahead. 'Twas a huge room, it was like a big dance hall, and there was no microphones, no amplification. We done a few things, and there was muttering and talking going on, but at this time there weren't that many people in. But on towards the middle of the evening a big audience gathered and voices got louder.

When we were going for about an hour or so, Felix thought he would do his party piece, and started playing a very nice slow soft Irish air called *Róisín Dubh* (The Little Dark Rose), and somehow or other the people decided they would listen, and why they listened I don't know, because there was hardly any Irish people in the place. Felix was piping away like a good one and there was a bit of a hush in the hall, and this clown came up and put a tanner in the one-armed bandit and pulled the handle. It was like thunder, and worse than all, he must have got the jackpot, and you know what noise one of them things makes when all the coins are dropping down.

Felix stopped playing. He started taking off the pipes. He opened all the buckles, took off the pipes and put them down on his knees, folded the bag, wrapped it up and put away the chanter, put them into the box, closed the box, locked the catches, put on his overcoat and trilby hat, fixed the overcoat nicely, and stood up on the stage. He looked down the hall and said,

'Well f— the lot o' ye!'

Felix was a very easy-going bloke, and usually he never got excited about anything. Well, he was angry that time, but he was so much of a gentleman, with his pinstripe suit and a white shirt! It was the first time I ever heard him come out with a four-letter word. I think the worst he ever used to say was 'damn'. 'Well damn that,' he would say if you were telling him a story that he didn't believe. But he really put a bit of venom into it this time. Some of the audience giggled, and some of them got frightened. Felix could say that, for unless there was some bloke who could handle himself, he wouldn't tackle him, because Felix was a very strong man. And we never got paid.

Felix was a nice fellow. He died in Newton-le-Willows. His son Michael, who was about fourteen when Felix and me worked together, was the makings of a very nice piper; he came to a few gigs with us and played very nice, and his sister Kathleen was a smashing good step dancer. They were very nice, well-mannered kids. But I'm told that Michael packed up the pipes altogether, which is such a pity.

Felix had some tunes. I've heard a story about the Dorans in their heyday, and they were playing somewhere around Dublin. A marathon piping session, and they played for I think it was fourteen hours and never repeated a tune. They weren't both playing together all the time — one would have to stop to eat and smoke and fill his pipe and things like that, but the music carried on for fourteen hours. They must have had a good memory! I know I wouldn't remember four or five tunes back, never mind fourteen hours.

But they lived for that. They'd rather talk about playing pipes or talk about tunes than they would about tomorrow's work, or what I was doing yesterday. The work they did kept them going and made money, but it wasn't all that important to them. The important thing was the Irish music. I was often in Felix's house when we lived in Manchester, and he would talk about nothing else. 'Twould be all music from I would go in till I would leave.

There were a lot of good musicians around Manchester. There was Martin Lynagh, a very nice fiddle player; he used to come around with my brother-in-law Patrick Keeney (Anna's husband — after she died he moved with his family to Manchester), and Des Donnelly from County Tyrone, who was one of the greatest fiddle players — he later had a fatal accident on a building site. I can't remember them all, but there was a world of good musicians. But funny, like our area back home, the fiddle was really the most important instrument around Manchester. Fiddle players had a kind of a season ticket to everything that was going.

Martin Carthy and Dave Swarbrick used to stay with me when I lived in Manchester, and one time they had a Saturday night free we went down to The Swan. Dave walked in with the fiddle case, and left it down, and was going up to the bar to get a drink, but he never made it to the bar. Some bloke got in before him.

'You're not buying any drinks, what are ye drinking?'

Because he had a fiddle. He produced a fiddle and from that back he was one of the gang.

There was a happening that turned out nasty in another pub that musicians used to gather in. There was a very deaf bloke that used to play there. They reckoned he was so deaf he couldn't hear his fiddle. Now my brother-in-law was deaf, but he could hear his own music. But this bloke couldn't even tune the fiddle. Someone had to tune it for him and then he could play it beautifully, because he was so practised and 'twas in the fingers.

Something happened one night that there was a bit of a row in the pub, and a friend of mine got a bit eaten out of the side of his face! Some bloke bit him like a dog would bite ye, just right on top of his cheekbone. There was a great commotion going on, and the poor fellow that was playing the fiddle didn't hear it, and he still carried on playing. Now because he carried on playing in an atmosphere that wasn't one hundred per cent social, he got roughed up, the poor so-and-so. That's how they felt about music in those days. They gave him a hard time — shook him and shoved him about — because he was desecrating the Irish music by playing it in a rowdy atmosphere. Oh, they took music pretty serious, and mind you, to an extent — but not to that extent — they still take it pretty serious in places back home. The Irish music is a kind of a sacred thing, next to religion. Religion is number one, and music is number two.

One of the greatest Irish musicians was Séamus Ennis, of course. I can't remember where I first met him, but Séamus and me used to stop with the same family in Liverpool. Florrie Brennan was a very well known Irish traditional singer, and her husband was a building contractor, and they lived in Liverpool. Séamus used to stay there for weeks at a time, and so used I, when I would have nothing to do. Florrie's husband Val is a very nice fellow, and very fond of music — likes a drink, and so on. If you got Florrie started on songs, you could sit there, and you would really have a good day and night listening to her, she would sing one song after another.

Now Séamus was fantastic fun and pastime. A night listening to him was really something to remember. He could be a very sensible bloke, and he was extremely intelligent. He had the most alert brain I think of anyone I ever met. And then, if he wanted to, he could be the most unsensible character in this world. I never met anyone who could go from one extreme to the other so fast. He would be telling you a very sensible story about a happening going back into old history, and he would come out with something so daft then, in the middle of it.

I remember one night in Florrie Brennan's he was telling about Oisín, Cú Chulainn — these Irish giants of years ago. He was telling this very sensible story, without a smile, and we were all ears listening to him. This chap was called Cú Chulainn (which means 'Culann's hound') because he could run faster than anyone in the world. It seems there was a big race coming on, and a whole castle and estate was promised to whoever would win this race, and at this time Cú Chulainn wasn't even heard of, but he just appeared out of the blue to fit the story. It appears that someone decided that some other one, who was called Murchú, would win, and gave him senna seeds to make him hurry up along the way. The race was going on fine, and this Cú Chulainn started gaining on the others, and Murchú, who had the physic in him, started gaining on them too. The chase went on, and Cú Chulainn was going as fast as he could go, and Murchú didn't seem to be exerting himself but was keeping up with Cú Chulainn. And then Séamus said,

'And Murchú would have won, only he had to stop for a ——' [to relieve himself].

No smile, no nothing. That was the end of the story. He just spoiled the whole long half-hour story with one sentence. I

remember Florrie was laughing so much you'd think she was crying, wiping the tears away from her face with a handkerchief.

Ah, Séamus was a very very bright fellow; he had an answer
for everything. It happened that he didn't like a certain well-known
Irish musician. I don't know why, there was something about it
that he just didn't like him. I remember once I mentioned this
particular man playing some tune, and Séamus said,

'Aha, well, aye. Ah, ——. You know it surprises me that somebody didn't set a mousetrap for that little so-and-so years ago!'

And you could just fancy this player — who was a medium-
sized kind of a bloke — in a mousetrap!

Séamus wasn't doing all that much at the time. He used to
do little bits in the Irish centre in Liverpool, and do a few pub
gigs. In fact he got very lazy the last few times he was there. He
would just stay in bed, and Florrie used to carry his food to him.
Really the chap wasn't well and it was playing on his mind that
he wasn't well. Towards the end he wasn't fit to play or sing, but
he could tell these stories better than anyone I ever knew.

The other great piper of the age was of course Willie Clancy,
but I didn't know as much about Willie as I did about Séamus and
Felix. He only came out during *fleá cheoil*s and that. But I met
him quite a few times. The first time was down in Gorey in County
Wexford. Ciarán Mac Mathúna introduced us. Willie was just about
to go into this place to do a session for some American visitors,
and they were going to tape him. It was only the chosen few would
get into this room, but being introduced to Willie, he told me to
come on with him. I was as proud as a peacock sitting beside him,
and him playing away for these Americans. But I never had much
to do with him. He lived in County Clare for all his life — he might
have been out of it for a while, but Willie was a Clare man, alive
and dead. Felix, Séamus, Willie, Johnny and the Doherty brothers
are all dead now — may they rest in peace.

One night during the Manchester years I was doing a club in Liverpool where I met an American. His name was Bob Long, and on
first meeting I thought he was a little bit crazy. But after a time,
when I got to know him better, I discovered that he was a complete raving lunatic! He could do a perfect accent and dialect from
any part of the world. And he had dozens of sketches and funny
stories: one of his best sketches was a London policeman trying
to arrest a drunken Irishman and his wife who was also drunk and
came from Yorkshire. He could change accents so fast that some-

times you'd think all three were talking at the same time. He was also a brilliant ventriloquist, and sometimes when he was talking on stage, a Scottish voice would keep interrupting him from the other end of the room — much to the annoyance of the club organiser; and most of the audience didn't know it was Bob himself who was doing it.

I'll never forget one club in Manchester. It was run by a huge Irishman the name of Michael Donnigan, known locally as 'Big Mick'. I'm sure he was one of the nicest, mildest and most even-tempered men you could meet — until he got annoyed. Then he turned into a cross between an elephant and a tornado. I wouldn't say he had a great ear for music, because he thought there was only one thing in the world worth listening to, and that was yours truly playing *Sliabh na mBan*. So towards the end of the evening I announced that I was going to play an old Irish air especially for Mick. He sat on the floor right in front of the stage and I don't think I've ever seen anyone look so happy: the corners of his mouth were almost touching his ears. Bob was sitting a few rows back, and I knew by his looks he was planning some mischief. The room was packed to capacity, but there wasn't a sound other than the music. When from the back came this very Irish voice,

'Ah, t'hell wid dhat, play dhe Irish Washerwoman!' All six and a half feet of Big Mick shot towards the roof, turned and headed for where he thought the voice was coming from. Most of the people standing along the wall saw him coming and managed to get out of his way. A few weren't so lucky and found themselves in a row of laps or sprawled on the floor. Mick knew most everyone in the room, especially the Irish patrons. And being convinced that the voice he heard was Irish but not knowing its owner, he decided to give them all the same treatment. I don't know how many he threw across the pavement or how many ran for their lives, but in a very short time there was a large vacant space inside the door.

By this time I had stopped playing — well, where was the point of going on. Everyone was turned towards the door watching Big Mick do his bouncing job, so I sat on the edge of the stage. When he decided that he had the right ones thrown out, or when his temper cooled down, I don't know which, he came up on the stage apologising to everyone. And he tried to make a speech about how he could never hold up his head again because Packie Byrne, the greatest gentleman that ever stepped off an Irish boat, was insulted in his club and made to feel a second-rate musician while playing an Irish air that would take tears out of a granite rock. Then he started crying, real crying, like a baby, and said he'd never come into the club again. While all this was going on Bob the culprit just sat there, dead-pan face, nodding agreement to everything Big Mick said. Only two people in the club knew who caused the ructions, and we both knew it wasn't me, so it had to be Bob. Anyway, two girls took Big Mick away, still crying.

That was the last I ever saw of him, although I did get news of him a few years after at a festival in Scarborough. A girl came to me and introduced herself as a friend of Big Mick. She was in fact one of the two that took care of him that night in the Manchester club. We had a long chat about him. It appears that he was brought up in a home for unwanted children, then done a few years fighting for survival on the Dublin streets. He came to England and after some training took up wrestling and went to live in France. It appears that during one bout he crushed his opponent so violently that he crippled him for life. When he realised what he had done he took to drinking and became mentally disturbed. He never got over what he done to that Frenchman and maybe he never will. In between his attacks of mental disorder he was the most good-natured and kind-hearted fellow I ever knew. This girl told me that he kept his word and never did go into that club again. It folded up a few months after.

Getting back to Bob: when I first met him in Liverpool he was on his way to Ireland to collect folk songs and stories but he changed his mind and came to Manchester with me instead, for a day or two as he put it. But the weeks passed and Bob was still at my place, drinking my beer, smoking my tobacco and wearing my clothes, which fitted him perfectly. He stayed in bed most part of the day and came to gigs with me in the evenings. But he just would not do shopping or washing up or anything to help in the flat. I was getting more and more fed up with him. He expected me to supply the food, but never offered to pay for any. The same with the rent, coal, laundry, and all. After about two months I found I had had enough of him, so I said,

'Don't you know that you should contribute something towards your expenses here?'

He didn't even look at me, just muttered to himself, 'So much for Irish hospitality.'

Well, that done it. I ran for the bread knife, he ran for the door. He had some papers and song books here and there in the sitting room. I gathered them up and pitched them out on the pavement where he was standing. His shirts and socks got the same treatment, also his haversack. When I was sure that all his gear was dealt with I picked up the bread knife again, and I went out and said,

'Now get away from here, and if I ever see you in this street again, I'll rip you open!'

I know he thought I was serious, because he was trembling and his hands were shaking while he was trying to stuff all his belongings into the haversack. I kept a straight face all the time, although I almost laughed more than once, thinking of how often he fooled and annoyed people by throwing his voice around. And now he was being fooled by someone he didn't know as an actor. He went off up the street and didn't even look back. I'll admit to feeling a little bit sorry for him. He had such stage personality and his acts were so original and clever I'll bet he could make himself famous as a one-man show. But he preferred being a layabout and scrounger. Anyway, I got rid of him. But I know I only passed him on to some other unsuspecting fool like myself.

25

A NEW LEAF IN LONDON

When I was living in Manchester I used to travel a lot to folk clubs. I often went as far as Penzance, and up into Scotland. I went wherever there was a gig to be done. Distance wasn't an object because for most of them years I had nothing else to do. I could leave at eleven o'clock in the morning and do a gig that night.

I enjoyed those years very much, up until about 1970 or 71. Then I started getting a bit lonesome, and feeling, this is not a great life: go a whole day without talking to anyone. Then I would arrive at the club and talk and sing continuously — knowing me with my love of yapping I would be going steady maybe for two and a half hours. As soon as that was over, fullstop. Mightn't talk to another human being till I would go to some railway station the following day, and the first I would talk to would be the ticket clerk, telling him where I was going, and then no more talk till I would get to the club and then go like hell for another couple of hours.

So I started feeling not very settled down and not being a very stable character; I was just hanging around in Manchester for a time, and maybe I would work for a week or two somewhere, and the next thing I would just forget that I should be working, and I wouldn't turn up. At that time, believe it or not, because it's something that I haven't done before or since, I was drinking pretty heavy. As soon as I got money I was away to The Swan. I was friendly with Bill Leader at the time, and I think he started thinking the same as me — that I should get out of Manchester because I was doing no good. So I came down to London with Bill, and I stayed with him for about three months. I had the firm intention of going straight, of turning over a new leaf. I had the one idea in my mind that I was going to get a job, which I did, the very first day I went out to look for one.

I got a job in a solicitors' office down in Westminster — Lee, Bolton & Lee. And I stayed there for eight and a half years. Now that is amazing, because before that about three months was my limit in one job. When people heard what I was doing, they said,

'You work in Westminster? Ha, you won't be long there boy!' But I made up my mind I was going to stay, and I stayed, and every day got better.

I enjoyed my time in the solicitors' office. It was a very big concern: at one time there was as high as fourteen partners, and there were lesser ones — up to a hundred people I suppose. But I was my own boss, and I could do as I liked. If I had a gig to go to I could leave any time of day. As long as I was in the door — and I always was — before eight o'clock in the morning to meet the postman and sign for the registered post. Then I would open it all and see what was inside it and put the contents in the proper place and distribute the money and cheques to the proper authorities inside. There were people so dense that they would put a roll of fivers in an envelope, and maybe there wouldn't be a name, it would just be addressed to Lee, Bolton & Lee, where there was over eighty people in the same office. I would have to go around our office on five floors with a couple of hundred pound in my fist, and ask people, 'Is this for you?' That happened no end of times. We used to call them dead letters.

I had good times in the office, and we were all very friendly. I used to always use the head when it came to the girls coming in in the morning late. I could get them out of that fix because I was working down in the basement where there were two big photocopying machines. The girls would come down, get out of their coats and leave the handbag there, and I would give them a piece of paper and they would start away up the stairs; if any of the partners met them, they were already at work, but in fact they were only on their way in. We had capers of every kind going on. The management knew of course: Commander Williams, the office comptroller, was a very bright bloke, and he knew this was going on. But it was done in a way that didn't cause offence or trouble to anyone, so he closed his eyes to a lot of things. He was a very nice gentleman; he retired shortly after I did.

Lee, Bolton & Lee's offices were right at the door of Westminster Abbey — once upon a time it belonged to the Abbey. The very office we were in was where the monks used to live, and it was No. 1, The Sanctuary. When I started there it was all as it was two-three hundred years ago, with a stained-glass window up the stairs, like you would see in a church, and there was big, heavy furniture, beautiful big desks. They started modernising the place then and they got in the nearest thing to prefab furniture. If you sneezed behind it it would collapse. They changed the place around and the atmosphere went. But they were a smashing company to work for. To this day they send me a cheque at Christmas.

I was happy there because I wasn't doing exactly the same thing day after day. I was out through the town more than half the day. I would be sent with a message who knows where — maybe down to their office in Canterbury, and all around the place like that. One time one of the partners came down to see me and said,

'Packie, could you do me a favour? Would you take the day off?'

'Oh,' I said, 'Aye, I'll take the day off!'

He said, 'There's a bundle of papers I want you to deliver in Edgware. You'll have to go to the bank first and hand in this letter and collect the papers. Now you'll do all this by taxi.'

I often used to go by taxi, especially if I was carrying valuables or money. So I started up to Drummond's bank in Trafalgar Square, handed in my letter, and didn't think anything of it. The clerk read the letter and asked me, 'Will you wait here Mr Byrne please?'

After a while a bloke came out with a bundle of papers. I thought it was a big land deal. I put it into my briefcase, came out. Of course I was supposed to take a taxi, but it was a nice day, and I thought, I'll walk up the Oxford Street and have a look at the shops. I was given the whole day to go out to Edgware and come back again. So I waddled about down Piccadilly and up Shaftesbury Avenue. Finally I thought, I'd better head away to Edgware. I hopped on the Underground as far as I could, then I walked another bit, swinging the briefcase. I got out to this office of solicitors about three o'clock in the afternoon with my bag and a letter from the bank. So I handed in my letter and they opened it.

'Oh, you're Mr Byrne from Lee, Bolton & Lee. Come this way.'

I was ushered into this mighty posh office, and I sat there, quite important with my briefcase on my lap. This other fellow came in and said,

'I'll relieve you of that now, Mr Byrne. Cigarette?'

'No thanks, I don't smoke.'

'Drink of something?'

'Hmm, yes.'

'Follow me please.'

I thought, this is funny! I had a very large measure of whiskey; then the old man came out to the street with me, shook my hand

and wished me all the very best. By this time I was feeling very important indeed, although I didn't know why.

I came back to the office just before the five o'clock lot were coming out. Of course my man was there waiting for me.

'How did you get on?'

'Oh, fine. I have a letter for you here somewhere.'

He opened it and read it and said, 'Good work. Look, you'd better get away home now, you've had a trying enough day.'

'I've had a lovely day.'

'Did you take a taxi?'

'I did.'

Next day the phone went. It was my man again. 'Can you come up?' So I went on up.

'Now,' he said, 'I'm safe enough at this distance because I'm far away from you, so don't come any nearer, because you're going to kill me when you hear what I've done.'

So he explained it all to me. It finished up that I was carrying one hundred and eighty thousand pound in the briefcase. It sounds incredible but it's true. The deal had to be clinched that very day, otherwise it would fall through. The chap that owned this premises away out above Brent was going off to Australia. There was another firm very anxious to buy the premises. Now the firm I worked for had a client that they knew wanted this particular kind of premises, and money was no object. The seller wanted cash, and he was leaving the next day. So they sent me up to Drummond's Bank with a letter to put £180,000 into a paper bag and hand it to me, and send me away to Edgware to this firm that was taking care of the sale.

I had no idea what was in the briefcase. I wouldn't take a taxi, I wouldn't behave myself and get on a bus and stay on it. I was going down Oxford Street and Piccadilly, leaving down the briefcase. In fact I went into Lewington's, the music store, left down the briefcase inside the door and went away looking at musical instruments!

When I heard what I was carrying I took a fit of the shakes. But I knew he was wise not to tell me, because if I knew how much I had in that briefcase I would be looking in three directions at the same time and give the game away.

In 1974, while I was working at Lee, Bolton & Lee, I had a heart attack. I was on my way to bed one night and I collapsed in the corridor. I was rushed away to hospital and put into intensive care, with people creeping around me! But I got over it, and came back out of hospital. I was only out three weeks or so, and then I took bad again. I was living off the Tottenham Court Road at the time, staying with Martin Winsor and Jenny Steele, who were both folk singers, and Jenny and me started away to the hospital. It was only about three or four hundred yards to the hospital, but it took us over an hour to walk that far. She laughs about it yet. I was just walking with the wall, and there she was, trying to keep me on the pavement — I was weak, I was all over the place.

As soon as I went into the hospital I got the feeling of safety and I started improving. I was only in a couple of days when they had to keep chastising me for being a damned nuisance! On one occasion the ward sister and a nurse came to my bed with a trolley, wrapped me up in blankets, put me on the trolley and wheeled me away. I thought I was going for an x-ray or cardiac test, but they took me to the nurses' sitting room to watch meself on the television! I was doing 'Pebble Mill at 5'.

Funny what a bit of confidence and reassurance can do. When you find nurses round you and doctors on call — you relax. A lot of going to hospital is as much psychological as medical.

Other than the time I was in hospital and when they sent me away to recuperate, I lost two days' work in nearly nine years when I was working in the solicitors' office. And nearly all that time I was doing a lot of gigs in the evenings. It was often a hell of a strain getting home from a gig, get an hour or two's sleep, and be up and in the office at eight in the morning. When I got out of hospital again I was thinking, I'll never go back to doing the clubs. I'll settle down and concentrate entirely on my job at Lee, Bolton & Lee. But that didn't last very long.

When I became reasonably fit again after this heart attack I went to a folk festival in Loughborough, in 1975. I remember that festival well, because that's where I first met Bonnie Shaljean. I saw her playing a harp, and that was the first harp I saw on the folk scene. Of course I made it my business to go and enquire who she was. She said she would like to hear some Irish airs, so we sat down and I played a couple for her, and one or two other people came over and we finished up with a very nice little session.

A little time after that there was a festival held at Bedford College. I went over and there was Bonnie doing a Carolan harp workshop, which was something entirely new. She mentioned one or two Gaelic phrases in a song, and admitted that she didn't know what they meant. So me with me big mouth shouted up from the audience what they meant, and we had a talk afterwards, and got to know each other. She invited me round for a meal, and got the tape recorder going, and I was putting Irish airs on the tape while she was cooking.

But it was a chance happening that we started working together. Bonnie wasn't doing very much around the folk scene. She worked at Cecil Sharp House, and she had one harp at the time. Roger Holt was running Dingle's folk club, and on two or three occasions he asked me to come and do the club. So I said, I will — on one condition: that there's somebody doing it with me, because I didn't know I would be fit to carry on and do the whole night myself, and it would be very useful to have someone there who could step in if I gave them the nod. So I thought of Bonnie. I'd only met her a couple of times before, but we done the club together. And we worked together for the next ten years.

Having discovered that we could work with each other, we formed a partnership, bought a car and some instruments and got on the road as a folk duo, doing clubs, concerts, festivals and any-thing in entertainment. Nothing spectacular, but enough to keep us going. We made a couple of LP records, and appeared on ra-dio and television.

As a matter of fact now — and this is not blowing my own coals or anything — we found quite soon after we started that we could get more gigs than we were fit to do. To start with, I would not pack up my job and go full-time into the folk scene, and Bonnie would not pack up her job while she was working. Along with that, I found that my health was going to get so bad that I wouldn't be fit to do either my job or the clubs. The arthri-tis was starting at that time, and the gammy hand started playing up on me, and my fingers used to get so sore that I wasn't fit to play the whistles. So we took it pretty cushy. Then when Bon-nie's eyes started playing up we cut down a lot. We had to em-ploy a driver, because she couldn't see the road to drive, and I had stopped driving long years ago. But working with her was a great experience, because she is a brilliant musician. A wee bit strict, but that wasn't a bad thing when trying to work with me.

I think Bonnie really suffered trying to work with me at the start until she got to know me, because I'm very haphazard. Like I don't play the same tune in the same way twice, because I can't remember how I played it the first time. Bonnie's a bit of a per-fectionist, and she would like a tune played note for note. Well,

I wasn't brought up with them kind of ideas. I was brought up that you played the tune the way you felt like playing it, and hard luck if the person listening didn't like it. If they did, well fair enough, but that wasn't going to change your mind. You played the tune your way, anyway. So Bonnie and me used to have little disagreements about that. People would often think when they were sitting in a club, oh crikey, Packie and Bonnie's having a row. Well, 'twouldn't be a row: it would be on stage a way of explaining to each other that we were going to do things our way, and she was going to do things her way. But they all ended up friendly, it was all forgotten immediately it was over. They were business arguments — we never had a stand-up fight or anything.

To this day, I feel a little bit proud of the fact that I think we were the first duo to get a harp and a whistle to correspond very well, because they are two very awkward instruments: they are both meant to be played with some other instrument other than each other, if you know what I mean. We didn't know if it would work, and we tried it and liked it ourselves and thought, well, if we like it maybe there's a hope that some one or two in an audience would like it, and it finished up that everyone did like it, and it kind of grew on them. People would come up and say, that's the first time I ever heard a harp and whistle played together, and it's really lovely.

It wasn't easy, really, getting them to correspond. The harp is fantastic for filling in, because as I said before, I'm a very haphazard musician, and I can play notes that was never meant to be in the tune, and I sometimes let a note slip, but the harp is always there to fill up all this. We played better together than one of us at a time — that was until she got into owning better harps than she had that time. I think the whistle took something out of the harp too, put a sharpness in the continuous ring. People thought that it took us months and months of practising: we often played tunes that we never practised, that we never even mentioned until we would just start and play them.

When Bonnie and me first met she was living in Golders Green and I had a place off Tottenham Court Road. It was a bit inconvenient for rehearsing, we couldn't get together as often as we should, and as she did all the driving the car was always at her place. We at last found a nice quiet house in NW2, with Sam Stephens and Anne Lennox-Martin, another very popular duo on the folk scene. We rented a room each. It's a very nice arrangement: we can hide away when we want to, but the other is always there to help out. If there's a spider in the bath I'm on hand to deal with it! We moved in in 1977 and so we've been there ten years now. That is the longest term I ever spent in one house since I left home — by a long way. Before that, a year was a long time for me to stay in any house!

Bonnie and me had many good times on the road. One thing that helped us along was the fact that we were both fairly broad-minded. And we didn't need drink or drugs to keep us going. I'm not saying that I don't like a pint of beer or that Bonnie is teetotal, but when there's work or driving to be done we would both draw the line.

It used to be great when inquisitive people would try to find out what our relationship with each other really was:

'How did you two meet', 'What brought you two together?' or 'Do you have a house or a flat?'

We knew that they were dying to know but too well-mannered to ask the vital question, 'Do you *live* together?' We managed to give politician's answers, which didn't make them very much wiser. I suppose if I was roughly half my age they wouldn't take a bit of notice, but a well-educated young woman from California and an aged, not very healthy man from the back hills of Donegal having the same address, sharing money, car and work, and being so opposite in appearances, background, culture and upbringing set their minds a-boggling! Do you know, there are still people who find it hard to believe that two people as close as Bonnie and me could go through life by being just friends, which is how we both preferred to live.

We had our ups and downs as everybody in showbusiness will have. But we were happy working together. We put up with each other for ten years on the road anyway. I retired from performing completely at the end of 1986. I'm very glad that Bonnie is continuing though. Being young and dedicated she has a worthwhile life before her and a lot to offer the world of music.

26

BLACK JACK, AND A HAUNTED HOUSE

One of the most enjoyable things that happened during my time in London was acting in a film called 'Black Jack', directed by Ken Loach. Now I was no stranger to acting, because I done plenty back home in Ireland when I was younger — I was telling you that I nearly ended up in the Abbey Theatre in Dublin — and when I was in Munn & Felton's roadshows. But that was a long time before, and when one day at work in 1978 I got a phone call from a woman who introduced herself as casting director of Kestrel Films I hoped I wasn't dreaming.

She went on to say that they were casting the principals for a full-length film and were considering me as one of the principal actors — two down from the leading stars, and could she call around or make an appointment to meet somewhere? It seems that Ken Loach had been looking for an aged man with an Irish accent who could act a little, and handle horses, preferably a musician, and a damned good liar! So he went over to Ireland to find this bloke and he couldn't, but whilst he was over there he met Ciarán Mac Mathúna, who told him there was a man in London who was the very man he was looking for. Ciarán didn't have my address or phone number, so Ken got in touch with Bill Leader who gave him my number.

I told this lady that I had a full-time job, and that I had bookings to do clubs and festivals; yes, she knew all that, and no, I would not have to cancel any gigs, the film-making would wait for me. So we arranged to meet in a West End hotel and have a meal. So, well-dressed and scrubbed I turned up thinking, there must be a catch in this somewhere, the whole thing seemed to be too much in my favour! I was shown into a room with seven or eight youngish people, and my telephone friend introduced me to Ken Loach, Tony Garnett, the producer, and a few others. I knew nothing about film people; I thought they should all be middle-aged, wearing three-piece suits and talking a load of bullcrap, but I was wrong again. I felt embarrassed because I was the only one in the room wearing a tie!

Ken gave me a kind of an audition. He had an actor in there to start an argument with me, and he outlined the story first that we had to talk on. It was that my son and this actor's daughter were thinking of getting married, and my son was a useless lie-about and I was all for the marriage, but he wasn't, because he thought too much of his daughter to let her waste her life on my son. So, off the cuff I had to sort of convince him that he had the wrong opinion about my son and that my people were every bit as good as his, in spite of the fact that he was rich and I wasn't.

I was to play the part of Dr Carmody, a soft-spoken old Irish rogue; he was a quack doctor, selling sugar and water as a sort of an elixir of youth. So Ken's idea was that if I could convince him that I was gaining on the bloke that was the father of the girl, I'll be fit to convince people to buy the dud medicine. There was another bloke there who never muttered a word; he was just sitting back and staring at me and listening to my carry-on, and I kept wondering, who the hell is he? Well, he was just brought in off the street probably, as he would be one of an audience looking at this as a film. And if he enjoyed it in the raw, by the time it was polished up and on the screen maybe others would enjoy it too. I had to have a kind of a broken, half-Scottish, half-Irish accent, which fitted pretty good with my accent, and I can be a very convincing talker. So Ken offered me the part if I could get the time off work.

I went to Commander Williams the next morning and poured out the whole story. He was almost as excited as me, and gave me a couple of months off. I went up to Yorkshire a few days after to the farm where the horses were, to get accustomed to the horses. I didn't forget how to lead a horse around or what to do with one if it got unruly. They gave me a beautiful big mare and a covered wagon. She was called Ruby, a real Shire, and she was rented from Jeff Morton's farm for the film. She was seventeen and a half hands, with feet the size of a milk crate, brown with a white strip on her face. She was lovely, and we got along grand. When she got to know me and understand my accent she'd do anything I asked her. She was coming along four years, never was anyone on her back, but she knew how to pull a cart. So I worked away with her during the film, and she was lovely to work with.

The cast and the other people working on the film were all staying at a motel in Bedale, North Yorkshire. The first night there we had a right old session in the bar and got on first-name terms with each other. Next day we were taken on location and I was

told what I had to do in the film. Dr Carmody reminded me a little bit of my stage act — he had the gift of the gab and the ability
to make people believe the impossible. I was part of a travelling
fair which consisted of ballad singers, jewellery makers, crooks,
fortune tellers and women of other trades, not all reputable. We
also had four dwarfs doing old English dances and making a
nuisance of themselves as part of the act. They were really smashing little fellows, very witty and highly intelligent. The leading
man, Black Jack himself, was a French giant, Jean Franval. He had
only a few words of English but he was a nice man and a big star
in France. His co-star was Louise Cooper, a teenage beauty from
Doncaster. She had all the makings of a very fine actress. I often
wonder what she's doing now, and hope she's doing well. Steve
Hirst played the part of Tolley. It would be nice to meet them
all again.

Working for Ken Loach was both interesting and educational. He didn't harass us — just gave us a good idea of what to do
and then let us ad-lib our way through. We worked long hours
— breakfast at 6 a.m. and straight into make-up. Some days we
spent waiting for a call to take places, others working real hard.
We usually got back to the motel about nine in the evening, had
a few pints and off to bed. It was great fun to see the visitors and
customers that didn't know we were filming staring at us. We were
a scruffy-looking bunch, especially the ones that handled the
horses: dirty hands and faces and covered with horse's hairs, and
after nine or ten hours working with horses you don't smell exactly like roses and lavender, especially in September when they
eat a lot of soft grass. The people that didn't know us tried to keep
as far away as possible, but the ones that did know us, like the
staff and a few of the regulars, made quite a fuss of us. This annoyed the toffee-noses very much, they looked proper disgust-
ed. They maybe thought we belonged to the travelling class and
wondered why we were let in at all, not to mention getting V.I.P.
treatment from everyone connected to the building!

The film was taken from the book of the same name by Leon
Garfield, a good story, well adapted and directed by Ken,
produced by Tony Garnett, with superb camera work by Chris
Menges. I saw it at a West End cinema, and others who saw it said
it was an enjoyable film. But thanks to one film critic in particular
it didn't get a great review. It's my opinion that this critic and Ken
were not good friends, because the slagging he gave it was really
disgusting. I didn't keep the review, so I can't remember the ex-

act words, but he said something like, the only one that done any
kind or shape of acting in it was Packie Byrne, and no-one understood a word he said! But the film was quite popular abroad, and
it gets shown occasionally on the telly.

When the shooting was finished I came back to London and
into the familiar atmosphere of the office. After a couple of months
away I almost forgot my old routine and had to be careful not
to do the right thing at the wrong time. Everything seemed so quiet
and peaceful after the hectic time in Yorkshire. You don't find
many horses wandering through a solicitor's office. I think I missed
them, and I know I missed all the people connected with the film.
They were a great bunch to work with and to drink with. I hope
they're all doing fine.

Earlier on when I was talking about my father and the old people
back home telling ghost stories I mentioned that I had an experience that started me thinking about those old stories. It was
one time when Bonnie and me went to Italy. It was a tour — good
old Taffy Thomas arranged it. Quite a few of us went over and
done six concerts. Bonnie and me were staying in an old house,
about four hundred years old or so, which was a sort of a museum. There was old farm implements, and instruments of torture,
displayed around the walls, and there was the old watches with
one hand, and the strangest-looking clocks you ever saw. The
Italian organisers probably thought, for an old Irishman and a
young American girl, we'll do something different, put them up
in there. And really, it was a lovely place. Beautiful, comfortable
beds and we brought in food and cooked for ourselves and had
a smashing time. We were there a couple of weeks, but one night
a few days before we had to leave a strange thing happened that
kind of changed our minds about the place. We came back from
doing a concert in a place called Canale, which is down towards
the centre of Italy. We were home about one o'clock or so. It was
a beautiful night with a nice big full moon. Bonnie said to me,

'Packie, would you go in and make the tea? I feel like sitting
outside for a while.'

The house was set in beautiful countryside stuck into the side
of a hill, with vineyards as far as you could see, right away into
the foot of the mountains. So, she pulled two armchairs outside
the house and sat down in one of them to enjoy the view. I was
inside, making the tea, and she came in and said,

'Have you been playing about with the lights?'

'No,' I said.

'The lights were changing colour!'

There was a big bulb on the corner of the house, shining down into the gateway out onto the main road.

'Ah,' I said, 'your eyes are playing tricks.'

'No', she said, 'it's true! the lights are definitely changing colour.'

I wouldn't even go out to see. I thought, oh she must be drunk on the quiet.

Well after a while we went to bed. And about half-two or three o'clock a breeze started blowing through the room I was in. Now, I was in the last room, away at the very back of the house, with bars on the windows. It looked like a jail room. Bonnie was in the first room at the top of the stairs, with quite a long corridor between the rooms. This breeze was blowing about through my room very strongly, and I thought, what a storm! Someone must have left the windows open. I got up to close them — and the windows weren't opened for maybe two or three hundred years. They were stuck with paint. I looked out, and there wasn't a leaf moving in the vineyard outside. That's funny! Suddenly the breeze through the room stopped. I got back into bed, and it started again.

There was a rocking chair over in the corner — a very old, decorative antique rocking chair, and the bed I was in was an antique too, with carved tops. The rocking chair started moving. The breeze carried on, and the door leading out into the corridor was moving. There was another door leading from my room up to a room where there were a lot of feathers from birds all over the world, all pasted into nice big frames, and antique watches and stuff like that. And that door was even going crazy — the breeze was so strong that the latch was clicking. I got up and put on the light, and something happened that I got cold, and I got shivery, and I got afraid. And I left on the light all night and sat on the bed.

In the morning Bonnie came to me and said,

'Do you know, a strange thing happened last night. You know that pin that belonged to my grandmother?'

She had a brooch that was pretty valuable, and she was very fond of it. She left it down on the little table beside her bed, and when she got up in the morning it was gone. She searched everywhere, and she knew that she put it there. We thought, oh well, it can't be helped. And at that time I didn't tell her about the breeze that was going on in the room I was in.

The following night the man that owned the place came in. His name was Franco Ferrero, and he was a smashing bloke. He worked in a safari park — he was the man that took charge of the wild animals when they were brought in from jungles in Africa and places, and he cooled them down and trained them and handled them. We couldn't resist the temptation and had to tell him about this happening.

'Well now,' he said (he could talk enough English that we could understand), 'I'm very, very sorry that this happened to you while you were here. I didn't want to tell you, but I was so afraid it might happen. Things do disappear here, and breezes do blow through the rooms. Very often I might lose a scarf, and I would find it tucked behind a picture, or wrapped round the banister. It's something that no-one can explain. That is why I will not spend one night in this house alone.'

And he was no coward, because he could handle lions and tigers. He told us very weird stories about the house. He got it from his mother's uncle; it was willed to him. Why he fancied it, there was very good grape-growing land around it — a nice slope, facing the sun, and very good soil for growing the grape trees. He grew quite a lot and made a lot of wine, but he was always shaky about the house. Franco told me that before it became a museum, the house was the headquarters, if that is the right word to use, of the Italian witch burners, and the room I was in was the room where they used to keep the witches before they burned them! After he got the house he began to notice strange happenings. Things started disappearing, and the doorbell started ringing and there was nobody there. The lights started changing colours, and the furniture moved about. He would get up off a chair and go to bed, leave the chair in front of the fire — big open fireplaces that he had — and the chair might be at the door in the morning. He got so frightened that he would not stay in the house alone. The only time he would stay there was when his girlfriend, who was a doctor, came and stayed with him all night, or his brother came and stayed with him. If he had to stay there at other times — to make an early start in the morning — he had an arrangement with some people down in the town of Bra to stay with them overnight.

Then I got really afraid, and Bonnie started getting shaky. I was scared stiff, but keeping up the appearances, I wouldn't tell him that, I was giggling. But he wasn't giggling, he was dead serious, and he said about twenty times that he was sorry that that had to happen when we were there. He said the brooch will probably turn up somewhere, maybe years from now, and if it does he would make sure to send it on to Bonnie. But it never turned up from that day to this. That was two or three nights before we left there, and to tell you the truth, I never slept no more! In fact I left my light on all night after that.

Franco's girlfriend was there several times, and she was very very nice. She really took Bonnie under her wing, because at that time Bonnie's health wasn't so good all through, and this doctor lady was examining her day after day and getting for her certain kinds of medicine — Franco would go away in the van and bring them back. They were the nicest couple you ever met, but no way would one of them stay in the house alone. In fact, Franco wouldn't even sit at the fire from evening until bedtime. Soon as it got dark he was out like a shot and away.

That's a real ghost story, and if you read it in a book you would say it was a fairytale, but the thing is it happened, and both of us are witnesses to it. I've been listening to ghost stories since I was about the height of a bob of coppers. I never believed any of them, even when I was a kid and my Dad was a good ghost-story teller. He could tell stories that'd make your hair curl, and I laughed at them all and went away to bed in the dark. That experience in Italy taught me a lesson, to not be so damned sceptical, to not think too much of my own opinion and bravery and all, because when it came down to the point I wasn't a bit brave.

I retired completely from singing and performing at the end of 1986. Having reached the age of seventy, I thought it was maybe time to settle down! Some people think that I'm wrong to retire, and that after more than twenty years on the folk scene I'll miss the clubs and the people so much that I'll crawl into some corner and stagnate. Well, maybe they're right, I don't know, but there are two sides to every story. I know I can't put on a show like I used to, my voice has become so weak I cannot sing so well, my fingers are painful and stiff so I cannot play very good, and the cogs in my brain don't grip so fast owing to the quantity of tablets I have to consume to keep breathing. In spite of all that I still get many offers of work in the folk scene and general entertainment, so I reckon I'm very thankful for that. But the time to get out of showbusiness is while you're still in; that way you can make yourself believe you're still popular and capable. I know that may sound like stupid pride, but overstaying your welcome is never wise and the thought that you're not wanted any more could be fatal.

27

CONCLUSION: SOME REFLECTIONS
FROM BACK HOME

When I retired eight or nine years ago from my daytime job, I
never intended coming back to Ireland. I thought I would spend
out the remainder of my life about London; but things had to
change, and I had to change with them. The landlord of the house
decided he wanted the place to himself and we were all told to
leave. I happened to be the last one out, and I didn't know where
I was going to go. I couldn't afford anything at all around where
I was living, and the council couldn't promise anything other than
bed and breakfast if I was on the street.

Then some friends of mine from back home came over on
a surprise visit to London, and when they heard what was going
on they first put the idea into my head that I should come back
to Donegal. They went back and a few days after they found this
little house for me; I came over in June to see the place, and now
in August here I am living in Ardara about six miles from where
I was born! Things are quite comfortable, and I'm very happy that
I was told to get out of that house in London, because otherwise
I wouldn't be here. It gets colder here in the winter than it does
in London, but I think I'll put up with that, because there's other
compensations. The view's a lot nicer here than in Kilburn High
Road! And to keep warm in the winter I expect I'll be burning
turf here on the fire just like we always did in the old days —
although, mind you, I won't be cutting it myself!

A couple of hundred yards from this house is the old fort
(that's what gives Ardara its name: *Ard an Rátha*, the mound of
the fort); from the top of that you can see all the way into the
mountains of Sligo and right the way down to Inishowen, and
I can picture myself in my younger days driving cattle and sheep
along the roads between them mountains. Where I was born is
just directly over that mountain that I can see from my front window, and that's the way I used to come into town, straight over
the mountain.

When I first left here fifty years ago, Ardara was a poor little place with nothing to recommend it. There was no street sweeping or anything like that — papers lay on the street till they rotted. But not so now. Ardara has changed a lot, and Glenties has changed even more. Ardara's a booming little town now. But there are some aspects of life that haven't changed. There is still a very good communal spirit. You go into any pub in the town and keep your ears open: the next man or woman that'll walk in after you is on first-name terms with every one in that bar, excepting a few visitors. It's Frank and John and Mary and Bridget and Paddy.

I can't walk down that hill into town without meeting someone that knows me, someone that I haven't seen for fifty years maybe. Coming back from Cashel the other night in the car, we met an old man pushing his bicycle up the hill. When we stopped he stuck his head in the window and said to me,

'Ah, I've met you before!'

And I hadn't seen him since maybe 1936 or 1937: he was on the committee that used to organise concerts in the hall out that way, and I used to come and sing at those concerts.

Lots of other people remember me from those times too. You know, sometimes it can be kind of difficult to get people to talk about business or things that I want done, because they are more interested in talking about old times! That's the way things are still in this part of the world — and I can't pretend I'm complaining about it.

That will eventually die out in Ardara, because there are a lot of outside influences, which isn't a bad thing: like there's Germans owning factories around the town. They'll be bringing in people who'll maybe not want to be on first-name terms with the locals, and that'll wash off on the locals. But when I left there was no foreigners: everyone in Ardara was an Ardara man or woman.

West Donegal, and maybe one or two other little parts of Ireland, is one of the very few places in Europe that you can say has not been completely spoiled by progress. Not completely. Say on the coast road from Killybegs to Carrick, there's definitely some nice unspoiled areas in there, but there's many that have changed a hell of a lot in my lifetime, been spoiled as far as the traditional view and customs and all is concerned. But some of the old ways survive.

You can still see the older folk out in the hayfields making the grasscocks, or an old fellow out with his scythe mowing down the hay. He's far removed from a combine harvester, but he gets there just the same — feeds a few cows.

One of the things I miss most is the old cattle fairs. They were fantastic in several ways, because along with being educational to someone that wasn't used to them, they were exciting too. I can remember the square here in Ardara on a fair day, and you couldn't move for people and sheep and cattle. The sheep would be tied up along the road towards our place for maybe a couple of hundred yards, whereas nowadays the most you'll see is a couple of stalls selling shirts and dresses and a few things like that. The hubbub and the noise was going on, and I would be buying from somebody over there, and that fellow was trying to sell to me but keeping his eye on an animal he saw somewhere that would suit his flock. But the rule is nowadays, you drive your cattle into the mart or auction and you get a cheque so many days later. That has taken away all the education. You don't have to talk one word. Tell the price to the auctioneer's clerk that you want to get for them, and that's it, you could go home and go to bed.

Times have changed a lot — probably in many ways it is for the better. Financially people are better off. But the same friendship or the same tenderness towards each other is not to be found no more. Everything got a bit commercial.

I remember when my father would take a springing heifer or a cow into the fair to sell, that would be one that would be coming near the calving and we didn't really want her. So if the market was bad for cows and nobody wanted to buy, he would be in the pub having a chat with somebody that had a couple of calves, and the next thing was he arrived home with a couple of calves — he had a swap! There was no money exchanged either way!

I don't think really that the people nowadays would trust each other enough to do that. You had to really trust somebody to do a swap like that, because anything could be the matter with that cow; but if there was, my father would say,

'Now look, Francie, she mightn't fit you.'

That was a hint. You would sell her to someone from Pettigo or County Fermanagh or so far away you'd never hear from her again if she wasn't a good one, but the neighbour didn't get her. No way.

When I was back here in 1985 I was talking to quite a few of the older people, and they all had the same story. 'Times are not like they used to be.' They still haven't learned to live with the modern world. If they're going anywhere, they won't be let walk: there's a car at everyone's house, and they're driven anywhere, and they don't meet anyone along the road or see anyone's crops like they used to. In my father's day, when he'd be going to meet somebody, he'd take his stick with him, and he'd probably walk about five extra miles, doing detours, to see someone's cattle or someone's fields of hay. All that's over and done with.

During that visit I also went to see the Campbell family, who live in the Glen of Glenties, right back in the hills. I was doing a gig with my gang at the Harvest Fair in Glenties, and the young men of the house, Vincent and Josie, invited us out, saying their father would like to meet me again. Old Peter Campbell is a lovely old gentleman: he was eighty-five then and still looking after sheep and cattle. His hands were bad, and he couldn't play the fiddle for us, but his son Vincent is one of the best fiddle players in the county.

I knew Peter sixty years ago, when I was just a short time at school, when the Campbells started bringing their sheep up to our place for the winter. Being on a mountain, they hadn't a lot of winter grass. But we had sheep and a very good winter place, where we could take Campbell's sheep for the winter, and look after them, and dip them, and treat them. And then in the summertime we'd send ours away down to Campbell's. The mountains were great for growing wool and they'd come home as healthy as dogs. From the very start I don't think one of us knew what we owed the other, because no-one took a blind bit of notice. The sheep came back — sometimes on their own: they were all mountain horned sheep, and they're clever, ewes in particular. When the winter was coming on, they'd know there wouldn't be much grass in the mountains, and they'd head away, straight over the mountains and land at our place and stay there for the winter. Come the spring again they'd get fed up in the lowlands and start away to the mountains, a few today and a few tomorrow. They were branded, of course, our initials branded into the horn and a blue spot of paint on each side of the body. It was a very useful arrangement, because we were all sure that the sheep were well fed, summer and winter. But that's all done away with.

Traditional music is still being played here and there. You'll find little sessions in the pubs in town. But nothing compared to what it used to be, when there was music and dancing in the country houses all over the county. There aren't many fiddle players left. All the Doherty brothers are dead now, and Mickey and Francie Byrne died just recently. There are a few good fiddle players around, like Vincent Campbell, and John Gallagher of Ardara, and James Byrne, who I met at a very nice session the other night over at Carrick. But they are all excellent musicians: nowadays a lot of other musicians don't bother — they hear the best in sessions or on radio and on records and they reckon they're not good enough. In the old days you'd often find the worst fiddle player you ever heard in your life, but he played the best tunes you ever heard. Old Paddy Boyle and Big Pat were a bit rough and ready compared to the good fiddlers today, but they played such likeable music, you know.

Of course, country and western is the in-thing in all the bigger places, where the admission is anything up to £6. There are up-and-coming Johnny Cashes and Dolly Partons and even a Slim Whitman. But I don't care how progress advances, it will never blot out the traditional music completely. The media is still trying to put a black cross on the traditional music, and in the more modernised areas they've succeeded in brainwashing the children into believing that the traditional music was some kind of a foreign language and not clean, but there would be no point in anyone going away back into the hills of Glencolumbkille and West Donegal and trying to preach their modern-music gospel.

In the area where I was born, nearly all the people left. Walked out and went to England and America, or into better land areas or into the towns. They just scattered. The old folk died and the young ones wouldn't take over the land no more. There's no old thatched cottages left, or at least none of them occupied in those areas. In Corkermore there are a number of these new-fangled bungalows in place of the old thatched cottages. The old house where I was born has been bulldozed. A German bought the house site from John Boyle, and he's built a house on it. He has his own private plane and he intends to build a runway where we used to cut turf! But the townland of Meenagolin is completely vacant, no-one at all living in it now, and I remember six families living in one little cluster, and there was children in every house, and in fact there were over twenty kids going to Croagh school from Meenagolin, and quite a few from Meenacloy, that's the next townland further down near the river. Meenacloy is completely a waste now.

So other than to visit John Boyle and his family, I won't be spending much time up that way. I'll have a few visitors myself, no doubt. As a matter of fact I'll have a lot more visitors now than

I would have if I never left around here, because I'll have a lot of visitors from England. Over the last few weeks before I came over here, I don't know how many little addresses did I hand out. In fact, yes, it has started already. But that's my life, like; I live for that, because I'm a bit of an oddity, I cannot live without people, and preferably young people. Because when I'm out with a lot of young people, and I always am, I feel I'm one of them — it knocks a lot of years off for me!

Maybe there'll be a bit more musical activity yet; the only trouble is I cannot sing very well, and with the crooked hands I can't play very well, but, I'll bet if I went out tonight and tomorrow night and the night after somebody would remind of something that I used to do away donkey's years ago, and ask me about it, and sure as hell I would swear first that I wouldn't remember it. I probably wouldn't, until I would start it: like Molly Bawn, that's a song I don't sing no more, not for long years, but last night someone asked me to sing it, and I thought I'll try a bit of it, and as soon as I did it all came back, the flow came back.

It's been a good life, of course it has. I've always done what pleased myself, and anyone that can go through life doing that hasn't much reason to grumble. Being free I think is one of the greatest advantages any human being could be offered. I don't mean not having a care in the world — you need a few cares to keep you on the straight and narrow path — but to be tied down in a job from you're 18 till you're 65 and working for the same company all the time, and see the same people around you day and night (there are people who thrive on that, of course, and good luck to them, I don't say they're wrong): to me that would be soul-destroying. I would like to see a bunch of people tonight, and a different bunch tomorrow, and try to analyse them as best I could and figure out the best way of talking to them that I wouldn't insult them!

I have no regrets at all. Some people you know, they have a sort of pity for me: 'You had a kind of an unlucky life, a hard life.' And they really mean it, through kindness, because I had so much illness, and deaths in the family, but funny, I take that as something that just has to happen anyway. And if you do get a bad run of health or misfortune, then it'll change sometime. After that, it's possible that the next phase of your life coming along may not be any better, but it's so much in contrast from the bad times that you imagine it's the greatest thing ever happened to you. You kind of balance one against the other, and it usually works.

Afterword by the Editor

A VISIT TO CORKERMORE

Packie returned to live in Ardara in August 1987, and I was able to visit him for a few days very shortly after his arrival. Packie was in excellent spirits and evidently happy with his decision to return to Donegal, as were his friends and acquaintances in the area, who greeted him with delight. Packie's old friend and neighbour Packie McGinley spared no pains ferrying us all around southwest Donegal. I was thus able to visit most of the places I had heard so much about, drink in the spectacular beauty of the county, and incidentally enjoy the company and music of some of the finest fiddle players to be found in the country. It was a hugely gratifying visit, but on my last day the one place we had not been to was the one I wanted to see more than any other — the old townland of Corkermore.

'Och, you don't want to bother going *there*,' said Packie McGinley. 'Why, there's nothing to see at all.'

I explained that I thought I might take some photographs for the book. Packie Manus doubted whether there were any subjects of interest, and pointed out that the light was dismal. This was undeniable: for most of the night and the morning it had been raining with a ferocity that was unusual even for Donegal. The river flowing through Ardara had swelled to a raging torrent, and one of the houses at the edge of town was flooded. Photographs, however, were only a small part of why I wanted to see Corkermore, and when I showed no sign of abandoning the idea, the two Packies readily agreed to visit the place with me.

As Packie Manus mentions in the opening lines of Chapter One, Corkermore does not today figure on most maps of Donegal. Even the Ordnance Survey Map, scale half-inch to one mile, reveals no clue to its whereabouts other than the Corker River. Meenagolin, however, is shown — oddly enough, since unlike Corkermore it is now totally deserted[1].

---

1 The spelling used on OS maps is *Meenagolan*, but I have used the form Packie felt was correct throughout.

From the inland road between Ardara and Inver we could see what remains of Packie's home townland about a mile away across the brown, barren moorland. This amounts to a couple of modern bungalows and a barn close to the tumbling ruins of some old thatched cottages.

From a distance I was struck by the contrast between what Packie called 'suburban dwellings in the middle of a mountain' and the traditional cottages (of which quite a number of well-kept examples are still to be seen in southwest Donegal). Built with stone and timber dug out of the ground, and roofed with straw from the fields, the old houses seem to have grown out of the land itself and blend snugly into the landscape, encircled by trees and surrounded by fields of hay and crops. The new bungalows, with their huge windows, harsh lines and perfect symmetry, look as though they have been plucked from a modern suburb and arbitrarily planted down here by some giant childish hand.

As we drove into Corkermore through Meenadreen, I asked Packie for his feelings about the fate of the old farm. 'Why should I be sad about it? I couldn't wait to get off the place and get rid of it when it was mine,' he said airily. However, this nonchalance contrasted with his firm refusal, when we parked the car at the bottom of the track leading up to the house, to accompany us up the hill to inspect the ruin of the old house and the new one for which it was demolished.

The atmosphere of desolation was overpowering. Water from the morning's rain was cascading down the neglected track. The new house was almost completely hidden from view by the firs Packie remembers his father planting all around the old cottage, which have now grown into tall and strong trees. At the back of the house site they grow directly on top of the high earth banks ('ditches') that served to protect the dwelling from storms. The new house, a large chalet-bungalow with a steep slate roof, was finished but showed no signs of having been lived in. A few yards away stood all that remained of the old cottage: a single gable-end wall, crumbling and overgrown with grass and nettles, which the new owner had decided not to bulldoze with the rest of the property. It was completely dwarfed in scale by the new building.

It seemed a cruel irony to see the remains of this tiny cottage that had housed a family of six in Packie's youth — and perhaps many more in earlier generations — overshadowed by the new house, which may be inhabited for a few weeks of the year by two or three people. If the single-storey modern bungalows that

have been built nearby are out of place enough, the incongruity of this new house in size and style seemed far greater and quite ludicrous in the setting.

Walking back to rejoin Packie Manus, who was waiting by the car, I looked at what had once been 'green land' used for cropping and grazing. It was now distinctly brown, because without careful attention it had soon been overrun by rushes. Packie remarked that he remembered when there wasn't a rush to be seen on the land from where we stood to the brow of the hill several hundred yards away. Generations of care lavished on the land by men like Packie's father, working long hours with his spade, draining, manuring, digging, planting and harvesting, seemed to have evaporated within the span of one generation, leaving no trace.

During Packie's boyhood, at this time of the year there would have been freshly built haycocks, ripening oats and a healthy crop of potatoes. The slurry draining from the cowsheds used to form a bed of rich soil inside the stone wall that had run around the front of the house and outbuildings; in spring and summer, Packie recalled, self-seeded wildflowers had turned the patch into a blaze of colour. There was no trace of any of this now to relieve the barrenness of the landscape, which is used only for sheep and the mechanical excavation of turf.

I asked Packie where Meenagolin had stood. He pointed to a hilltop some two miles distant. After the last of the people had left, the land was bought by the forestry commission, and the site of the townland is now buried beneath a swathe of conifers. Meenacloy had been just across the river from where we stood. Here nothing had been planted, and yet there was not a trace of any building or structure to show that people had ever lived on the spot.

We wandered around the ruins of a farm nearby. Among a group of crumbling buildings stood one that had last been used as a dairy, now abandoned and full of scrap. When I asked Packie what it had been originally, he replied gently, 'That was Big Pat's house.'

Phrases from a song sung by Packie's fellow traditional singer Paddy Tunney came to my mind as we surveyed the scene. 'The Green Fields of Canada' tells, like so many Irish folk songs, the sad story of emigration and the depopulation of the countryside. One line laments that 'the land's gone to rushes', and another the loss of 'fiddlers that flaked out the old mountain reels'.

The song seemed to sum up the fate of this valley. Rushes were everywhere and the home of the best fiddler had become an abandoned cow byre. Not a soul was to be seen, although it was the time of year for building haystacks. The contrast between the present desolation and the vivid images of life conjured up in Packie's recollections could not have been greater. It occurred to me as we looked back up the hillside that we could perhaps have stood on the spot for years without seeing anyone pass by on foot, here where people used to walk at all times of the day and night.

Nobody could blame the men and women who left this poor land for opportunities elsewhere — least of all a city dweller who has known nothing approaching the crofter's endless round of toil and meagre living standards. But anybody can see that so much that was good has passed along with the backbreaking labour and unhealthy living conditions. The loss of the 'art of survival' seems a heavy price to pay for any of the benefits of modern life.

A feeling of loss remained with me for a long time after that visit. Back at Packie Manus's house in Ardara he too remained pensive. He remarked that every one of the ruined houses we had seen had been a rambling house, full of dance, stories, and music.

Characteristically, however, he could not remain downcast.
Perhaps to cheer us both up, he said,

'Well, you know, it was never a very pretty place.'

Then, after a thoughtful pause, he added,

'But it was a thriving place, and it was bloody good fun living there. Aye, it was.'

APPENDIX: DISCOGRAPHY

Solo recordings

Packie Byrne. EFDSS LP 1009. Published 1969.

This record, comprising songs and ballads, a humorous narration, whistle solos and lilting, gives a good sample of Packie's varied traditional repertoire.

> *Barbara Ellen; The Skylark; My Lagan Love; Story; The Frog's Wedding; The Rambling Pitchfork; Blooming Caroline; Foyne's Legacy and Away And Over; Paddy's Green Shamrock Shore; Slieve Gallon Brae; Derry So Fair; The Foggy Dew.*

Packie Manus Byrne: Songs of a Donegal Man. Topic Records 12TS257. Published 1975.

This album consists solely of ballads, including several of the rarest gems of Packie's repertoire; the excellent sleeve notes provide much detail about the songs and where Packie learned them.

> *John and the Farmer; The Rich Man's Daughter; The Holland Handkerchief; Molly Bawn; The Jolly Ploughboy; Young Alvin; Johnny o' Hazelgreen; Lament to the Moon; The Creel.*

Compilations

Singing Men of Ulster. Innisfree/Green Linnet Records SIF 1005. Published 1977.

This collection is of particular interest because it consists of field recordings made between 1956 and 1962. Eight singers are represented, including John Doherty and Paddy Tunney. Packie contributes The Frog's Wedding and an excellent performance of Molly Bawn.

With Bonnie Shaljean

These two records comprise airs and dance tunes, and traditional songs sung by both Packie and Bonnie, with whistle, harp and harmonium.

The Half Door. Dingle's Records DIN 302. Published 1977.

Captain Taylor's Air and March; I Will Lay Ye Doon; Min an Erin; The Drummer Boy at Waterloo; German Barn Dance; The Recruited Collier; I've Got a Bonnet; The Munster Buttermilk; The Ghost's Welcome; Our Ship She Lays in Harbour; The Half Door; Miss Hamilton's All Alive; The Lark in the Clear Air; The Red-Haired Man's Wife; Hanigan's Hooley.

Roundtower. Dingle's Records DIN 311. Published 1981.

An Culin; The Bantry Girl's Lament; The Blooming Meadow, Paddy the Dandy; Billy Reilley; Father Murphy's Topcoat, Drops of Brandy; Ramblin' Irishman; Rosie's Brahan, The Fernden Polka; Donal Og; Madame Bonaparte, King of the Fairies; Poor Dog Tray; Johnny Leary's Polka, The £42 Cheque; Shenandoah.